Civilization and Violence

BORDERLINES

A BOOK SERIES CONCERNED WITH REVISIONING GLOBAL POLITICS
Edited by David Campbell and Michael J. Shapiro

For more books in the series, see p. vi.

Civilization and Violence

Regimes of Representation
in Nineteenth-Century Colombia

CRISTINA ROJAS

FOREWORD BY MICHAEL J. SHAPIRO

BORDERLINES, VOLUME 19

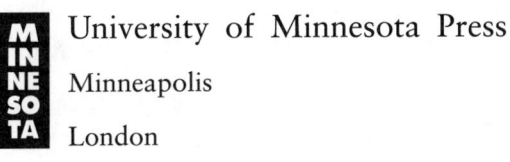

University of Minnesota Press

Minneapolis

London

Copyright 2002 by the Regents of the University of Minnesota

An earlier version of chapter 5 was previously published as "The Will of Civilization and Its Encounter with Laissez Faire," by Cristina Rojas de Ferro, *Review of International Political Economy* 2, no. 1 (1995); published by Taylor & Francis, P.O. Box 25, Abingdon, Oxfordshire, OX14 3UE, United Kingdom.

All rights reserved. No part of this publication may be reproduced, stored in a retrieval system, or transmitted, in any form or by any means, electronic, mechanical, photocopying, recording, or otherwise, without the prior written permission of the publisher.

Published by the University of Minnesota Press
111 Third Avenue South, Suite 290
Minneapolis, MN 55401-2520
http://www.upress.umn.edu

Printed in the United States of America on acid-free paper

Library of Congress Cataloging in Publication Data

Rojas, Cristina.
    Civilization and violence : regimes of representation in nineteenth-century Colombia / Cristina Rojas ; Foreword by Michael J. Shapiro.
        p.   cm. — (Borderlines ; v. 19)
    Includes bibliographical references and index.
    ISBN 0-8166-3430-0 (hc. : alk. paper) — ISBN 0-8166-3431-9 (pbk. : alk. paper)
        1. Violence—Colombia. 2. Colombia—Civilization—19th century.
    3. Elite (Social sciences)—Colombia—History—19th century. 4. Power (Social sciences)—Colombia. 5. Capitalism—Colombia—History—19th century. 6. Colombia—Economic conditions—19th century.
    7. Colombia—Social conditions—19th century. I. Title. II. Borderlines (Minneapolis, Minn.) ; v. 19.
    HN310.Z9 V5663 2001
    303.6'09861'09034—de21

The University of Minnesota is an equal-opportunity educator and employer.

12 11 10 09 08 07 06 05 04 03 02   10 9 8 7 6 5 4 3 2 1

To my sons, Gonzalo and Rodrigo,
whose love gives me confidence in a peaceful tomorrow
for Colombia,
and to the memory of Magdalena and Ernesto, mis viejos,
whose example inspired me.

BORDERLINES

Contents

Foreword

MICHAEL J. SHAPIRO

Cristina Rojas's *Civilization and Violence* defies singular classification. Certainly it is about nineteenth-century Colombia. But the conceptual scope of the study takes its significance well beyond the character and political history of one state during its key nation-building century. The investigation seeks, first, to address an issue that transcends a particular period and place: the answer to the question "Why violence?" The pursuit of this answer leads Rojas into a highly original analysis of the civilizational commitments that Norbert Elias has shown to be central to European practices of distinction (or, more specifically, of invidious comparison). Rojas treats the Colombian version of civilizational commitment, notably in terms of its authorization of violence.

But Rojas's investigation is not limited to a critique of ideology. She articulates Colombia's civilizational commitment, which was integral to its "regime of representation," with an innovative and elaborate analysis of the relationship between political economy and political culture. The destructive "will to civilization," which Rojas discerns in the Colombia of the nineteenth century—"a place of encounter between the colonial past and the imagined future"—is shown to have a delegating effect on the development of both political and economic subjects.

In addition to the pattern of effects that she maps in the Colombian case, Rojas provides a way of reading paradoxes that disables any attempt to render political developments as linear narratives. She shows how attention to the "violence of representation" impugns traditional readings of political development in states that claim to be democratic polities. Moreover, Rojas weaves in the story of capital expansion and addresses the complexities of the interrelationships among political, economic, and cultural registers.

Finally, in sympathetic resonance with its contributions to history and theory, *Civilization and Violence* is an exercise in the politics of what Jacques Rancière has called subjectification. It makes voluble alternative voices—those that have not been legitimate parts of the dominant political history and political economy of a state aspiring to democratic nationhood.

Acknowledgments

Like many scholars born and raised in Colombia, I could not escape the question "Why violence?" I am indebted to all the people who helped me to understand the complexity and multiple dimensions of violence. I benefited from my early encounter with the work of Michael Shapiro, whose thoughts on representation and violence inspired important parts of this book. I thank him and Carrie Mullen for making possible the publication of *Civilization and Violence.*

I acknowledge and thank for their comments my professors at Carleton University: Jane Jenson, Rianne Mahon, and Lyn K. Mytelka. I am especially grateful to Arturo Escobar for his sincere advice and guidance, to my friend and colleague Fuat E. Keyman for his intellectual and personal support, and to Valerie Howe not only for her time spent in editing, but also for providing moral support that was so much needed. I also want to thank Benedict Anderson, Ivette Cárdenas, Elvia Caro, Mauricio Ferro, Larry George, Catherine LeGrand, Jesús Martín, Antanas Mockus, Craig N. Murphy, Doris Sommer, Rob Walker, Cynthia Weber, and two anonymous readers for their valuable comments.

More than an individual contribution, this dissertation is a familial venture. No page of this book has not been carefully examined and touched by my sister, María Magdalena Rojas; I have no words to express her generosity and dedication. Juliana Rojas and Ariel Pakes provided me with the wisdom I needed to keep writing without confusing the trivial with the substantial. I am very thankful for the rich dialogue that we had, together with my family, about politics and violence. The love, confidence, and support of my two sons, Gonzalo and Rodrigo Ferro, also kept me writing, even in those moments when I was not able to see the light at the end of the tunnel.

Finally, I thank my students and colleagues at Carleton University in Canada, Universidad Javeriana and Universidad Nacional in Colombia, and the David Rockefeller Center for Latin American Studies at Harvard University, where I concluded this book.

Introduction: Civilization as History

When one examines what the general function of the concept of civilization really is, and what common quality causes all these various human attitudes and activities to be described as civilized, one starts with a very simple discovery: this concept expresses the self-consciousness of the West. One could even say: the national consciousness.

NORBERT ELIAS, *THE CIVILIZING PROCESS* (1939)

Norbert Elias's history of civilization in Western Europe points to one of the major dilemmas for a scholar dedicated to the study of violence and civilization in a Third World country. Toward the end of the eighteenth century, when European nations believed that they had achieved civilization within their own societies, they saw themselves as "bearers of an existing or finished civilization to others, as standard-bearers of expanding civilization."[1] The process that made "civilization" an element of the national self-consciousness of the West was the same process that authorized violence in the name of civilization. The self-consciousness of civilization authorized bringing civilization to others by violent means. As he set off for Egypt in 1798, Napoleon announced, "Soldiers, you are undertaking a conquest with incalculable consequences for civilization."[2] Europe's passion for conquest in the name of civilization caused the percentage of the earth's land surface that it controlled to increase from 35 percent in 1800 to 84 percent in 1914.[3]

Civilization was enhanced not exclusively by military means, but by the ideological construct of what Mary Louise Pratt calls a "planetary consciousness," global-scale meanings whereby the planet was re-visioned from a unified European perspective.[4] Once in contact with local realities, these global meanings were transformed and adapted to national projects of domination by local elites. Subordinate groups also contested them. As a result of this struggle, old meanings appeared under a new form or new meanings emerged. Spanish America was no exception. The struggle between civilization and barbarism has haunted the imagination of Latin America from independence to the present.[5]

European mastering in the name of civilization had incalculable consequences for understanding violence in the Third World. Therefore, civilization and violence may not necessarily have been the antagonists scholars presume, with civilization taming violence and violence unmaking civilization. In the history of colonization, civilization and violence intertwined and supported each other. I argue that narratives of civilization and violence play key roles in the formation of racial, gender, and class identities. These narratives also provide pivotal logic both to the formation of the nation and to processes of capitalist development.

I contend that those representations that define hierarchies, those that exercise authority and define legitimacy, and those that support dominance and silence the dominated are integral to the production and reproduction of violence. The analysis of violence presented in this book challenges views in which violence is seen merely in its phenomenal, external manifestation, views of such things as war, open conflicts, or physical violence. Violence also exists in interpretation. Therefore, this perspective is as much about narratives, interpretations, and meanings as it is about violence in the restricted form in which it is usually understood.

VIOLENCE AND DISCOURSE

The analysis of the discourses on the Third World provides a basis for analyzing the way violence "is put into discourse" and the effects that this discourse has on relations of power and domination.[6] In virtually all schools of thought that examine the global political economy, a hallmark of the distinction between the functioning of capitalism in First and Third World countries is the coupling of capitalist development in the Third World with violence. "Bloody Taylor-ism," "savage capitalism," "praetorianism," the "development of underdevelopment," and "bureaucratic authoritarianism" are some of the conceptualizations of Third World capitalism that allude to its distinctive element of violence. In the view of some theoreticians, violence is an essential instrument by which capitalism is able to ex-pand to precapitalist, backward, or traditional Third World coun-tries, whereas for others it is an inevitable by-product of the arrival of capitalism.

Adam Smith's and Karl Marx's shared belief in the peaceful ex-pansion of capitalism was called into question once capitalism en-countered the Third World.[7] Theories of imperialism were about the need for violence if capitalism were to be expanded. For example, Rosa Luxemburg argued that capitalist expansion to other nations was a condition for accumulation, and violence was a necessary re-sult. In her view, the global drive to expand leads to a collision be-tween capital and precapitalist forms of society, resulting in violence, war, or revolution.[8] The articulation of modes of production, as for-mulated by P. P. Rey, also accepts that violence is a necessary condi-tion for transition to capitalism in those social formations where capitalism "arrives." There capitalism takes "the form of 'dirt and blood' rather than flowing peacefully from 'rigorous laws of eco-nomic processes.'"[9] Both theories of imperialism and those based on modes of production are good examples of approaches that see vio-lence as an inexorable law of development.[10] Different streams with-in a world system perspective also presume the inevitability of vio-lence, not as a condition for transition to capitalism, but as a means to reach socialism. Gunder Frank's "development of underdevelop-ment" theory, for example, argues that development of the core and underdevelopment of the periphery are caused by the same economic structure, which encompasses both. Violence is called for in order to destroy the pattern of underdevelopment in the periphery.[11] Theories of the peripheral state, similarly, see the exercise of violence as the permanent characteristic of such states. The state is given the respon-sibility of furthering capitalist expansion, and this accepted role must be accomplished through violence. For example, Mathias and Salama argue that in the Third World the establishment of relations of production is accomplished through violence.[12] Scholars who focus on the internal process of accumulation are also prone to a functionalist presumption of the inevitability of violence. In Guillermo O'Donnell's influential conception of "bureaucratic authoritarianism," the emergence of authoritarian regimes in the 1960s is attributed to difficulties in the process of "deepening" the productive structure.[13]

Notwithstanding the centrality of violence in histories of capitalist development, the linkage between capitalism and violence has remained obscure. Violence is often called upon to fill a theoretical gap and to explain the failure of capitalism to follow its own general laws of expansion. Violence has come to be seen as an inevitable characteristic of the Third World. Its normality has helped to obscure rather than to clarify the linkages between violence and the development of capitalism. Perhaps, however, the distinction between the trajectory of capitalism in the First and Third Worlds is not best understood in terms of the existence of violence on one side. Perhaps, as I argue in this book, the global political economy of capitalism is better understood if the formation of meanings that have accompanied the expansion of capitalism, particularly meanings about differences, identities, modern civilization, and violence, is factored in.

DIFFERENCE AND VIOLENCE

Beyond the previously mentioned epistemological flaws in the conceptualizations of violence and development, these modes of analysis are also characterized by fissures that touch the ontological domain, the way that reality is constructed. Violence has come to signify Third World reality as a result of the incapacity to deal with difference. Violence results from a tendency to interpret difference from a position of privilege, generally the position in which the interpreter is located. I borrow Bakhtin's concept of monologism to describe this tendency.[14] In a monological understanding, the identity of the Other is deduced from a single position, the interpreter's field of vision. The interpreter is located outside the represented world and, from the vantage point of his or her external position, provides a definitive meaning for this reality.

In the previously described literature on development, the "precapitalist mode of production," "traditional," or "underdeveloped" countries are seen through the experience, needs, or practices of European capitalism. Third World historical and cultural differences are conceived of as an imperfect Other whose meaning is revealed by way of an already constituted identity known as "modernity," the "capitalist mode of production," or "development." Ethnocentrism and androcentrism are monological interpretations as well. In them the experience of Western civilization is provided a special status as compared to those of women or non-Westerners. We can say, as Dorothy Smith did, that all those historical narratives and analyses "represent the world as it is for those who rule it, rather than as it is for those who are ruled."[15]

The monological construction of reality applies both to the way in which the Other is defined as different and to how its difference is discursively constructed in order to legitimize the exercise of violence and domination. Said's criticism of the way the Orient was constituted as well as dominated by Europe and Escobar's concept of developmentalization charge that the disciplines of development served to reproduce imperial pretensions.[16] As has been argued by Slater, modernization theory provided a discursive legitimization for practical interventions and penetrations that saw the Third World as an Other to be subordinated and assimilated.[17] Postcolonial critics, such as Gayatri Spivak, have argued that the representation of what is called the Third World is linked to imperialist interest.[18] Feminist scholars have disclosed the way violence against, and domination of, women are not independent from the hierarchical construction of gender differences. Therefore, the institutionalization of power relations in the state and the division of labor are secured by fixing differences between men and women or between native and foreign.[19]

Illustrative of the problems behind monological readings of the Third World is the modernization school, whose theoretical development is related to the Cold War years. Discussions of the role of violence among scholars of modernization clarify the way that a discourse about violence can structure the reality that is the object of intervention. The attainment of political order was identified by political scientist Samuel Huntington as a primary step on the path to development of Third World nations. Non-Western politics were represented as "potentially explosive," continuously threatened by instability.[20] Following this line of reasoning, violence came to be equated in common discourse with revolution or the disruption of order. The main strategy for attaining political order was defined as the containment of revolution. Chalmers Johnson provides a good example: "To make a revolution is to accept violence for the purpose of causing the system to change; more exactly, it is the purposive implementation of a strategy of violence in order to effect a change in social structures."[21] The identification of violence as the disruption of order, in concert with other components of the discourse about Third World violence, played a vital role in the First World control of the Third World.

Samuel Huntington proposes a paradigm for interpreting world politics around civilization in the post–Cold War world.[22] He sees the rivalry of the two superpowers during the Cold War being replaced by a clash of civilizations along a fault line that divides the world between a Western one and a non-Western many. Unlike the expansionist tendency to spread Western civilization in the name of universal values, Huntington sees the current danger as ensuing from a "revolt against the West." In his view, rivalries between civilizations are not new; on the contrary, "the civilizational 'us' and the extracivilizational 'them' is a constant in human history."[23] Following the realist tradition in international relations studies, he sees conflict as arising from an alteration in the balance of power in favor of non-Western civilizations. He also aligns himself with those responsible for security studies where difference is seen as translated into fear, distrust, and feelings of danger. Huntington's analysis is a reminder that a narrative of civilization remains prominent in twenty-first century world politics. Although civilization previously served to mask Imperial pretensions in the Third World, in contemporary world politics civilization is invoked to disguise what Huntington sees as the "de-Westernization" of the West. Analysis of previous representations of civilization and their effects may allow us to appreciate the dangers of an interpretation of history whereby others are used as instruments to reassert the West's desire for recognition and coherence. I argue that the real wellspring of violence is not the danger coming from the Other, but rather this internal desire for recognition and coherence; it lies within.

We can conclude that, methodologically speaking, it is equally misleading to elevate violence from a contingent situation to the level of an inexorable law and to reduce a general problem to contingency status. It is also fair to suggest that an analysis of violence in the Third World should incorporate the formation of meanings as well as what has been traditionally understood as "material" factors. An augmented political economy should also analyze the way civilization and violence have been "put into discourse."[24] In addition to these methodological problems, the focus has to be placed on deeper ontological questions posed by the conceptualizations of the Third World. Therefore, the relationship between violence, civilization, and capitalist development must not be considered as a question of exceptionality or anomaly; it must be related to the way in which narratives about the Third World are produced. As Said has argued, the Orient was appropriated by the West in complicity with representations about the Oriental.[25]

THE REGIME OF REPRESENTATION

In this book I suggest an abandonment of monological interpretations of both "political economy," in the restricted sense of the production and circulation of "things," and of violence, in the restricted sense of observable manifestations such as wars. I examine processes of production and exchange as explicitly embedded within broader systems of meanings. Political economy encompasses production, circulation, and exchange, not solely of things but also of meanings. As Shapiro maintains, the production and circulation of meanings are "repressed economies" that are immanent in cultural practices even though they, and the systems of power and authority to which they are related, remain concealed and fugitive.[26] As with the concept of political economy, the notion of violence is broadened here so as to formulate a relationship between violence and the production of narratives about the Third World and between these narratives and processes of capitalist development.

In order to capture the linkage between actors and their interpretations, in this book I propose a method of analysis centered on the notion of a regime of representation as an alternative mode of historical interpretation. Epistemologically, an interpretation of history in terms of regimes of representation supposes a dialogical process facilitating encounters and exchanges between local and external interpretations. Regimes of representation are spaces of desire and violence. They are also spaces of cessation of old orders of representation, and therefore spaces where violence has to be resolved. An emphasis on regimes of representation calls forth a different political economy that incorporates the formation of desires accompanying diverse forms of accumulation. I hypothesize that in the dissimilar coupling of narratives of capitalism and civilization in the First and Third Worlds resides one of the secrets of the contradictory nature of capitalism.

As a topological trope, the concept of a regime of representation allows us to present on stage local actors, their desires, and the context where events take place. In this sense, the past is re-presented in the present. A regime of representation is the space of encounter between the past, the present, and the future—the space of encounter between the self and the Other and between selves and the external world. Therefore, a regime of representation emerges from the interaction of a diversity of actors and from the interaction between these actors and their context. It supposes the presence of actors struggling for recognition.

As an epistemological device, the concept of a regime of representation is dialogical.[27] Dialogism brings different languages in contact with one another. Against the monolithical tendency to deduce one identity from a single position, the interpreter's position, dialogism allows the self and the Other to reveal their own interpretations. A dialogical epistemology opens space for the accommodation of heterogeneity, contradiction, and resistance.

A regime of representation is a space of presence and absence, and therefore a space of desire. Regimes of representation are structured around a lack. Representation requires the articulation of something new.[28] This is part of the dialogical character of representation. Because representation is an "unlimited horizon," the subject is not identified completely with this representation; there is always something missing.[29] A regime of representation allows for a re-visioning of history as an account of the multiple ways to gain ontological presence within an open horizon of possibilities.

The concept of a regime of representation has ontological, normative, and political dimensions. Ontologically, processes of identification and differentiation occur in representation. Both subjects and historical events are constituted in representation through the attribution of meanings. Gender, racial, and class identities do not correspond to fixed differences in sex, skin color, or positions in productive structures. Subjects and historical events are constituted in representation. To acknowledge that representation of the self and the Other has an effect on the constitution of subjectivity entails a recognition of the place of fantasy in the constitution of the self and the Other.[30]

A regime of representation is a space of intersubjective recognition and desire as long as the subject depends upon recognition by other subjects.[31] The self and the Other each seek to unify themselves by means of the response of the Other. However, the subject is not confident of this response. This is reflected in the importance of the question *"Che vuoi?"*—What do you want? What do others want from me?[32] Fantasy is used by the subject in an attempt to fill the gap between desire and the inability to translate this desire into a positive interpellation.[33]

In this book I use popular literature as well as constitutional and political debates to bring actors onto the stage and let them reveal their own play and their struggle to work for and against the rules governing their interpretation. The emphasis on regimes of representation invites us to relinquish the tendency to deduce reality from concepts such as laissez-faire capitalism, modernity, or development. This method discourages granting privileged status to the economic over the political, to external over internal factors, to the structural over the intentional, or to class over ethnicity or gender. On the contrary, an analysis centered on regimes of representation asks for an exchange among different voices and a disclosure of the efforts to give salience to one interpretation and to suppress alternative ones. Instead of asking why laissez-faire failed or how the political influenced the economic, the analysis of the regime of representation looks at the form that these concepts had once they entered the universe of local interpretations.

Therefore, violence is understood beyond the restricted sense of observable manifestation or phenomenal manifestation, as in Charles Tilly's definition of violence as "observable interaction in the course of which persons or objects are seized or physically damaged in spite of resistance."[34] When violence is restricted to "observable interactions," more subtle aspects of violence, such as the violence implicit in naming, interpreting, and silencing, are ignored. Violence is approached neither as a derivative nor as a purely manifested phenomenon. Recognizing violence in representation and elaborating the linkages between this dimension of violence and its manifestation and possible resolution (the capacity to end violence by means other than force) avoids the establishment of a direct relationship between a cause and violence as its external manifestation.

Therefore, different regimes of representation exhibit a diversity of manifestations and representations of violence. Intertwined with diverse forms of production are a diversity of meanings accompanying the formation of racial, gender, and class identities. Certain identities could be considered more civilized than others, and also more capable of striving toward the goal of progress. Like race and gender, regions are distinguished on the basis of the extent to which they are imagined as violent, their place on the scale of civilization, and their role in the international division of labor. In this book I trace the linkages between the formation of individual and regional identities, as well as capitalist development.

This is not, however, an approach to violence and political economy that allows no space for resistance. On the contrary, as the story of violence in Colombia reveals, the dominated are rarely content to be silenced. Wars are fought, constitutions rewritten, poetry criticized, and labor structured in the constant struggle for representation and voice. It is in this story of struggle and the desire to be recognized that we can best see the interplay of meanings and violence and that we can come to understand the failures of capitalism in the "uncivilized" world.

To illustrate this point, I have chosen the history of Colombia, often considered anomalous for its paradoxical marriage of a state of continuous violence with the hallmarks of democratic civilization. Rather than considering the Colombian case an exception, this analysis offers an opportunity to reflect upon the hybridity of civilization and violence in the postcolonial world. This analysis also offers the opportunity to reflect on the epistemological and ontological premises that have underpinned studies of violence in the Third World. Traditionally, the scholar's role has been to explain, control, or predict the sprouting of violence. Therefore, violence has been taken for granted. The manner in which narratives on violence are embedded in representations of the Third World is less often put into question.

VIOLENCE AS REPRESENTATION

In Colombia "violence" has been used to designate historical periods, name particular actors, and legitimate counterviolence strategies. Entire periods in the history of the country have been called *la(s) violencia(s)*. *La Violencia* is used to designate a period of eight years (1949–1957) in which it is estimated that 180,000 people (1.5 percent of the population) were killed, nearly 400,000 plots of land were abandoned, and 2,000,000 people were displaced from their land.

Like the civil wars of the nineteenth century, *La Violencia* took the form of a bipartisan conflict between Liberals and Conservatives, but it lacked the military structure of a civil war. Contemporary violence is referred to as *las violencias,* the plural expression emphasizing the diversity and changing forms of violence. It has been characterized by its "multivariety," having socioeconomic, political, cultural, regional, and lately, drug-related dimensions.[35] A government commission referred to the situation in the 1980s as a "superimposition" of violent acts whose forms included the organization of private armies; the private settlement of accounts; an increase in the number of so-called self-defense groups, incidents of terrorism, and death squads; and the organization of "cleanup" operations against juveniles, petty criminals, prostitutes, vagrants, and homosexuals. The commission distinguished at least ten different types of violence: criminal violence against the state and private citizens; guerrilla violence against the state and private citizens; state violence against guerrillas, social movements, and ethnic minorities; private, nonorganized violence; private, organized violence; and private, family violence.[36]

The Colombian discourse on violence subsumes a number of infrequently encountered, unrepresented, or invisible types of violence. An element of elusiveness regarding the authorship of violence appears both in popular discourse and in fiction. Violence has taken on an identity of its own, turning itself into an actor: *la violencia* is represented as an overwhelming subject capable of causing painful and devastating events. In popular expressions, for example, violence has been personalized in statements such as *"La violencia* killed my family. . . . *La violencia* took my land."[37] Fiction has also revealed the "subjective" aspect of this violence. Gabriel García Márquez, in his novel *The Evil Hour,* concludes the search for the author of violence with the attribution: "It's the whole town and it isn't anybody."[38]

These passages from the history of Colombia suggest a relationship between the circulation of narratives about violence and civilization, the process of identity formation and the development of capitalism. The discourse on civilization and violence has altered the identities of individual and collective actors by transforming their representation and the definition of the sites where violence occurs. The depiction of certain acts as violent, as well as the designation of the subjects and objects of violence, reveals a regularity: not only are certain acts and qualities repeatedly distinguished as more violent than others, but, at the same time, the identity of actors participating in the political arena has been subject to a process of transformation and stigmatization by traditional depictions of history. The boundaries between civilizers and barbarians and between legitimate and illegitimate violence are the product of a struggle over representation. Classifying an action as "violent" cannot be automatically taken as a replication of events: on the contrary, the term *violence* may be employed only to describe the resistance of the dominated groups, such as women, workers, blacks, or Indians. The violence inflicted upon them—the root of their resistance—may be designated using a term that obscures and dilutes its oppressiveness.

The unifying elements in situations of violence call into question subjectivist accounts where violence appears only as the sum of scattered events or as the result of a single individual who invented or precipitated them. The very diversity and number of events, actors, and places where violence is manifest is a problem for those who would explain violence as a symptom of contradictions or dysfunction in the social system in the form of either the opposition of feudalism and capitalism or of tradition and modernity. Therefore, the uneven distribution of violence across space, the discontinuity between the conditions under which violence becomes apparent and between its representation and its resolution, the diversity of the ways in which violence is experienced—all these elements call into question a purely phenomenal understanding of violence. To restrict our vision to only the most easily observable dimensions of violence, the tip of the iceberg, is to sanction its accidental, casual character and hence to place a shadow over the more permanent, subtle forms of violence.

CIVILIZATION AND VIOLENCE IN NINETEENTH-CENTURY COLOMBIA

The unfolding of events in nineteenth-century Colombia suggests that history is not always driven by the dictates of economics. For various reasons, economic referents do not provide the basis upon which to ground historical analysis. On the one hand, a mixture of religious, ethnic, educational, and regional objectives motivated the numerous civil wars that followed independence. These wars are better explained when the struggle for civilization is taken into account. The abolition of slavery and religious measures constituted the main motives for the war of 1851; in 1854 Conservatives and Liberals joined forces to depose a general who had overthrown the legitimate government to protest against the constitution approved in 1853; in 1861 Liberals went to war in the name of the federal constitution of 1853, alleging that their Conservative opponents had infringed on the principles of federalism; religious and educational reforms generated the war of 1876. Racial issues also contributed to conflict and to the ritual of war. The abolition of slavery was a main element of the war of 1851, and racial tensions were present in the war of 1861. These constitutional, religious, racial, and educational interests cannot be reduced to class conflicts or economic forces.

The strong divisions that existed between the two political parties, the Liberals and the Conservatives, make problematic an analysis that explains political cleavages by means of underlying economic conflicts of interest. A common tendency among students of Colombian politics has been to depict the profound enmity between Liberals and Conservatives as part of the subculture of the political system, where each party is presented as having its own vision, memories, and traditions. Conservatives are depicted as believers in Catholicism, order, authority, and a centrist model of state organization; Liberals are portrayed as defenders of federalism, as less concerned with the problem of order, and as opposing control by church or the state.[39] Once the existence of a fundamental division is established, this conflict becomes a main explanation for the unfolding of Colombian history. Historical causality is ascribed to political "hereditary hatred" as if it were a natural characteristic of Colombian democracy.[40] Social beliefs, cultural practices, and ideologies are kept alive by reinforcing certain practices and avoiding others. Part of the historian's task is to disclose these practices and the means by which beliefs emerge, are transformed, or disappear.

The Colombian case also challenges conventional understandings of the development of capitalism. The history of the development and geographical expansion of capitalism has been told as a story about how "things" are produced, exchanged, appropriated, and consumed. Concentrating on the world of things encouraged a mode of reasoning wherein commodities and labor were studied in abstraction apart from their social context. In Colombia, the period between 1849 and 1878 has traditionally been labeled as a time of "unchallenged hegemony" of the principles of economic liberalism.[41] The economic policies put in place after the mid–nineteenth century seem to confirm the consolidation of laissez-faire principles: the country strengthened its integration into the international market through agricultural exports. There was a broad consensus among the country's leaders about the desirability of freeing the market from governmental and institutional constraints.[42] Nevertheless, civil wars, regional conflicts, and the use of force in the appropriation of surplus labor paralleled the country's integration into the world market. The unfolding of these events suggests that capitalist development cannot be studied independently of the system of meanings and the local practices supporting them.

In this book I suggest that postindependence Colombia (1849–1878) was characterized by a desire for civilization on the part of an enlightened creole elite. In nineteenth-century Colombia, the "will to civilization" was related to the prospect of the disappearance of old systems of hierarchy and power and the emergence of new forms that would imitate the ideal of European civilization. The ideal of civilization materialized in the privileging of certain economic practices, in religious and educational ideals, in habits and dress practices, and in the dream of a *civilización mestiza* in which whiteness would remove the traces of a black and indigenous past. The desire for civilization did not impede violence. Rather, it went hand in hand with civil wars, the use of force in labor relations, and brutal sexual and racist practices. It is the relationship between civilization, violence, and capitalist development that I endeavor to explore in this book. An important part of this endeavor is the tracing of discursive practices: how differences are established, which contradictions are generated, and the effect of what is said and what is silenced.

The construction of identities (racial, gender, religious, regional, and class) was an important component of the civilizing project. The disappearance of slavery was accompanied by a fear of manumitted blacks who were considered a threat to the white population. This fear was reflected in the attempt to regulate the black population through the vagrancy law of 1843. Religious freedom went hand in hand with claims about the priesthood's potential threat to republican institutions, leading ultimately to the reexpulsion of the Jesuits from New Granada in 1850 by the Liberal president José Hilario López. Jesuit allegiance to an international order was seen as a threat to the construction of a national and liberal order. There was also a fear of the loss of self-identity on the part of the Colombian elite. This fear was reflected in the debate over the adequacy of British liberalism as the model with which to replace colonial institutions, which was defended by the Liberal "Generation of 1849."[43] In opposition, the Conservatives defended the view that the Spanish legacy of religion and morality represented the real pillars of civilization. A more widespread fear among the mid-nineteenth-century elite was *el miedo al pueblo* (the fear of the people).[44] The fear of mestizos, Indians, and blacks shaped the project to be pursued by the Colombian elite. These fears accompanied the establishment of the economic basis as well as the foundational myths of the nation, the state, and the constitutions.

The new political parties, Liberal and Conservative, concurred that the most important goal was to promote and defend civilization, which was seen as fundamental to material progress. Party leaders unanimously proclaimed that the source of civilization was the European continent and that the independence gained in 1810 was not the beginning of a new civilization. Civilizations could be neither invented nor improvised, they agreed. European civilization furnished the model to be emulated, whereas indigenous practices were considered vices to be eradicated.

The consensus reached by the Liberals and the Conservatives did not extend to *how* to forge civilization. The Liberals, who had gained the presidency in the elections of 1849, envisioned a civilization ensuing from "sovereign individuals." They were inspired by the image of the individual proclaimed at the heart of laissez-faire doctrines. The sovereign individual was embodied in the dream of a *civilización mestiza* in which the colors of Indians and blacks would fade in their encounter with white descendants. Economically, the Liberals endorsed the division of labor in which Europe produced manufactured goods and Colombia specialized in agricultural exports. Politically, the aim of civilization suggested to them the need for an enlightened democracy where both intelligence and wealth would guide the people's destiny. The Liberal Party, which was able to retain power during most of the three decades following the 1849 election, introduced reforms intended to make the individual sovereign: it abolished slavery, restricted corporal punishment, decreed press and religious freedoms and free trade, abolished state monopolies, and lessened the intervention of the state.

For the Conservatives, the best means by which to achieve civilization were, in order of importance, Christian morality, enlightenment, and wealth. The Conservatives centered the quest for civilization on the dissemination of "good" doctrines, which were those coinciding with the principles of Christian morality. Laissez-faire and the

emphasis on the sovereign individual became the epitome of pernicious doctrines whose dissemination threatened Christian civilization. The Conservatives were more prone than the Liberals to restrict
the circulation of printed material, to restrict legitimate religious practice to that of the Roman Catholic faith, and to advocate more government intervention. Like the Liberals, they tended to support freer
trade, although they strongly supported the central organization of
power.

Finally, the analysis of the period between 1849 and 1878 is also
crucial for an understanding of the relationship between violence
and the formation of the nation-state. At this time, the Colombians
were engaged in the task of imagining the nation: forty years had
elapsed since independence in 1810, and there was a feeling that
colonial institutions still remained in the form of economic, social,
cultural, and political institutions. Slavery and the maintenance of
the state monopoly over tobacco, legislation regarding Indian common lands *(resguardos)*, ecclesiastical *censos* (i.e., church liens or
mortgages), and *patronato* (special power ceded by the pope to the
Spanish Crown to orient Christian civilization) were some of the
colonial practices that survived independence. The Generation of
1849, whose leaders were born and raised in the republican era, defined their struggle as one between these colonial institutions and
democracy. Several reforms were instituted in an attempt to replace
the old colonial institutions with republican ones. Slavery and communal Indian lands *(resguardos)* were abolished in 1851 and 1850,
respectively; the state's monopoly on tobacco ended in 1850; freedom of the press and religious freedom formed part of the constitution of 1853; universal male suffrage, federalism, the abolition of the
fuero ecclesiastico and of compulsory tithe collections were also introduced in the constitution of 1853; and the correctional and judicial processes were reformed. The Liberal and Conservative Parties
were both consolidated during this period and became the catalysts
for launching or opposing programs of change.[45] The Liberal Party,
which remained in power most of the time from 1849 until 1884,
was identified as the motor of change, whereas the Conservatives appeared to be halting the processes of reform.

MAPPING THE BOOK

The encounter between civilization, desire, and violence in a regime
of representation provides the content of this book. In chapter 1,

"The Will to Civilization," I argue that the mimetic desire to attain civilization was the predominant regime of representation in Colombia during the period from 1849 to 1878. The will to civilization was a place of encounter between metropolitan and local representation. Different articulations between knowledge, gender, and race allowed creoles born in Colombia of Spanish parents to consolidate the power over mestizos, blacks, women, and Indians.

In chapter 2, "Civilization and Violence," I argue that uncovering and exposing the will to civilization allows us to understand the violence of representation where the premises of antagonisms, violence, and the numerous civil wars of the past century lie. This violence is related to the disappearance of a system of differences and identities inherited from the past. Political antagonism between the Liberals and the Conservatives was also embedded in the mimetic desire to civilize the Other. Furthermore, the suppression of alternative histories into a universal history overruled the creation of a common space in which recognition might supersede violence.

In chapter 3, "The Political Economy of Civilization," I trace the production, accumulation, and exchange of desires around the will to civilization. This makes it evident that in the nineteenth century the regime of representation based on the exchange of things, separate from the realm of individuals, had not yet been universalized. The political economy was organized around the process of production, exchange, and circulation of "civilizing" capital. Power was concentrated in those who possessed civilization's secrets: male creole literati. Words became valuable commodities that motivated struggles over their mode of circulation (free or restricted), their authorization (divine authority or legal foundation), and strategies to control and shape them.

In chapter 4, "The Subalterns' Voices," I retrieve the voices of the subaltern and therefore overcome the monologism frequently found in the attempt to understand the positions of the self and the Other. In it I argue that the regime of representation is built out of a process of exchange, in time and space, of several languages. Regimes of representation imply the presence of actors with different points of view, bringing different voices in contact with one another.

In chapter 5, "The Will to Civilization and Its Encounter with Laissez Faire," I focus on the contradictory encounter between the two regimes of representation. Contrary to the arguments that contend that laissez-faire held a hegemonic position, I argue that the will to civilization was the prevalent representation. The will to civilization presupposed ethnic, gender, and class hierarchies that collided with laissez-faire principles. The idea of a self-regulatory principle did not prosper.

In chapter 6, "Representation, Violence, and the Uneven Development of Capitalism," I inquire about the relationship between the two moments of violence: representation and manifestation. There I illustrate how diverse representations of violence coincided with diverse manifestations of violence in relations of production. A relationship is found between the use of force in the relations of production and a hierarchical conception of identities. By comparing several regions in terms of the degree to which labor was perceived as undifferentiated, in this chapter I establish a relation between identities and processes of accumulation in capitalist development.

1

The Will to Civilization

Neither Indians nor Europeans, but a race between the original natives and the Spanish usurpers; in short, being by birth Americans, and our rights those of Europe, we are obliged to dispute and combat for these rights against the original natives, and to persevere and maintain ourselves there in opposition to ours invaders, so we find ourselves placed in a most extraordinary and embarrassing dilemma.

SIMÓN BOLÍVAR, *CARTA DE JAMAICA* (1815)

The mid–nineteenth century in Colombia has been commonly characterized as a period of economic liberalism. In this period Colombia opened up to external markets and adopted laissez-faire principles.[1] There is a strong tendency among historians of the nineteenth century to take for granted that the incorporation of the country into the world economy was the predominant desire on the part of the local elite.[2] The desire to open the country to external markets as an explanatory mechanism does not acknowledge the presence of parallel or substitute desires that may have had a greater effect on the relations of the mid-nineteenth-century elite with the external world and with their fellow countrymen. To see history as open to the dictates of other forces, not just economic ones, allows us to establish which social practices mattered most, which regimes of representation were unifying these practices, and who was the Other that was opposed to the accomplishment of the desires of the country's elite. This is a crucial task in studying the period under scrutiny, since the elite fought

1

not, as it was initially thought, over issues of free trade, but rather over religious, educational, and moral issues. The question to be asked is "Why was this group ready to go to war over education, the most appropriate university text, freedom of the press, or religion in the school system?" To answer these questions, we must recall the mimetic nature of desire implicit in the struggle for recognition.[3] An analysis based on the regime of representation allows us to explore the encounter with Others, which incited the emergence of a civilizing desire, and the strategies for reaching the desired object.

A closer look at the past reveals that what was at stake and what divided Liberals and Conservatives was the desire for "civilization." The will to civilization was the dominant regime of representation from 1849 until the crisis in 1878 and also the unifying force in whose name the main political reforms were made. The will to civilization was the desire for an orderly European civilization and paralleled the struggle for accumulation of capital. The former entailed as much violence as the latter.

CIVILIZATION AND COLOMBIA'S HISTORIOGRAPHY

The desire for civilization has not been totally absent from interpretations of the history of Colombia. However, historians have overlooked the force of the will to civilization in the period of consolidation of political institutions. This lack of consideration reflects the monological character of these interpretations that privilege economic motives as the motor of history. Or, when the force of noneconomic drives is recognized, scholars have paid attention only to the elite's ideals, which has prevented them from capturing the ambivalent, and therefore contradictory, desires of those mastering the world. That has been the case in the best analyses of Colombian history: Marco Palacios's *El Café en Colombia, 1850–1970*[4] and Frank Safford's *The Ideal of the Practical: Colombia's Struggle to Form a Technical Elite.*[5]

As Palacios has noticed, the adoption of economic liberalism during the second half of the nineteenth century was related to the desire to overcome Colombia's "barbarian" stage and to achieve "civilization."[6] Palacios depicts *hacendados* as Eurocentric individuals whose desire was "to impose civilization in the hollows of the Andes through growing coffee."[7] *Hacendados* were "men without rural ties and traditions, [whose] aspirations tended towards city life and civilization."[8]

Although Palacios stumbled onto the force of the desire for "civilization" relative to the actions of the nineteenth-century elite, he did not fully recognize its significance—nor could he, given his theoretical preoccupation. Due to a restricted view of political economy, he equated the desire for civilization with economic motives. In his first chapter of *El Café en Colombia,* entitled "The Road towards Civilization," he states that in the nineteenth century "no other word surpassed in circulation the word *civilization.*" Yet he interpreted the desire represented by this word solely from an economic perspective and, as a consequence, saw the desire for civilization in a wholly economic context. In his view, the word *civilization* was "the nineteenth-century equivalent of our expression *economic development.*" To equate the will to civilization with economic development is to obscure the richness of the debate and the struggles surrounding the desire for civilization.

Frank Safford's analysis focuses on the struggle of the nineteenth-century elite to pursue the "ideal of the practical" or the ideal of technical progress, in addition to the changes that were put into practice to encourage discipline and improvement of work habits. Liberal reformers changed the previous methods for "coercion of the lower classes in favor of market discipline."[9] These changes included the provision of support for technical training, the development of teachers' training and primary schools, and even the establishment of a military school to form "scientific officers."

Safford reviews the central role of the ideal of progress in explaining divisions between Liberal and Conservative elites. From early in the nineteenth century, members of the Colombian elite were concerned about how to bring about the "moral development" of the population, an aim that included fostering the discipline of labor.[10] Furthermore, a main divisive issue was the orientation of university instruction toward upper-class students. On one side were those who wanted to channel students away from the study of the law, medicine, and literature and to increase scientific education. On the other side were those who wanted to channel students into the study of the law and the humanities. Also at stake was a struggle over whether control of education would rest with the main provinces, such as Bogotá and Popayán, or with the small cities. The ideal of a scientific and centralized system of education gained support during the period from 1821 to 1845 but declined in the years following the Liberal triumph of 1849. The Liberals sought to destroy the centralist, elitist, and repressive character of the previous system.[11] As Safford points out, Liberal reforms provoked violent conflict and civil wars. The Liberals encouraged turbulence among certain elements of the lower classes, and their reforms irritated their Conservative opponents to the extent that the army attempted rebellion in 1851 and instigated several wars between 1859 and 1863.

The major flaw in Safford's analysis is his reliance on the universal and nonviolent nature of the elite's desire for progress. Safford's sympathy for the elite's adoption of the North American quest for progress does not allow him to uncover the relationship between desire and violence. In his view, conflict resulted because the passion for political life was stronger than the commitment to progress. As he concludes with reference to the nineteenth-century elite, "What one hand built up with enlightened policy, the other devastated with the sword or undermined with political machinations."[12] This assertion assumes that the quest for progress or civilization did not involve violence, and it does not recognize that the quest for civilization was inextricably linked to the passionate character of political life. The universalism of Western ideals is presumed rather than scrutinized. This explains Safford's difficulty in dealing with conflict within the elite and between the elite and subalterns.

Attempting to understand the nineteenth-century quest for progress without taking into consideration its repressive practices has also served to perpetuate the myth in Colombian history that liberalism's philosophical base for reform has been inspired by a utopian vision. In this view the belief in the emancipative character of the law and the primacy of legislation over coercive forms of domination led to the desire to open the country to the modern, enlightened world. If any vices are attributed to the liberal program, they relate to its excessively "spiritual" or utopian character.[13] Sanctioning the consideration of material or economic forces for analysis forecloses consideration of the force of the will to civilization in the period of consolidation of political institutions and laissez-faire capitalism. The reading of history based on the desire to accumulate wealth has led to inadequate consideration of the importance of the struggle for civilization, in whose name civil wars were fought and political conflict occurred.

THE WILL TO CIVILIZATION AS A SPACE OF DESIRE

The second half of the nineteenth century was a decisive period in Colombian history. Forty years had passed since the country had achieved independence in 1810. Those who had struggled for independence and formed part of the first generation born in the republic shared a feeling of the persistence of a colonial past that needed to be superseded and an image of a future to be constructed. The years to come would be years of reform endorsed to override the past or to precipitate the future. In the evocation of past and future was condensed images of "who we were" and "who we will be," power images of who should be responsible for the rite of passage from the past to the future, how it should be done, and spatial images of the sites where the transformation should take place.

Underlying these images was a strong will on the part of the group that emerged with power in the postcolonial period. The mimetic desire to be European became an organizing principle, the nodal point, and the basis for the republic.[14] This will was stronger than the will to accumulate wealth, because it was considered a prerequisite to the latter. To defend the cause of civilization, the recently born Conservative Party created a newspaper named *La Civilización*. The aim was clear: "With the publication of this paper our purpose is to promote and defend civilization in Nueva Granada and Spanish America."[15] The universal character of civilization was clearly stated: "We call civilization the means accumulated by humanity in the search for perfection and happiness."[16] The idea of the universal character of civilization concurs with the belief held in Europe until the eighteenth century.[17] Between the eighteenth century and the twentieth there was a shift in priority from humanist ideals applicable to people in general, to nationalist ideals. The idea that civilization determined the hierarchy of nations inspired the desire for civilization among mid-nineteenth-century Colombian elites:

> We call a society civilized if it has an advantage over another in knowledge, morality and wealth. From the horde of savage nomads, without laws, authority, principles, almost without distinction from animals, to those nations admired by all because of their enlightened and material development, there is a vast hierarchy of nations, each

one naming, as civilized, those with a better condition and, as barbarian, those behind.[18]

The encounter with a hierarchical concept of civilization was problematic for nineteenth-century elites. At the imaginary level the elites identified with the European model as the one they wanted to imitate. But at the symbolic level they rejected the place from which Europeans observed them.[19] Being named "barbarians" placed them in an "embarrasing" position; it appeared as if they were not worthy of esteem. Furthermore, the coupling of civilization and nationality was problematic as long as it collided with the elite's desire to govern the nation. The ambivalent character of civilization, as explained in the following section, arises from the desire for recognition coupled with the refusal to be governed in the name of civilization. The method to be followed is to concentrate on the contradictory encounters between different forms of representation: What were the predominant global and local systems of meaning? How did global meanings encounter local systems of representation, and how were they received within them? How did this encounter result in the will to civilization? How did it affect distinctions among people and hierarchies? Whose identities were excluded from this regime of representation? How was violence exercised?

THE ENCOUNTER BETWEEN METROPOLITAN AND LOCAL REPRESENTATIONS

To examine the process out of which the will to civilization emerges I analyze the formation of what Mary Louise Pratt calls "metropolitan representations," which are global-scale meanings built around the European construct of a unifying global or "planetary" consciousness.[20] The spread of a universal, Eurocentric civilization formed part of this metropolitan representation. The will to civilization resulted from the encounter between metropolitan representations and universalistic and imperial pretensions and from particular meanings that, in an ambivalent manner, opposed and eventually succumbed to these imperial pretensions.

In Mary Louise Pratt's history of "imperial meaning-making" she notes that travelers and explorers played an important part in imperial making.[21] She distinguishes two main narratives accompanying European expansion: the narrative of natural history, which was present in travel writing in the second half of the eighteenth century, and the narrative of a capitalist vanguard that arrived in Latin America after independence, in the mid–nineteenth century. Through the narrative of natural history, the European's global presence and authority were naturalized. The encounter with nature, as an ideological construct, allowed the appropriation of the planet and then its redeployment from a unified, European perspective. The landscape was depicted as "uninhabited, unpossessed, unhistoricized, unoccupied even by the travelers themselves."[22] This picture served to legitimize the European geopolitical expansion and at the same time conferred an aura of conspicuous innocence.

According to Pratt, in traveling to South America, Alexander von Humboldt sought to reinvent popular imagining of America and, through America, of the planet itself. Humboldt's thirty-volume *Travel to the Equinoctial Regions of the New Continent in 1799, 1800, 1801, 1802, 1803 and 1804* included sixteen volumes of botany and plant geography, two of zoology, two of astronomical and barometric measurements, seven of geographical and geopolitical descriptions, and three of travel narratives. America was represented as "a primal world of nature, an unclaimed and timeless space occupied by plants and creatures (some of them human), but not organized by societies and economies; a world whose only history was the one about to begin."[23]

The mid-nineteenth-century Colombian elite encountered the "natural history" vision. Metropolitan and local visions were set against each other in a contradictory and ambivalent manner. Elites generally attempted to resist the imperial vision; however, most of the time they remained imprisoned by the ideal of a European civilization that condemned them to a weak, fragmentary hegemony. The writing of José María Samper provides a clear example of the encounter of imperial and postindependence elite visions. Samper's major political treatise, *Ensayo sobre las Revoluciones Políticas i la Condición Social de las Repúblicas Colombianas (Hispanoamericanas),* written in 1861, clearly targets the European audience with the aim of correcting the European natural history vision of America.[24] The essay's introductory heading is "Mistaken European Ideas about Colombia." The European, according to Samper, "had more interest in the study of our volcanoes than our societies; they know our insects better than our literature, our alligators better than the actions of our statesmen.

They have more knowledge of quinine and leather processing in Buenos Aires, than knowledge of our infant democracy."[25] His argument was based on the belief that the feeling of hostility and disdain on the part of the European resulted from this ignorance: "They have disdained us, by dispensing with the obligation of understanding us."[26] Samper's goal was to fill with human presence the empty scenery captured by the European's eye.

Postindependence travelers to Spanish America in the nineteenth century, Pratt's capitalist vanguard, also reinvented the Americas as backward and neglected. The reason, Pratt argues, was to encode "its non-capitalist landscapes and societies as manifestly in need of the rationalized exploitation the Europeans bring."[27] The goal was to transform America into an industrial zone and its population into wage laborers and consumers of metropolitan-produced goods.

Mid-nineteenth-century Colombian elites engaged in a debate about this metropolitan understanding of Third Word development. The European vision, in the eyes of the Colombian elite, menaced something more than their self-image; it struck directly at the elite's right to govern the recently liberated country. To accept the vision of the European capitalist vanguard would mean to surrender to governance by the civilized nations. This dilemma appears clearly in the rejection by Miguel Samper,[28] José María's brother, of the interpretations of the Latin American region by the British sociologist Benjamin Kidd in his book *Social Evolution*. According to Samper's own summary, Kidd acknowledged the richness in natural resources of the Central and South American continent, but pointed to the danger of their possession by an inferior race. Samper quotes Kidd's vision: "[These countries] have exhibited a general absence of the public and private feeling characteristic of the countries with highest social development. . . . The lack of the most elementary qualities of social efficiency on the part of the races would lead to the waste of natural resources of one of the wealthiest regions on earth. We can acknowledge the right of property, but not the right to impede [our] use of the vast amount of resources under their custody."[29] To accept Kidd's premise about a lack defined as a "general absence of the public and private feelings characteristic of the countries with highest social development" would mean to surrender to governance by Europe, making the struggle for emancipation in 1810 superfluous.

Nevertheless, creoles did not call into question the desire for civilization. They took on the task of completing the European project. They desired civilization because they wanted to be recognized by Europeans. The regime of representation in place after independence was, and still is, overwhelmed by the European narrative at whose center was the desire for civilization.

THE CREOLE'S "EMBARRASSING DILEMMA"

The postindependence period entailed this assessment of the past and the present in relation to a desired future based on the European model of civilization. It also entailed an assessment of the images of the self in relation to the civilized European and the barbarian Other. Civilization appeared in a contradictory way: regarding the past, the War of Independence had emancipated the country from a colonial regime whose domination for over three hundred years had been exercised in the name of civilization. Regarding the future, the struggle around civilization would involve a process of encounter with a "civilized" European culture. This would give rise to what Bolívar called "a most extraordinary and embarrassing dilemma," in the passage quoted at the beginning of the chapter.

The elite's discourse, using Homi Bhabha's terminology, "was uttered between the lines and as such both against the rules and within them."[30] The narrative of Sergio Arboleda illustrates the "between-the-lines discourse" chosen by the Colombian elite. Arboleda disassociated himself from the European discourse about America, observing that Europeans "blinded by the light of civilization surrounding them . . . declare in a peremptory manner 'that the barbarian race, a mix of all races, living in America, lack the inability (sic) for productive occupations and cannot be a free and well-governed nation.'"[31] Arboleda replied with an ambivalent discourse, distancing himself from the authority of the European vision of America while at the same time endorsing the use of this authority by the creole elite. His discourse on racial mix accomplished both:

> If those who in an unjust manner have asserted our lack of ability for productive occupations had observed the character of our conflicts, they would discover that in this mixed race there are not only fervid passions, but also heroic virtues and both evil and good feelings. On the one hand, we see the enthusiasm that results from a rich imagination. On the other, the faith and sacrifice of men struggling to improve the political and social conditions of their fatherland, countering the

savage spirit . . . the ignorance of the masses, the milliard obstacles of nature in America, and last, the utopia of European demagogues . . . and the mistaken policy of Western imperialism, which worsens the already difficult situation of these countries with their hostile interventions.[32]

The nineteenth-century elite's thought found the European coupling of civilization and race problematic. The "embarrassing dilemma" was solved not by entirely rejecting the European vision, but by the creation of a sense of equality and a distancing from Europeans, as is reflected in the double mission of "countering the savage spirit" and "the ignorance of the masses" and, at the same time, struggling against "Western imperialism." The nature of creoles, being of European parents but born in America, suited well both objectives. The crucial role was played not by race alone, but by the "knowledge" of the European civilization to which creoles were entitled by their European origins. Male creole literati enjoyed the privileged position of dictating the how, who, and what of civilization. Their power stemmed from being the "owners" of civilization in what they depicted as a barbarian society. However, meanings related to race, gender, knowledge, and civilization were not fixed. They were fluid constructs that were articulated and mobilized in different manners. What it meant to be an Indian, a woman, or a creole varied from one historical period to another. As the next section demonstrates, identities as well as the roles of knowledge and civilization were articulated differently in the preindependence, independence, and postindependence periods.

KNOWLEDGE, RACE, GENDER, AND CIVILIZATION

Several factors explain the preeminence of knowledge as one of the foundations for the regime of representation in Colombia in the second half of the nineteenth century. The first factor to be considered is the presence of institutions of higher education as early as the seventeenth century and the place of education in the colonial period. In 1602 the Jesuits founded in Bogotá the Colegio Mayor de San Bartolomé, which, together with the Colegio de Santo Tomás, became a university in 1639. In the same year the Jesuits created the Universidad Javeriana, which was closed in 1767 when the Jesuits were expelled from the country. In 1810, the year of independence, there were three universities, five high schools or *colegios,* and five seminaries. There were two *colegios* in Bogotá, two in Quito, and one in Caracas. Cuenca, Panamá, Cartagena, Santa Marta, Popayán, and Mérida all had *colegios-seminarios*. Bogotá, Quito, and Caracas had universities.[33] Education was almost entirely in religious hands. Primary schools, attached to parishes and convents, were private and restricted to the elite: only 1 percent of the school-age population attended elementary school. The masses, especially Indians, blacks, and mulattos, were illiterate. Many observers estimate an illiteracy rate of 90 percent.[34]

The creoles' pride in their equality of knowledge with the Europeans, coupled with the discrimination they experienced from them, fostered a desire for emancipation. The resulting dilemma is what Anderson calls the creole's "fatality of trans-Atlantic birth." For the creole "the accident of birth in the Americas consigned him to subordination—even though in terms of language, religion, ancestry, or manners he was largely indistinguishable from the Spanish-born Spaniard."[35] Science and education played an active role in fueling the desire for emancipation by subverting the colonial order based on place of origin.

As has been illustrated by McFarlane, during the preindependence period Spaniards introduced notions of enlightenment and science as a support for Spanish authority.[36] The Botanic Expedition (1783) conducted by scientist José Celestino Mutis and the educational reform led by Moreno y Escandón (1774) were two important attempts to introduce enlightened ideals among the creole elite. The effect, however, was contrary to the colonists' intentions. Enlightened notions of the primacy of knowledge over social practices, such as inherited class position, came to play an important role in the subversion of the hierarchical system that had long structured Spanish society. The creole's strategic reversal of the enlightenment discourse on knowledge illustrates well the ambivalent effect it had on colonial discourse by subverting colonialist discourse in favor of emancipation.[37]

Creoles and Spaniards were divided over intellectual issues, and this division took on political connotations. One of the issues at stake was the creole's plea for the advancement of the sciences instead of the colonial advocacy of scholasticism. The value attributed to science by young students from San Bartolomé is seen in a letter sent to the Spanish viceroy in the preindependence year of 1791. The students asked for approval for the hiring of a "professor to teach elements of physics and mathematics, botanics and natural history, in one word, a professor from whom we can learn about the land where we live and the wealth surrounding us."[38] They even opted for paying the professor by giving up bread supplied for the school. The reason was obvious to them: "We prefer to commit ourselves to the rigor of hunger and to give primacy to the nourishment of our souls over that of our body.[39]

The esteem given to knowledge came to replace the Spanish notion of nobility based on birth. Creoles organized scientific societies such as the Economic Societies of Friends of the Country (Sociedades Económicas de Amigos del País), and they created the creole newspaper the *Papel Periódico de Santafé* aimed at fostering new ideas.[40] These societies not only promoted the economic and social transformation of the country, but also legitimized the view that knowledge was more important than birthplace. The newspaper set the groundwork for the establishment of an "imagined linkage" among readers across the territory. The criticism of Spaniard domination and the emergence of the nation were made possible, as suggested by Benedict Anderson, through the creation of a printing community.[41]

During the preindependence period, this printing community did not embrace all equally. It was divided into the enlightened and the wretched masses (*miserable multitud*). The newspaper's public was the "enlightened minority" in charge of the direction of the *muchedumbre*. The newspaper stated its mission as follows:

> This minority of individuals, endowed by nature of enlightenment differently from the wretched masses, has a right to a privileged position with respect to the remaining men, because only their judgment and thoughtfulness have the capacity to recommend human proceeding. . . . Therefore we must write for them, and we must work according to them, without fear of contradictions with the others.[42]

Before Colombia won its independence, creoles also put forward proposals for the elimination of racial differences as part of their attempt to build an imagined community. Contrary to the goal, envisioned in other Latin American countries, of preserving racial purity through "selected" European immigration, they envisioned a strategy centered on racial amalgamation. Perhaps this was because in the eighteenth century (1778) mestizos were almost half of the total population (46 percent), with the rest classified as white (26 percent), Indian (20 percent), and black (8 percent).[43]

The creoles' desire relative to the Others of their society in the pre-independence period mixed economic and sexual exchange. Furthermore, sexuality was seen as the means by which creoles could appropriate the territory. Racial amalgamation rather than purity would well accomplish this goal. The idea of interracial sexual relations was put forward by Pedro Fermín de Vargas around 1790: "It would be very desirable for the Indians to be extinguished, fusing them with the white, declaring them free of tribute and other fiscal burdens peculiar to them, and giving them property rights to their land. Greed for their property will lead many whites and mestizos to marry Indian women."[44] Fermín de Vargas openly contradicted the Spanish law put in place in 1776, by which parents had the right to veto the marriage of their sons or daughters because of racial differences, even if the contracting parties were more than twenty-five years old.[45]

The differences in the preindependence period between the enlightened creole minority and the "wretched masses" broke down during the battle for independence and were revived again in the post-independence period. Since the struggle for independence required the mobilization of popular support, the distinction between enlightened creoles and the "stupid" masses was masked. The independence movement favored an identity between creoles and Indians who were opposing a common European enemy.[46] Before 1810 Indians were referred to as primitive barbarians. During the independence period the discourse centered on Spanish oppression and the Indian was used as a symbol of identity and solidarity against Spaniards. The creole Francisco José de Caldas identified himself with the Indian as a victim of European oppression: "The abject condition of Indians is the result of the Spanish government, which has kept us ignorant (embrutecidos) during three centuries."[47] The use of "us" to refer to the identity of Indians and creoles was common at that time, as in the following passage written by the creole Ignacio de Herrera: "From the moment of Conquest they denigrated us, and in the Spanish Court they convened a meeting to decide if we were worthy to receive baptism. . . . Three centuries have proved the opposite. . . . Americans have no less talent than any other nation and they have capacity to receive any sacrament."[48]

The struggle for independence also disarticulated gender representations of power, as in the case of the mother as the symbol of the Crown's relationship with the colonies. Spain, known as *la madre patria* (the mother country) during the colonial period, was called a "stepmother" by independentists such as Antonio Nariño, who saw Spain in the same way cruel mothers "who treated their offspring like strangers and their children like slaves."[49] The true mother became the place of one's birth, the American territory. The feeling of creoles' brotherhood with Indians was also made possible by this change in representation. According to Nariño, the creoles' feeling of brotherhood with Indians was stronger than their feeling of brotherhood with Europeans because their "mother was not Europe, who despised them, but America, their birthplace."[50]

The mobilization of women in the struggle for independence also found problematic the stereotype of women's domestic role. As documented by Evelyn Cherpak, women's roles in the independence movement included activities such as sponsoring meetings to discuss and plan revolutionary activities, participating in public demonstrations, and serving as combatants on the battleground.[51] The fantasy of the *Amazona* was incorporated into the revolutionary image. In a speech to the revolutionary army, Simón Bolívar, founder and president of Gran Colombia, gave voice in an ambiguous masculine way to the representation of women warriors:

> Even the fair sex *(bello sexo),* mankind's delight, our Amazons, fought against tyranny, with divine bravery, although without success. Spanish monsters, surpassing the cowardice of their nation, have directed their weapons against the candid and feminine breasts of our beautiful women, spreading their blood, killing some of them, imprisoning others, because they were helping the cause of freedom for our beloved country.[52]

This praising of Indians and women materialized into the symbol of a female Amazonian Indian that was used on the coins, shields, and flags of the newborn republic.[53] The 1812 coin of the province of Cartagena depicts a seminaked female warrior Indian with a feather crown. In 1813, all coins replaced the figure of the Spaniard king with the face of an Indian woman accompanied by the motto *Libertad Americana.* Both the Venezuelan shield and the Colombian band bore representations of a female Indian sitting on an alligator.

Once independence was achieved, representations concentrated on the internal relations with the subaltern. The years from 1819 to 1926 were crucial for the consolidation of the independent republic. A congress met in Angostura to proclaim the union of New Granada (today's Colombia) and Venezuela under the name of the Republic of

Colombia. Simón Bolívar was made president of what has become known as Gran Colombia. By then, the patriarchal and autocratic character of Bolívar had replaced national representation by Indian women. The painting of Bolívar by Pedro José Figueroa is illustrative (see figure 1). Entitled *Simón Bolívar, Libertador y Padre de la Patria,* the picture portrays Bolívar as history's author and the new republic

Figure 1. Simón Bolívar con la América India *(Simón Bolívar with Indian America), by Pedro José Figueroa (ca. 1770–1838), 1819. The painting is also known by the title* Simón Bolívar, Libertador y Padre de la Patria *(Simón Bolívar, liberator and father of the country). Registry number 03-076, 1.25 × 0.95 meters, oil on cloth. Courtesy of Colección Quinta de Bolívar Bogotá, Colombia.*

as his daughter. Although America is still represented as an Indian, she has lost her combative appearance. She is represented as a delicate girl dressed in European clothes (but with an Indian headdress) and protected by the patriarchal figure of Bolívar.[54]

At the time of consolidation of the emergent republic, identities were disarticulated again. On the one hand, the process of unification of the republic sought a sense of shared identity for its fellow citizens. But on the other hand, basing hegemony on the civilizing desire invited a distancing between the creole elite and the "ignorant masses." Jesús Martín has characterized this double process of assertion and denial as "abstract inclusiveness and concrete exclusion."[55] Therefore, racial differences were seen as an obstacle and as a tool to legitimize the elite position of dominance. This explains why in 1821 the Congress of Cúcuta asserted civil equality for Indians, which meant that Indians could not be held for unpaid personal service and that they were capable of holding public office.[56] The congress also abolished Indian tribute and Indian *resguardos* and announced that they should no longer be named *indios,* but rather *indígenas.*

The process of "concrete exclusion" is evidenced in the resistance of *resguardo* members to this congressional law. In their view, as a result of the law they were losing communal land to whites. The Indians of Guane questioned the principle of "abstract equality" behind the legislation: in their view, taking the land without compensation was "contrary to our constitution and to the right of equality that it concedes to the Indigenes."[57] This passage well illustrates the contradictory meaning of equality mobilized by creoles and Indians. Although for the former equality meant a sense of sameness that did not acknowledge difference, for Indians equality without the recognition of difference was not what independence was about.

The sense of distancing is also reflected in the attempts to reverse the policy granting the status of citizenship to Indians, to reestablish the practice of Indian tribute, and even to implant a modified, republican version of *corregidor* control of indigenous labor. The reasons were related to a supposed incapacity on the part of the Indians to fulfill their duties, plus a tendency toward idleness and drunkenness. The creoles also accused the Indians of refusing to work for the *hacendados,* causing considerable losses to the latter as well as to the state.[58]

The view of the elite in charge of devising the basis of the new nation was extended in a different relationship with blacks. The internal antagonism was projected into the figure of the black. In the discussion of the abolition of slavery in the 1820s, fear was used as the main argument by the groups opposing abolition: the supposed criminal nature of blacks became a central issue, and often blacks were accused of crimes such as assault, abortion, infanticide, and suicide.[59] In 1843 the proximity of liberation increased the fear of the manumitted, as is shown in the following passage written by the governor of Buenaventura:

> We must seriously consider the growing number of blacks that have left the power of their master and become members of society, bringing with them the seed of all kind of vices, indolence, and African wildness. Very soon there will be almost no trace of the white race; instead of the virtues proper to the Republic we will observe barbarism, the habits of slavery or ignorance, and the savagery of the black race . . . a race that must be separated from us. We must ask Congress for a law demanding that all emancipated blacks, without distinguishing the means through which they reached freedom, be directed to begin new populations in the uninhabited land dividing Colombia from Venezuela or in Central America.[60]

The Congress of Cúcuta approved a manumission law tainted by these racist views whereby blacks were to be kept under the tutelage of whites. Changes in legislation did not favor women, either. Therefore the law for the abolition of slavery signed in 1821 declared only "freedom of wombs" *(libertad de vientres)*. The law made the freedom of children born of slaves obligatory, even though it established that these children must work for the same proprietors as their mothers until they reached eighteen years of age.[61] If the change had any effect on violence against women, it was the lessening of the corporal punishment that had resulted from declaring a female slave's womb to be the property of her owner. Therefore, on President General Mosquera's own estate, slaves were punished with twenty-five lashes for disciplinary faults, but "a pregnant women could only be punished using the stock for punishment."[62]

It was no coincidence that a law of October 6, 1821, replaced the image of the Indian female on coins and the Colombian shield with a female face with Roman headdress as a symbol of freedom. The word *Libertad* was engraved in a band on the female's head.[63] This illustrates the ambivalence of the creole elite's discourse after independence: once the menace of Spanish domination eroded, creoles sought to identify more openly with the European civilization. The "embarrassing dilemma" began to be solved in favor of the creole's identity.

CONCLUSION

Creole men concentrated the desire for civilization around them, granting themselves a privileged place in the building of the emergent nation. Different articulations between civilization, gender, and race allowed creoles born in Nueva Granada of Spanish parents to consolidate the power over mestizos, blacks, women, and Indians. A system of hierarchical differences based on sex and the color of one's skin was established. The civilizing process was depicted as a process of achieving whiteness, a process whose highest stage was the fusion of races, ending racial heterogeneity. What had been seen in the colonial past as a hierarchical structure of colonizer and colonized appeared in the postcolonial period as a racial hierarchy. Race and gender became historical explanations and *mestizaje* its culmination. This mixture, however, was posed not in an egalitarian order, but rather in a hierarchical order, following a "natural" path:

> It could be said that in the same way that mountains are from their base up to the summit natural thermometers, society forms a living stratification, whose layers are the diverse races or castes, resulting from complex mixtures, all located in the most convenient environment according to the convenience of blood, traditions, industry, and energy of each one.[64]

The will to civilization as a place of encounter between the colonial past and the imagined future, as a passage between barbarism and civilization, was a place of violent encounter. There was a violence of representation in acts of suppression of history: native, local, and female histories did not find a place in the civilizing project. There was also violence in the establishment of differential hierarchies and strategies of civilization imprinted on the bodies of creoles, mulattos, *zambos,* blacks, Indians, men, and women.

2

Civilization and Violence

The relativity of human desire in relation to the desire of the other is what we recognize in every reaction of rivalry, of competition, and even in the entire development of civilization.
JACQUES LACAN, *THE SEMINARS OF JACQUES LACAN* (1988)

A significant paradox of Colombian history is the long history of violence and conflict that had been inserted into the democratic process. In the nineteenth century, after the War of Independence in 1810 there were nine civil wars and nearly fifty regional or local conflicts, most frequently in the period from 1863 to 1865. The questions frequently asked are "Why were the most notable proponents of civilization and progress also disruptive politicians?" and "Why was conflict mainly among the Liberal and Conservative elite?" Furthermore, the nineteenth-century history of civilization and violence is to a certain extent writing the history of the present. This is so, first, because there are some elements of continuity between violence in the nineteenth century and that in the twentieth century, such as partisan rivalry. As Oquist remarked during *la violencia* (1949–57), "Party identification became a question of life or death. One's fate was often decided by a one-word answer to the question of which party one belonged to, and there was no such a thing as neutrality."[1] Some scholars attribute the continuity between past and present violence to the nature of the nineteenth-century party system. According to

19

David Bushnell, there were no strong differences between the two parties in the nineteenth century, except in ecclesiastical matters.[2] The violence of political contest increased, in his view, because people believed that differences were more clear-cut than they really were and because there was competition for bureaucratic positions. Therefore, the cumulative effect of injuries was passed down from father to son to grandson, inclining the rank and file of one party instinctively to expect the worst from the other.

Second, there is a feeling that a violent past has created a predisposition to violence, despite the fact that the shape and content of violence have not remained the same. Daniel Pecaut, a well-known French student of Colombia's violence, found local and family memories of the nineteenth century in modern Colombia in the period of *la violencia*. According to him, the civil wars of the past century transformed the party system into subcultures, and political parties became collective identities linking individuals to prepolitical and political affiliations.[3] As a consequence, party identification overwhelmed any other social division, and the state was unable to guarantee the symbolic unity of society. Therefore, violence is linked to the autonomy of politics, named by the author "political availability."[4] Without social content, there is only the feeling of a fundamental difference between the parties: a Conservative essence linked to the spiritual aspect of human nature and a Liberal essence that denied that spiritual foundation. According to Pecaut, from the logic of exclusion and difference emerges the representation of politics as violence. Violence follows from this representation. At this moment emerges what he calls the prepolitical content: in 1948, during the period of *la violencia,* there was an emergence of a prepolitical discourse about the lack of civilization and the regression of Indians toward their violent nature.[5] Undoubtedly, Pecaut advanced the understanding of violence through the introduction of elements of identity formation and exclusion into the political discourse. However, his explanation of nineteenth-century violence based on its prepolitical nature is inadequate as long as it assumes an identification of tradition with violence.

Carlos Mario Perea has also sought the reason for the effect that the traditional political culture has had on the Colombian violence of the mid–twentieth century.[6] Perea does not refer to this traditional element as "prepolitical," nor does he see the two major political parties as two subcultures with different approaches to modernity or tradition. In his view, in the 1940s there was a unique political culture in which the two parties were using the same discursive grammar, such as religious differences and a segmented citizenship. During the period of *la violencia* there was a new representation of the political as the term *violence* invaded the political discourse. It is Perea's conclusion that the symbolic war preceded and announced the subsequent violence.

In nineteenth-century Colombia, the recurrence of partisan rivalry, the religious and moral content of the disagreements between Liberals and Conservatives bring to the forefront the relationship between violence and representation. Furthermore, violence during the nineteenth or twentieth centuries did not occur as a result of conflicts over material objects, such as wealth or land. Rather, the formation of identities, especially partisan affiliation, points toward a relationship among violence, desire, and representation. Therefore the need to establish the link among party identification, violence, and desire for civilization.

VIOLENCE AND REPRESENTATION

In order to deal with this symbolic dimension, I broaden the notion of violence so as to formulate a relationship among violence as an act of interpretation, violence in its "physical and observable" dimension, and violence as reinterpretation. I call these dimensions the three moments of violence: the representation, manifestation, and resolution of violence. These three moments of violence replace the conception of violence as a phenomenal event, a manifestation. Violence is not simply manifestation; it also involves representation and the resolution of violence. When restricted to observable interactions, more subtle aspects of violence such as the violence implicit in naming, interpreting, and differentiating are ignored.

The Violence of Representation

The first moment of violence, *representation,* refers to the act of fixing identities. To name an action rational, to designate an actor as legitimate, to describe a process as efficient is to condemn another as irrational, illegitimate, or backward. The moment of representation is crucial to understand the violence inherent in processes of identity formation. This is because identities are constituted in relation to difference and exclusion.[7] Identities (gender, class, race, and nation) are constructed in processes of encounter: how one defines the Other is not independent of the definition of the self. To conceive relations of identity or difference as encounters between the self and the Other is crucial to avoid an "essentialist" understanding of identity and to acknowledge the mutual constitution of identities. Relations of exclusion and the establishment of hierarchical differences mark the definition of self-identities and relations of antagonism. All relations of identity or antagonism are forged out of the tension between the self and the Other.[8]

The Manifestation of Violence

To understand violence as manifestation, we need to recall the place of desire in the constitution of identities and then demonstrate how desire is constitutive of violence. In the mirror stage, the subject identifies with the Other. The Other represents the unity of a self that is fragmented. The subject fixes upon himself an image that alienates him from himself. From this internal tension, according to Lacan, emerges aggressiveness that is caused by the "desire for the object of the Other's desire: here the primordial coming together *(concours)* is precipitated into aggressive competitiveness."[9] It is clear that for Lacan the subject does not desire the object because it has an intrinsic property that makes it desirable or to satisfy an internal need. He or she desires the object because it is the Other's desire.[10]

This relationship of antagonism between the self and the Other is not expressed directly, but, as in Girard's postulate, takes a triangular form: the self and the Other converge in the desire for the same object, resulting in conflict.[11] Desire is mimetic, since one individual elects the same objects as his or her model. Two desires converging on the same object end in conflict, because the success of one prevents the success of the other, so rivalry ensues.[12] Therefore, hostility originates in the projection into the Other of my own fragmentation. I defend myself against my own division by transferring it to the Other. The more I depend on the image of the Other to constitute the unity of my self, the greater is my need to project my own fragmentation onto the Other.[13]

As a consequence, situations of rivalry emerge not from an awareness of difference, but from a perception of "doubleness." The mimetic nature of desire flows into a "double-bind" or dead-end situation. Reciprocal violence coincides with relations of antagonism: antagonists are not able to see the reciprocity of the relationship in which they are involved. From inside they see each other as identical, so the members of the community are transformed into "twins," matching images of violence; each is a double of the other.[14] The consideration of aggressivity as an inner tension within the self that is projected onto the Other makes it possible to understand war not only as a strategic calculation, but also as an ontological practice.[15]

Resolution of Violence

The presence of reciprocal violence points us in the direction of its resolution. If the violence of representation is an original moment and manifestation a phenomenal moment, resolution is a moment of ending, of cessation of an old order. Resolution of violence is the process aimed at ending manifested violence. Resolution is the moment when antagonisms have to be resolved and strategies are designed to provide a resolution to them.

Central to the problem of the resolution of violence is the overcoming of a rivalry where one party becomes the double of the other. According to Lacan, it happens at the level of the symbolic. Only the "pact of speech" can put an end to antagonism.[16] Therefore, violence is not resolved by the use of more violence; it is speech that puts an end to violence. Speech is already a pact of recognition: "Speech is always a pact, an accord, one comes to an agreement, one is of the same mind—this is yours, this is mine, this is this, this is that."[17] The paradox of violence is that it has to be resolved in representation by altering the original violence that gave rise to the manifested violence. It is in representation that antagonisms have to be reconstituted. Violence can be resolved in the symbolic order only by refixing meanings and recreating original relations of identity and difference.

Laclau and Mouffe have suggested that relations of antagonism can be resolved by reconstituting identities.[18] In their view, society is constituted as a chain of equivalences and of differences; which one is predominant is crucial to the resolution of violent situations. At some moments the social field is divided into two camps, with equivalent features represented on each side. An example is the situation between colonizer and colonized. Differences in dress, language, skin color, and customs are equivalent in that they rest on distinction between the colonizer and the colonized. All different features of an object become equivalent to the subject's features. The discursive space is divided into two camps, and identity becomes negative of the other. A logic of differences makes possible the subversion of the system of equivalences. This was the case with Disraeli's formula of "one nation" in the nineteenth century. He overcame the division of society into two camps, recasting differences as "positivities" and displacing the frontier of antagonism to the periphery of the social field.

Furthermore, as Žižek reminds us, in this process of displacement there is a dimension "beyond interpellation" that opens the space for desire and makes the symbolic order inconsistent.[19] This dimension is *enjoyment,* which cannot be symbolized. Enjoyment originates in the failed attempt to answer the question "What does the Other want?" It is at this point that interpellation fails. The subject knows what he or she wants, but does not know the desire of the Other. Fantasy is the screen "masking this void." For Lacan, the way to resolve the coupling of desire and violence is the law. The law allows for the detachment of the subject from the Other's desire.[20] Through the law the subject creates distance from the Other's desire and in this way becomes disalienated from the rule of the Other.[21] Therefore, the law protects the convergence of two desires on the same object and avoids violence.[22]

By examining the regime of representation known as the will to civilization, it is possible to understand the violence of representation where the premises of antagonisms, violence, and the numerous civil wars of the past century lie. This violence is related, in the first place, to the disappearance of a system of differences and identities inherited from the colonial period in a country whose memories of independence from the colonizer were still fresh. Second, violence originated from those pursuing the civilizing task. The desire for civilization was racial and also gendered. Third, political antagonism between Liberals and Conservatives was embedded in the mimetic desire of each side to civilize the other. In the Colombian case, each party was conceived as the Other's double, and so violence ensued. Fourth, the suppression of alternative histories into a universal History overruled the creation of a common space for recognition to supersede violence.

CIVILIZATION? YES, BUT WHOSE?

There was not a clear transition between the effacement of the system of differences inherited from the colonial order and the establishment of identities to accompany the search for civilization. The middle of the nineteenth century was characterized by a loss of identity in terms of the model to be followed as the most appropriate for the country. At the moment when the system of differences weakened, the meaning of civilization emerged as a problem. To create a new civilization was one alternative, as reflected in the following question: "Have the Granadine people been enlightened enough to be able to create a place for themselves in humanity, to search for the road to a new civilization?" An affirmative answer was out of the question, since the power of the creole elite rested on their role in maintaining continuity with European civilization. As Samper wrote:

> People have been isolated from the universal life, reduced to stupidity at the hands of the tyranny; they had been subjected to the pernicious influence of religion and slavery; without commerce, arts, schools, without habits and without a national character; these people are unable to produce a radical thought to guide their movements to a new social order.[23]

Both Liberals and Conservatives struggled fundamentally over the route to civilization. "The search for civilization against barbarism" was one of the pillars of the Conservative Party's program, and for the Conservative J. Caro, civilization was a moral question.[24] The acquisition of knowledge and morality were seen as the means to build civilization: "We must look for the motor of civilization in men's interior. . . . It is always a belief, an idea, knowledge, that pulls men out of barbarism and conducts them along the road to civilization."[25] For the Liberal J. Samper, civilization referred to the search for "individual sovereignty." According to Samper, the public spirit after independence was a progression "along the road of civilization searching for the advent of individual sovereignty as the final aspiration of politics and philosophy."[26]

The desire for civilization was haunted by what Louis Montrose calls a "subversive irony,"[27] one that it nowhere explicitly confronts, but does frequently, if obliquely, register. The destabilization of this discourse arose from the need to ground the credibility of the elite's civilizing power in the same civilization they wanted to discredit. If colonialism was conducted in the name of civilization, how could one vindicate the search for civilization in a recently independent republic? And whose civilization would that be—the one practiced by Spaniards who had been expelled in the recent struggle for independence or the British civilization which was seen as the epitome of capitalist development? Or would it be that of the indigenous peoples? The colonial past exercised domination through a series of symbols, institutions, and well-established identities. Were these to be retained, establishing a continuity with the new republic? What would happen to language and religion, the most important signifiers of civilization in colonial times; to the central state, the benchmark of colonial domination; and to racial and gender identities that had provided the mode of classification in the colonial past?

Since the conquest and during the colonial period, "civilization" brought with it an "external" character in the form of an opposition between the civilized character of the European colonizer and the savage, barbarian character of the colonized population. With the Revolution of Independence, the distinction between external and internal disappeared. "Civilized" and "barbarian" met within the same territorial space. Once the distinction had been lost, how was one to proceed? By what means was civilization to be implemented?

The capacity of the creoles to become the legitimate carriers of civilization depended on the balance between the feelings of continuity and discontinuity with European civilization. Discrediting Spaniards' capacity to install civilization was the road followed by the Liberal Party, which was in power. José María Samper's *Ensayo sobre las Revoluciones Políticas* (1861) provided a rationale for Spain's failure to accomplish civilization after four hundred years of domination. The situation in the Spanish colonies, according to Samper, was one of encounter not with a civilized people, but with an inferior race. That made it necessary to create a new society, "an entire civilization." Creating this civilization demanded "infinite resources and immense efforts." Spain was only an "atom in the enormous new world. . . . Pretending to overwhelm everything, the colonizer empire drowned in the immensity of the colonized, and instead of a vigorous civilization, engendered a grotesque semi-barbaric fetus."[28]

Liberals ascribed the economic, political, and social desolation of Colombia to the Spanish colonization. The way to solve the impasse was to create a divide within the civilized world. This solution was proposed by the Liberal J. Samper, who distinguished between the northern and Mediterranean worlds, attributing the quality of "civilization" to the former. By establishing a difference between colonization and conquest as two innate characteristics of race, Samper was able to deny Spain the ability to colonize:

In Europe we can see a curious contrast that the passage of time has never denied. German races, or Northern races, are the only ones having the spirit of colonization, that is, the creation of civilized societies where it was barbaric before. On the contrary, the Latin race or Southern races, are the only ones with the spirit of conquest, that is, of domination (through assimilation) over already civilized people.[29]

The exclusion of Spain allowed him to resolve this dilemma, thereby embracing the Anglo-Saxon civilization and rejecting the Spanish tradition. A different solution, associated with the Conservative Party, was to establish a continuity between the Spanish past and the new republic. The following is the evaluation of the situation of Colombia at the moment of independence by the Conservative Sergio Arboleda, a defender of the Spanish legacy:

> Certainly, the country was behind in the sciences and arts; industry and commerce were restrained by restrictions, and African slavery opened a dangerous wound. Notwithstanding we inherited from Spain good habits, families were solid, we had respect for authority and consideration for women, a virtuous priesthood, strong moral and religious beliefs, Indians and blacks instructed in the spirit of Christianity and the road toward civilization, and all the races were unified in a true fraternity which merged into one grand family.[30]

Arboleda summarized the Spanish legacy in one principle: religion. He attributed the postindependence condition of Colombia to the attempt to replace Catholic principles of authority with Protestant institutions. In an article entitled "Only Priests Can Save Us and No One Can Save Us but Priests," Arboleda identified religious feeling as the soul of Spaniard heritage; he saw the Revolution of Independence as an interruption of the road toward progress due to the disregard of religious beliefs.[31] His conclusion was that the formation of clerics was the only road to the formation of the nation.

VIOLENCE AND IDENTITY FORMATION

In Colombia during the colonial period, domination was exercised in such ways that power relations were institutionalized on the basis of certain identities: peninsulars (Spaniards), creoles *(criollos)*, Indians, blacks, and women.[32] The establishment of a "system of distinction" was perhaps the most crucial issue for the reformers of the New Granada in their aim to end a form of domination (the colonial one) and to install a new civilizing order. The form of government

and the role of party leaders hinged on the identification of hierarchical differences separating governors and governed, those able to
govern and those subject to being governed. The identification of
differences signals the how and the what of government and what
strategies were to be followed to guarantee good government. The
following question reflects this concern: "Can a person who is manumitted proceed suddenly out of the house of his owner to establish
industries? Can we deposit in the hands of the student who is learning the alphabet, who just became literate, a treatise of geometry so
that he can solve its problems?"[33] The answer presupposes a hierarchical difference between civilizers and those to be civilized, a differential capacity to know civilization's secrets, and a strategy to pursue
the civilizing task.

José María Samper drew a map of those who favored the Revolution of Independence according to "topography, tradition, social
condition of classes and crowds according to the degree of advancement in their relation with the external world and with the remaining Colombian cities."[34] The identity between creoles and Indians,
characteristic of the struggle for independence, was broken. Rather,
Samper envisioned strong differences among these groups, which
were summarized in a central plot that functioned as the point of reference: groups were differentiated by their capacity to "understand"
the meaning of the revolution. This capacity was graded according
to what Samper perceived as the distance of these groups from civilization measured temporarily and geographically. Male creole literati were located at the top of the classification. Priests, soldiers, and
artisans followed literati, in descending order:

> The *literati* (all creoles) comprised of lawyers, medical doctors, lite-
> rati, naturalists (like the scientist Caldas, the well-spoken Zea) and
> academics;
> the low clergy, the enlightened ones, most of them born in the
> Hispanic-Colombian territory and belonging to poor and plebeian
> families;
> young soldiers who, in small numbers, enlisted in Spanish schools, in
> military districts or in engineering headquarters;
> city artisans, with Colombian or creole origin, and small proprietors.[35]

Differentiation between creoles and others was accompanied by a
lack of recognition of agency that served a double purpose: it naturalized their marginalization from the construction of the new re-

public, and, more important, it granted their *disponibilité* in order to be molded to the creoles' own image, thus guaranteeing their subordinate status. Samper established this relationship between the capacity to act and skin color: creoles—whites whose parents were Spaniards, but who were born in Colombian territory, were granted the highest capacity for conducting the war of independence. In contrast, blacks, Indians, and mestizos were given a subordinated status. They were instrumental in the hands of creole literati:

> The slaves, unable to understand the Revolution and oppressed by their condition, enlisted simultaneously in the two causes, according to the opinion of their owners or the resources of the enemy army. . . .
>
> Regarding the Indians, *mulattos,* and remaining mestizos, it is evident that the first were always instruments of the enemy forces in the mountain region; free *mulattos* and *zambos* formed part of the revolutionary forces, and the mestizo of Spaniard and Indian descent were the most fierce contenders in both fields; those semi-barbarians were instruments to each party.[36]

Women were the last category mentioned, and their contribution was recognized not in their capacity to understand, but in their instinctual predisposition:

> There is an additional factor that deserves mention: women's support for the Revolution. It is certain that when we want to know *a priori* the character or justice of a revolution or of a social event, or at least the degree of popular support of a similar event, it is enough to know where women stand. . . . Why? The truth is that women do not understand the philosophy of revolutions, nor do they have the moral or intellectual strength to take care of political issues, in whose details they very often make mistakes. But instinct is more the base of their sense and insight to perceive *justice,* to have respectable feelings, and to exert piety.[37]

Geographical representations were built around the civilizing power of the nation's capital:[38]

> In addition, it must be clear that, as a general rule, urban populations were more accessible to revolution and the most enthusiastic in contrast with the rural population, who were more ignorant and subject to irresistible traditional influences. A difference was also noticeable by topography and climate: in the plains and warm lowlands, the revolutionary spark spread faster and stayed longer than in the cold mountain regions, isolated from contact with civilization, without

communication with the social centers where relative enlightenment concentrated.[39]

In Samper's typology of Nueva Granada, history becomes imprinted in the body, and intelligence, beauty, and knowledge are attributes of the white race, whereas ugliness, stupidity, and malevolence are attributes of races of darker colors.[40] The creole from the highlands was depicted as handsome and distinguished, of Spanish descent, white, and possessing a natural ability for academia, arts, and jobs. The Antioqueño was depicted as the most beautiful in the whole country; a mixture of Spaniard, Jew, and creole; a hard worker and a good businessman. In contrast, the Indian from the province of Pasto is depicted as half-savage, of primitive race; as living happily in the middle of affluence, without need of culture; as acting against civilization and passive toward progress. The Indian was also seen as easy to govern through religion, but indomitable once in revolt. The mulatto (with a mixture of black and Spanish blood) was depicted as exuberant and tempestuous: if provided with education in freedom and democracy, the mulatto could become a safe element of civilization. This was because his physiology was seen as being more black than white, but his moral qualities as more white than black. Posed at the other extreme of the ethnic composition was the *zambo* (with a mixture of Indian and black blood). The *zambo* was depicted as belonging to "the worst race of the country"; as the "voluptuous prince of solitude, a dreamer and indolent, free and savage as the shade of the tree where he is resting."[41] Samper also believed that the *zambo*, aided by civilization and education, could progress.

Creoles put forward the practice of miscegenation as the road to progress and civilization.[42] The civilizing process appeared to be an evolutionary process of whitening. The process of miscegenation had both a progressive and a regressive character: progress followed from mixing the blood of whites with the blood of people of "inferior" colors, whereas regression occurred if a person with some white blood mixed his or her blood again with that of a person of a dark color. Antonio J. Restrepo summarized in the following way the "scientific conditions" under which this process took place:

> The first fusion, between a white man and a black or Indian woman, is called mestizo; the name *zambo* is reserved for the mestizo of a black man and Indian woman, or its opposite. The second fusion is

[of] the mestizo man with another black or pure Indian woman, the result is called *cuarterón* (quadroon), because in reality one-fourth of the white race remained; the *cuarterón* man bred with another black or pure Indian woman, becomes a *tente en el aire* (nebulous), not being a fish nor a frog, nor black nor white nor Indian, and [in] the following fusion of a *tente en el aire* with a black or Indian woman, the pure black or pure Indian appears again, having wasted the half-white of the first fusion; this is the reason why Gumilla call this backward motion *saltatrases* (jump-backwards).

Notwithstanding, the ordinary and most likely thing to happen is that this fusion would occur in the opposite way from that of the above description, and within a period of five generations the black or Indian disappears with only the white remaining.[43]

This heterogeneity defined the situation as it was lived and also structured the institutions dreamed of—which were both similar to and different from European ones. The "will to civilization" became the dream of a *civilización mestiza* (métis): "A *civilización mestiza*, astoundingly, difficult to forge, turbulent and rough in its beginning, apparently contradictory, but whose destiny is to regenerate the world through the practice of the main principle of Christianity: fraternity."[44] Miscegenation embodied a fantasy of a white society that would not be split by racial divisions.[45] The dream of a *civilización mestiza* entailed the assimilation of inferior races by the white race, where the latter was the predominant one. Miscegenation was conceived of as a process of whitening. This rationale appeared clearly in José Eusebio Caro's statement: "The human race conforms to the same laws as the other living species. Inferior races are destined to disappear in favor of superior races. Indians in America are almost extinguished. African and American blacks will disappear in the same way. . . . It is the destiny of the white race to replace all human races. In the end, the white race will provide the most perfect attributes."[46] Mestizos were seen to embody all the ambivalences accompanying the dream of a mestizo civilization. In mestizos converged all the hatred against the different racial groups; they did not have the paternalistic protection granted, for example, to indigenous groups.[47]

ENGENDERING CIVILIZATION

The will for civilization was located in women spatially (in the womb), temporally (in the future), and in terms of desire. After the conquest, the process of *mestizaje* had a gendered character: it was exercised in a hierarchical fashion in terms of superior (white and male) and inferior categories (black and Indian women): Indians and blacks provided the subordinated women and Spaniards the conquering men.[48] During the conquest, Indian women were subjected to the rules of war and conquest, and the *mestizaje* had what Gutiérrez de Pineda describes as an "irregular character." The white man exerted direct power over the Indian women in a relationship of biological and economic exploitation. In a petition of chiefs of an Indian group against the behavior of the Spanish mayor *(corregidor)*, the three elements appeared:

> They complain that the *corregidor*, in addition to forcing the Indians to provide free labor, coerced their women to work in pottery and the young daughters to provide their domestic service; having in their kitchen four, six, and eight, to make bad use of them, using force and robbing women of their virginity. . . . If they do not consent, our daughters are severely punished. . . . If he does not want the women for himself, "he gives the women to his friends," and even more, "he does not allow our daughters to get married, only those designated by him can get married."[49]

During the colonial period, the possession of women changed from the concept of conquest to the concept of servitude *(servidumbre)*. The system of servitude has been considered one of the causes of the disappearance of the Indian groups.[50] In the case of black women, the *mestizaje* was also carried out through "irregular channels" (sporadic relationships, polygyny, or concubinage), since legal marriage between whites and blacks was not allowed by the Spanish Crown. In addition, unions between these races were surrounded by myths of cursed progeny, such as the possibility of being born with a stigma of color and other vices, that were often considered congenital or acquired in drinking "breast milk."[51]

As Joan Wallach Scott has argued, gender representations became implicated in the conception and construction of power that accompanied the will to civilization.[52] The divisions between public and private, feeling and reason, actor and subject of civilization became strongly entrenched. An otherwise unnoticed event, the recognition of women's right to vote by the province of Vélez as early as 1855, alerted male creole literati to the subversive possibility of women's entry into the public domain. The reaction to this subversive potential allows one to trace the containment of women in a devalued, private, sentimental sphere that at the same time enhanced the public status of men.

An article written by Emiro Kastos entitled "Something about Women," concerning the Vélez Constitution, reflects the problematic nature of women's participation in public life for the civilizing ideal put in place by creole men like him.[53] According to Kastos, the real issue at stake was the convenience and advantage of introducing women in public life and allowing them to participate in government. In order to dismiss the value of any advantage, Kastos assumed beforehand that women's vote would not change political outcomes: "She will carry the same opinion as her husband, father, brother, or lover, which means that we will end up with more ballot paper but not votes." The identification of women with feelings supposed that men were carriers of interest: "Men are dominated by interest, women by feelings." In men's own view, to be carriers of interest entailed not a positive, but a negative, connotation that entitled them to be the guardians of women and to expect their care once at home: "Public life is not women's place. Women must remain at home, softening with their care and smiles the bitterness we brought from outside. . . . [To women I say,] Stay at home. Allow us the pleasure of being president or dictators, to intrigue in elections, insult in Congress, lie in newspapers, and kill our brothers in civil wars."[54] The incursion of women into politics would mean the loss of love and feeling, and therefore their suicide as women: "Women must be women: if they become politicians, and wear vests and boots and make speeches, that would mean their suicide. We will not be able to stand the presence of a woman in the Congress, even in defense of the Republic."[55]

Women were not excluded from a role in the civilizing mission. But their role was such that it did not require public intervention, although it did require male protection, as seen in the following description by Kastos:

> To accomplish her beautiful and heroic destiny, a woman does not
> need political rights, nor emancipation and independence as claimed
> by modern innovators. This is her humanitarian and civilizing mission,
> her true and heroic destiny: to support those suffering, to sacrifice for

the ones she loves, to bring relief to the sick, to inspire compassion and virtue in her son's heart; to fully accept the responsibilities of mother and daughter; to practice charity in the middle of a society full of egoism and love for money; to smooth habits and to bring home poetry appropriate to her charm, beauty, grace, and tenderness.[56]

The limited role in the civilizing task assigned to women explains the concern among creole men for improving the situation of women, especially with regard to their capacity as moral guardians of civilization. Therefore, some changes were introduced in the institution of marriage. During a short period of time, 1853–56, civil marriage and divorce were accepted. Salvador Camacho Roldán saw the effect of liberal reforms on the situation of women this way: "They [liberal reforms] ended the feudal period, but most of the feudal habits still persist, among them the prostitution of the peasant's daughters for the desires of the proprietor, the despising of women's modesty within the organization of labor, their submission to degrading jobs."[57] He added that "the Revolution of Independence removed the domination of an alien power and the exploitation by a distant enemy; blacks, Indians, mestizos, and creoles were made citizens; but neither institutions nor habits have made the first step to end the humiliation of the daughters of the nation. Women's abuse on the part of the landlord, the *gamonal,* the soldier, the *tinterillo,* does not have any legal consequences for the abuser in the penal or civil code.[58]

Creole men saw in women the main guardians of civilization and morality. Therefore, the desire for civilization was located in women's minds and bodies. As documented by Patricia Londoño, creole literati organized public speeches advocating education and enlightenment among women, and several newspapers targeted the "beautiful sex" *(bello sexo)* as their readers.[59] For example, Rufino José Cuervo talked about the "jump into the charming world of women's society," since "are not women the foundation of good manners, . . . the praise of civilization, and neatness of our era?"[60] The lack of enlightenment and good manners among women was perceived by Cuervo as "slowing down the progress of culture and morality in our newborn country. . . . It makes it necessary that women enlighten their minds, cultivate their character, and refine their behavior."[61] In this line of thought, literatus Medardo Rivas organized several conferences at a school for women with the desire to "beautify your soul through noble and generous examples; beautify your heart through tenderness and passion; beautify your body through advice on good hygienic practices; and smoothe your manners by the practice of courtesy and good manners."[62]

Improving the condition of women through education was seen as requisite for civilization, and specifically as a better way to move women away from prostitution, as advocated by Manuel Ancízar:

> The population of the city is diminishing as a definite result of the negligence regarding the condition of the poor people, but especially of women. Most of them do not find within the city means to earn a salary to satisfy their needs, mainly because they do not have the knowledge or skills learned by rich women in special schools. Abandoned to their own destiny, without a pattern of good behavior to follow, they end up living a disorderly life until they die early. Several attempts have been made to submit them to the harassment of police, and in groups of ten or more, they had been sent to the jungle of Chucurí to die of misery and high fever, but this has not made things better. To kill is not the way to increase morality.[63]

Some scattered evidence suggests the ambivalence regarding the subordination of women and the dominance of male creoles. For example, the assembly of the province of Santander proposed to abolish the criminality of rape for the rape of a woman older than twelve years or for that of a woman less than twelve years old if the rape was committed by one man.[64]

Therefore, gender differences were crucial to the construction of a regime of representation in line with the "will to civilization." Creole men took for themselves the right to civilize those placed in lesser categories. Miscegenation became part of the strategy aimed to whiten and then to civilize the other segments of the population. Men's desire for civilization was located in women's bodies, and therefore, engendered.

POLITICAL ANTAGONISMS

A profound tension arose between the Liberals and the Conservatives regarding the civilizing process. The two parties had antagonistic views over law and religion as the ways to channel the civilizing desire. From the moment of their formation in 1848, they diverged concerning the religious question. The Conservative Party stated that one of its main principles was "*Christian morality and its civilizing principles* against the immorality and corruption common to materialistic and atheistic principles" (emphasis in original).[65] In contrast, according to the Liberals, religion should not be used as an instrument of government: "The two powers must revolve independently, each one in its own orbit, so that each one has its own object and different ends."[66]

A passage of the novel *Manuela* by Eugenio Díaz summarizes the kind of antagonism between Conservative priests (P) and Liberals (L) regarding their desire to civilize, where one group used religion as the main instrument and the other proposed the spread of laissez-faire principles. The important point, as Girard reminds us, is not that differences did not exist. The problem is that contenders were not able to perceive the reciprocity of their relationship. The Liberals and the Conservatives both believed that they were able to civilize the masses. Both were seen to "pursue the same goal, to make society" better. As perceived from inside, they saw only differences; but as perceived from the outside, each was the double of the other:

> P. Sir, if politics does not encompass morality, and if morality can't take roots without religious instruction; if politics were not concerned with happiness or unhappiness of men, then the priest should abstain from politics. But wherever men coexist, there is misery. . . . For these reasons the presence of priests is necessary, relieving pain, providing advice, teaching and preventing errors and crimes. Is it not necessary for the priest to be political? In this parish where no one is able to read, where nobody provides explanations and nobody remembers the written law, where no one provides schools, who is going to teach the route of goodness? Who is going to prevent robbery of the landowner? Who is going to preserve and encourage marriage, the base of political society?

> L. Society has always tended to perfection; and instinctively the people know what is better if we do not place obstacles in their way. The laissez-faire principles are worth more than all regulations in the world.

> P. Sir, I would believe in your theory if I did not know (because I have been in the Indian territory) that neither the Caribbeans, nor the Tunebos, nor the Guaque Indians, have advanced by themselves anything in civilization in three hundred years, while other evangelized people have gone further.

> L. Have they gone further than our liberal school? You must wait until our social principles are disseminated, and you will see that it is not the case.

P. The socialist of my school had already spread our message.

L. When? Who? How?

P. Have not Catholic priests crossed deserts defying arrows, animals, hunger, and infinite plagues, in order to accomplish their civilizing mission? Have they not suffered the odor of the hospital to alleviate suffering? Have they not dedicated their life to confession and preaching reform? Is not civilizing, feeding, and reforming work in order to make society better?

L. We write and deliver speeches.

P. How many listen to your speeches? How often are those speeches delivered? Among the poor people, how many read what you have written? And how many are convinced and take profit? They listen to us each week, and without being pretentious, they believe what we say. . . . Are you still uncertain about our initiative and our good results?

L. At least we pursue the same goal, to make society better. The difference is that your method is very slow; it has passed almost two thousand years, while with our method we conceive a reform, we publish it, and zis! zas! We go forward if our opponents do not bend it. From this discussion we must conclude that Golgotas [Liberals] and Catholic priests are similar.[67]

This polemic comprised two fundamental questions: who were the most legitimate carriers of the civilizing process, and what was the "political" power granted to their civilizing mechanisms? Two groups competed for the position of supreme authority over the civilizing process: those who claimed to derive the authority of their words from the divine mandate of Christianity and those who claimed the legitimacy of the "written word" in the name of law. The strength of the former is related to the role of the church in the process of colonization and the power invested in the church to accomplish the civilizing mission. During the period of Spanish rule, the church, in the name of *patronato,* enjoyed a monopoly in the process of cultural formation. This power was consolidated after independence: one-third of the signers of the Act of Independence were clerics; in 1823 clerics constituted one-third of the Representative Legislature.[68]

With the ascendancy of the Liberals to power, the conflicts with the church intensified, taking the form of a church-state antagonism. Although this antagonism has existed since independence, by 1849 it appeared under a new form. During the period from 1810 to 1848, the clash between the state and the church took the form of a desire on the part of the former to appropriate the control of the *patronato* that the Spaniards had exercised over the church. At this time the church was still considered an auxiliary of the state in the civilizing mission, as the following statement on the part of Secretary of the Treasury Florentino González makes clear: "The nation must take in its hand the livelihood of the ministers of the church, who are keepers of good morals, so we can infer that they must be considered assistants of public authority, in a religious civilized society."[69] The appropriation by the Conservative Party of the power to exert the civilizing mission in the name of God posed a serious threat to the space from which the Liberals exerted their power. The Liberals claimed a separation of the political space from the religious one, centering the debate on the restriction of clerics to the private realm of the family. As González wrote:

> I have proof that by proceeding in this way [with the intervention of clerics in politics] religion is deprived of its natural character, the morale of clerics diminishes, and the [morality] of believers is corrupted. The government has turned bishops and priests into political agents, by employing them in electoral matters, mixing them in partisan questions, sharing partisan passions, making them instruments of annoyance and oppression, and denuding religion of its character of family counselor and guardian of morality.[70]

At the time of this statement, González did not see in clerics the "assistants" of government. Like many of his Liberal peers, he exerted pressure so as to subordinate divine law to state law. Several measures taken by the Liberals reflect this tendency.[71] In 1851, the *fuero ecclesiastico* (ecclesiastical court) was abolished, which meant that clerics and bishops had to be judged by the Supreme Court of Justice and not by special courts belonging to the church. The same year, Jesuit priests were expelled from the country and the Congress issued laws abolishing the *diezmos* and other taxes benefiting the church. A decree called for the election of clerics in the municipal *cabildos*. In 1853 the church was officially separated from the state. Priests were declared enemies of constitutional order: "Most of the clerics had been involved in revolution, taking advantage of their pastoral position to invite the masses to rebellion against the constitutional government of the provinces; some of them have taken arms, reaching the scandalous situation of a priest being killed as the head of a *guerrilla* movement."[72] A decree was issued on *tuición de cultos* (tutelage of cults), calling for priests to swear obedience to state laws; otherwise, they would be expelled from the national territory.

Although the Conservatives' strategy was to embed the power of their words in the divine domain, the Liberals sought their power in the constitution.[73] Once the Liberals were installed in power, they wrote the constitution of 1853 to replace the older constitution, which had been issued ten years earlier. The new constitution allowed each province to dictate its own constitution, in an attempt to counterbalance the centralist character of previous constitutional arrangements. Between 1853 and 1856, sixty-one provincial constitutions were issued.[74] The coup d'état in 1854 attempted, among other things, to revive the constitution of 1843. In 1858, the congress approved the Confederación Granadina Constitution with the declaration: "Today is the end of the Revolution of 1810: our civic virtues have won."[75] In 1863, another constitution was born, La Constitución de Rionegro, which was considered the most liberal of the constitutions. It delegated to the provinces all those things not explicitly conceded to the federal government.[76] Under this constitution, each province could enact its own legislation and provide a definition of who was considered a citizen. The country's name was changed from Nueva Granada to Estados Unidos de Colombia. The Federal Constitution guaranteed freedom to individuals and established freedom of the press and speech, as well as the right to possess and sell arms and munitions even in peacetime. It abolished the death penalty and incarceration for longer than ten years. One of the authors of the constitution stated, some years later, that "this Constitution organized the central power as a simple host in the constitutional house."[77] The constitution of 1863 was officially declared dead in 1886, and a new constitution was born.

The substitution of religion for the law was depicted by historian Colmenares in this way: "For Liberals, the real ambition was to install in the place previously occupied by moral-religious consensus a system of loyalty based on an abstract deification of law."[78] The deification of law for Colombian Liberals is reflected in Justo Arosemena's title of his treatise on politics, written in the form of a religious instruction, *Principios de Moral Política Redactados en un Catecismo* (Principles of political morality written in a catechism).[79]

As a result of this convergence of Liberals and Conservatives on the object of the desire, they saw themselves as rivals. They were not able to see their identity in the situation in which they were involved; they saw only their differences. One's desire for the object of the Other's desire precipitates aggressiveness. Each party considered the other an antagonist and as an obstacle to accomplishing its desire, civilization. Therefore, the divide between Liberals and Conservatives was posed as a moral divide. In the words of José Eusebio Caro, "Morality is the only one and true query. This is the issue that explains the origin of the Conservative and Liberal party. It could not be other."[80] In an article entitled "The Moral Question," Caro stated the Conservatives' view: "We have expressed our commitment to defend the cause of civilization. . . . We have demonstrated that morality is the first element, the mother-element of civilization; [morality] is the essence of civilization. Who says immorality says barbarism."[81]

The important point is that morality became a "pure difference" between Liberals and Conservatives. To achieve self-identity, the Conservatives located the source of immorality in the Liberal Party. But this is not sufficient to explain the antagonism between the parties. Rather, as Girard recognizes, it is violence that makes the object of desire valuable. Therefore, violence becomes object and subject of desire, as reflected in the sentence "Who says immorality says barbarism." "Barbarism" (violence) confers value to morality, legitimates more violence, and produces violence. Therefore, party antagonism was defined in terms of morality (desire) and violence.

> This question, the moral question, is the only true question. This question explains the presence of the Conservative Party and the Red [Liberal] Party. It could not be any other. This question will be the last one. The day we can resolve this question we will be independent, settled, free, and moral. . . . And [the struggle to resolve] this last question, the moral question, will be the longest, the fiercest, and the most ferocious. It is more difficult to be moral than to be independent.[82]

Since, at least for the Conservatives, morality was seen to be absolute and unshakable, the struggle between the Liberals and the Conservatives was a struggle that presupposed the other's disappearance: "The last struggle over this question [morality] would not come to an end until the Conservative Party had annihilated completely and absolutely the Liberal Party, that is, until the lack of credibility would be so great that the party lost its capacity to appear. . . . The Liberal Party must disappear like crime and licentiousness."[83]

The desire to eliminate the Liberal Party was accompanied by the logic of equivalence, where all positive determinations belonged to the Conservative Party and everything in the Liberal Party was equated with violence, in the guise of crime and licentiousness. The two forces were seen as antagonistic: the triumph of one could not occur without the other's disappearance. As expressed by Gonzalo Sánchez, "In a society where political contenders are not conceived as rivals but as deviations from an originative belief[,] . . . political and social regeneration can only be achieved through the annihilation of the transgressors."[84]

This view also explains the representation of terror accompanying political contenders. The day the Liberal Party came to power was labeled the "Revolution of March 7, 1849." This revolution was presented as a continuation of the Revolution of Independence in 1810. In the words of Liberal José María Samper, "[The period] beginning March 7 1849, comprised the resurrection of freedom, the development of national prosperity, the progress of a republican civilization influencing the whole Colombian continent, and the real foundation of democracy as the government of the century."[85] The same date, March 7, 1849, when published in a Conservative newspaper, evoked terror. José Eusebio Caro, in an article entitled "March 7, 1849," anticipated, in the following way, the expected reaction on the part of his readers: "Nothing appears more neutral than the title of this article; however, its reading would cause a tremor in more than one reader, like the reaction of an injured person to the contact of the cold scalpel with his wound."[86] These images of terror on the part of the Conservative Party were attached to the fear of losing the part of civilization already gained under the Spanish colonization.

THE WILL TO CIVILIZATION AND THE SUPPRESSION OF HISTORY

The will to civilization entailed an assessment of the present in relation to the colonial past and the desired future. It also entailed an assessment of the images of the self in relation to the civilized Other. Therefore, civilization appeared in contradictory ways. Regarding the past, the War of Independence meant a difference with a process of domination accomplished in the name of civilization. Regarding the future, the struggle around civilization meant an identity with the European culture. At stake was creoles' capacity to impose a new system of differences that allowed them to turn old rules of colonial domination to their own favor and, at the same time, to distance themselves from the old rulers.[87] Political struggles were therefore about the appropriation of the origin of civilization's history.

The interpretation of the Revolution of Independence became crucial for this task. Interpretations of this revolution served to reinforce these feelings of identity with or difference from the colonial past. For Liberals the Revolution of 1810 appeared to have been a revolution in the name of difference: "Independence was an uncontested event; but it was necessary to build a nation, to inaugurate civil and political freedom, and to create a new society . . . amid the rubbish of an arbitrary and antisocial regime."[88]

For Conservatives, the colonial world, independence, and the republic formed one and the same tradition. Conservative Miguel Antonio Caro advocated this thought:

> 1810 does not mark a division between our grandparents and us; the political emancipation does not assume the improvisation of a new civilization; we cannot invent civilizations. Religion, language, habits, and traditions: we have not invented these things; we have received these things from generation to generation, from hand to hand, since the time of the Conquest and they will be transmitted to our children and grandchildren as the legacy of a civilized race.[89]

Identity was the feeling of Caro when he declared, "Our history from the moment of the Conquest until today is the history of the same people and of one and the same civilization."[90] Therefore, the will to civilization is the by-product of an originative violence, a violence that suppresses differences into identity. The narrative of a unique history accomplishes this goal by suppressing the histories of indigenous and black peoples. The act of disregarding the local history was an act of violence. This violence interrupted a continuity between different histories, and those left "without a history" were not able to recognize themselves.

The desire for civilization was not independent of the way differences in civilization were established and the way these differences empowered those possessing the knowledge, color, and sex identified as appropriate for leading subordinates down the road to civilization. Meanwhile, the creation of the self-image of one with a superior civilization meant a violent dispossession of the Other's history, culture, and identity.

The popular "Song of the Indian Who Doesn't Know His Distant Origin" provides an illustration of the denial of history to Indian peoples, what I have termed the "violence of representation." The song is composed of two parts. The first part, the popular song of an unknown author, makes reference to the denial of Indigenous history by the white colonist:

Romance del Indio que
Desconoce su Origen Remoto

Soy gajo de árbol caido
que no sé donde cayó.
Dónde estarán mis raices?
De qué arbol soy gajo yo?

Yo no sé donde nací
ni sé tampoco quién soy;
no sé de donde he venido,
ni sé para donde voy.

Song of the Indian Who Doesn't
Know His Distant Origin

Branch of a fallen tree I am
that does not know where it fell.
Where could my roots be?
Of which tree am I a branch?

I do not know where I was born,
nor know who I am;
I do not know where I come from,
nor know where I am going.[91]

The second part is a commentary by Octavio Quiñones's father or grandfather and refers to the effects of repressing Indians' history. This denial of history makes the linkage between the past and the future an impossibility. By ignoring a people's "roots," the link between their past and their future is broken. The violence of suppressing a people's history has another effect as well—the inability of that people to heal, which results from their lack of presence. Healing requires a symbolic presence. Without knowing the roots of his suffering, the Indian is unable to heal its scars.

El Indio ignora la historia
pero su alma la presiente,

porque ama la libertad
y al amarla se enaltece.

Sabe que su corazón
hondas cicatrices tiene;
sabe que nació con ellas;
sabe que con ellas muere,
y que ha querido borrarlas,
y que borrarlas no puede.

La historia que el Indio ignora
muchos crímenes envuelve;
es la historia de su estirpe
sacrificada vilmente.

La historia de la conquista
sobre cuyo horror se extiende
un manto de indiferencia
que mil delitos proteje;
la oprobiosa destrucción
del país de Nemequene.

The Indian does not know his history,
but his soul anticipates his history
in the love of freedom
and the praise he has in this love.

The Indian knows that his heart
has deep scars;
he knows that he was born with scars;
and with scars he is going to die;
and he knows he has to try to heal them;
and that healing has not been possible.

The history that the Indian ignores
is the history of many crimes;
is none other than his own history
sacrificed vilely.
The history of the Conquest
on whose horror has been heaped
a layer of indifference
covering many crimes;
the opprobrious destruction
of the nation of Nemequene.[92]

There is also in the song an explicit reference to the relationship between ignoring history and the power exercised on the Indian and between knowing and liberation.

Por qué se le niega al Indio
que su historia lo consuele?
Por qué se calla esa historia
que a los patriotas ofrece
ejemplos de dignidad
y de heroísmos alegres,
de valor ante el verdugo,
ante el bárbaro inclemente?

[. . .],

Tal vez se calla esa historia
porque la reacción se teme.

Si conociera algún día
la estirpe a que pertenece,
el Indio sentiría orgullo
de su origen, que se pierde
en un pasado glorioso
que por glorioso no vuelve.
Que el Indio ignore su historia
a sus verdugos conviene,
porque así su explotación
a nadie aflige ni ofende.

Why is the comfort of his history
denied to the Indian?
Why is that history silenced,
which, to the patriot, offers
examples of dignity,
and of joyful heroism,
of courage when facing the executioner,
in front of the ruthless barbarian?

[. . .],

Maybe this history is silenced
because of the reaction they fear.

If some day he would know
his own lineage,

the Indian would be proud
of his origin, lost
in a glorious past
never to come again.
That the Indian does not know his history
benefits his executioners,
so that the Indian's exploitation
is not to anyone offensive.[93]

The commentary on the Indian song explicitly states the relationship between the violence of representation—in this case, the suppression of history—and the manifestation of violence, that is, the capacity of whites to exploit Indian peoples.

CONCLUSION

The will to civilization was a contradictory, ambivalent space centered on a desire for, and a disavowal of, European civilization. It was a space of desire and violence. This violence was an originative violence, a violence of representation in which the indigenous civilization was disregarded in favor of an external, alien civilization. This analysis also reveals how exclusion operated in processes of identity formation and in the attribution of meanings, and therefore reveals violence in representation. In the will to civilization there was a violence in the form of representation of identities and a violence in the form of suppression of alternative histories. The will to civilization established hierarchical identities and differences. Blacks, Indians, and women were deprived of their alterity when compared to white males of European origin. In these acts violence was embodied (represented), later to become manifest. Processes of differentiation were imprinted in the body: skin color and gender were identified as the hierarchical criteria for establishing distances and exerting power relations. The will to civilization became the dream of a *civilización mestiza* in which all races would be fused into one, the superior white one. Civilization was engendered; therefore, violence was exerted on women. The gendered (male) character of a *civilización mestiza* explains the exclusion of women, along with blacks and natives, from civilization.

3

The Political Economy of Civilization

The passion for literary competition was so high that in the streets everybody signaled victors and defeated. The victor had ensured a place in the most distinguished families, and praised by everyone, entered into the aristocracy of talent, by then superior to the aristocracy of wealth, and a successful public career was open to him.

RUFINO JOSÉ CUERVO, QUOTED IN *LA VIDA DE RUFINO CUERVO Y NOTICIAS DE SU ÉPOCA* (1892)

The history of the development and geographical expansion of capitalism has been told as a story about how things are produced, exchanged, appropriated, and consumed. A concentration on the world of things encourages a mode of reasoning wherein commodities and labor are studied in abstraction from their social context. The discipline of economics assigns itself the task of uncovering and formulating universal laws that are held to regulate the world of things. Political economists have differentiated themselves from economists in their argument that the world of economic activity cannot be studied independent from the power structure that sustains exchange relations and other social relations that also constitute the economy. Some political economists, particularly those influenced by Gramsci, have also stressed that the story, which tells us that capitalist economic relations are self-regulating and unforced, creates the illusion that hierarchical ordering systems are not repressive, but rather natural.[1] A Gramscian approach to political economy acknowledges that things cannot be studied independent of the meaning systems supporting them. Even money, the most abstract commodity, is embedded in a world of significations that provide it with its value. What would money be without trust in social arrangements, without the enforcement of the state, and without distinctions and desires?

Recently political economists have pushed the boundaries of the discipline even further, redefining political economies as systems of value production, interpretation, and exchange. As Michael Shapiro explains, they are "repressed economies" immanent in cultural practices even though they, and the systems of power and authority to which they are related, remain concealed and fugitive.[2] This understanding of political economies accounts for the specificity of capitalism and for the existence of alternative economies that might accompany, resist, or complement capitalist relations.

Colombia's historiography has evidenced the limits of attempts to ground explanations in the productive structure and the elite position with regard to the structure of production or the international division of labor, as with Charles Berquist's economic history of the nineteenth century. According to Berquist, "The national fortunes of Liberal and Conservative parties and the fate of liberal political economy, paralleled the fortunes of export agriculture."[3] To sustain his point, Berquist poses a causal relation between the success of export agriculture and the Liberals' political preponderance.[4] Although he accepts a uniformity of class composition among the elite, he identifies each party with a different economic interest: the Liberals are identified with the export economy and Conservatives with nationalist tendencies oriented toward domestic problems.

Berquist is overly reliant on the derivation of elites' interests from their position in the occupational structure (those with import-export interests versus groups not involved with the export-import economy) and overly inclined to relate the ability to sustain these interests to the fortunes of export agriculture. Criticisms of the first tendency have been well formulated by Safford.[5] The economic interests of the upper classes during the nineteenth century tended to be complementary rather than contradictory. Merchants and landowners figured in the ranks of the Liberal and Conservative Parties. An analysis centered on the different positions held in the occupational structure has not proven more valid. In the nineteenth century the Colombian elite was not differentiated by its location in the agrarian, merchant, financial, or industrial realms. They rather tended to be in more than one realm and to move from one to the other. It would also be mistaken to presume that they had enormous financial capital. On the contrary, the local elites were poor when compared with their American neighbors.[6]

The elites' power as expressed in terms of their capacity for authoring the world did not come from a privileged position in relations of production, but rather, as I endeavor to explain in this chapter, ensued from their belief that they were the legitimate owners of civilization, based on their positions as literate male creoles. Therefore, as historian Malcolm Deas has pointed out, nineteenth-century Colombia was "governed by grammarians," and grammar was an important component of the power structure as reflected in the creation of divisions between those enlightened, and thus entitled to run the country, and those upon whom authority should be exerted and made subjects of civilization.[7] This power structure was premised on a political economy that made not things, but meanings, the center of the process of accumulation.

THE POLITICAL ECONOMY OF CIVILIZATION

The conviction that history is not shaped by a single and privileged category illuminates the search for alternative political economies. I have already mentioned the historical contingency that made possible the emergence of the political economy of capitalism. Civilization and wealth were bound together in such a way that the former was not seen as requisite for the development of the latter. On the contrary, the paradigmatic change was the belief that the expansion of trade would bring civilization to those nations trading with the civilized world. Nevertheless, civilization and commerce were articulated differently in those countries with a colonial relationship with metropolitan centers. At that moment the consciousness of civilization served as a justification for colonial rule.

The proposal for the analysis of a political economy of civilization raises the question of the identification of the object of desire. It has already been stated that it is not the materiality of the objects that determines their value, but rather the reciprocal desire for the object. This understanding of political economy provides room for the study of desire, independent of the materiality of objects. Tracing the production, exchange, and circulation of desired objects makes evident that in the nineteenth century the regime of representation based on an exchange of things, a regime separate from the realm of individuals, had not yet been universalized. In other words, economics was not perceived as a realm separate from the political. In the will to civilization the political economy was organized around the process of production, exchange, and circulation of "civilizing" capital.[8] The market or field of this capital was characterized by the distribution of those civilizing qualities that were accumulated by male creole literati: law, grammar, and morality. This market oriented the struggles and subsequent strategies put in practice by the creole elite to accumulate, control, and distribute these traits among different groups, at the same time ensuring their privileged position. This struggle over the same subjects created a strong rivalry between the Liberals and the Conservatives.

Law, grammar, and morality operated as spaces of recognition from which the literati constructed their worldviews. The power to impose particular visions is linked to the amount of civilizing capital a group claimed to possess. Therefore, the will to civilization was related to the construction of a political economy where the struggle centered on making certain interpretations more legitimate, as well as on defining political spaces that made some identities more visible and valuable than others. In the will to civilization, words were desired as valuable commodities. Words established the link between the regime of representation, the will to civilization, and its authors, the literati. Forms of circulation of words and their diverse forms of legitimization became the main points of reference from which authors defined their positions and struggles. These forms of legitimization included legal and divine authority. The Conservatives favored a restricted circulation of words and saw the Christian religion as the means by which to legitimize claims to truth.

The Liberals, on the contrary, made freedom of the press and constitutional law the foundation of their struggles and the foundation of their power. Some words were more valuable than others, and some voices were more authorized than others. The capacity to control the circulation and legitimization of words defined the basis from which power could be exerted. Wherever the legitimacy of words was threatened, actors were ready to fight in wars; wherever words needed to be protected, legislators issued laws to guarantee their proper value. In the building of the regime of representation, words and civilization were linked together as parts of the whole. Several strategies were used to ensure that some words were more authorized than others, and through different means words were caused to empower certain authors and not others. Grammar and education formed elements of the struggle for control of the production, circulation, and empowerment of words.

The Literati as the Authors of Civilization

Although the establishment of hierarchical differences addresses the questions "Who is civilized, and who is not?" and "Who will be civilized by whom?" the problem of an author has to do with the capacity to create divisions and with access to the power to oppose and impose these divisions.[9] The governing role that the literati exerted during the nineteenth century cannot be understood independent of the vantage point of a "surplus of vision" which, according to the literati, gave them a privileged position with regard to civilization.[10] Distinctions between the literati and others reflected the ideological struggle to gain legitimacy in validating a surplus of vision. Therefore, blacks, women, and Indians were discussed and their incapacity for civilization explained. The privileged space enjoyed by the literati in the will to civilization empowered their vision of the world relative to that of other groups. The creole literati enjoyed the power to "author" history and bring inferior people to their own image. The unequal distribution of power between categories stems from an interconnection between location and the capacity to see that was granted to the diverse groups. Those who were enlightened had a priority in the building of the new republic. Here is Samper's view:

> Everywhere the Creole is the brain of the Revolution, without any economy of generosity and sacrifice, while the Indian, black, mulatto, and the mestizo, are the material instruments. The Creole is at the same time legislator, administrator, popular leader, and chief. . . . He is the one guiding the Revolution and the depository of the philosophy of the Revolution. The remaining races or castes, especially at the beginning, did not do anything other than to obey the impetus of those possessing the prestige of intelligence, intrepidness, and even the superiority of the white race.[11]

The subordinate status conferred on the nonwhite races is even more explicit in the following words of Florentino González, a Liberal reformer:

We Creoles working for the progress [of Christian civilization] come from the European race. . . . Africans, when slaves, were in contact with the white owner but did not acquire their qualities. Liberated, [blacks] became what they were in Africa before.

If there is any hope for freedom in these countries, it has to come from the Creoles (including the mestizos with a predominance of European blood). Creoles are the only ones who have manifested in favor of freedom and civilization; the only ones possessing qualifications that are a clear example of having aptitude for the public sphere.[12]

This quotation epitomizes the discursive strategy followed by the male creole literati: once a clear boundary between civilization and barbarism had been traced, they proceeded to establish a continuity between this civilization and their creole origins. Traveling the road from barbarism to civilization was possible only under the guidance of the "only ones possessing" the qualifications necessary for civilization: the male creole literati. The literati were the architects of representation around the will to civilization. Their personal lives were united in an explicit way with the nation's destiny. This was the case of José María Samper, one of the most important architects of the will of civilization. His biography, "Historia de un Alma" (History of a soul) was described as "the inner history of a soul and also the history of several men and their events; It is also the history of the Fatherland."[13] By seeing everything from one position, the literati were able to exclude other fields of vision. Their position, however, was a weak and fragmentary one. To understand why, we should map the positions from where literati spoke.

Bogotá, a Lettered City

As Michael Shapiro has pointed out, spatial arrangements form a "ground plan" that situates the sets of authors eligible to produce meaningful and effective discourses.[14] In the Latin American context, the cities were privileged sites where the literati grounded their visions. Ángel Rama refers to the colonial cities as *ciudades letradas* (lettered cities) where power groups were specialized in the civilizing mission and whose "pleiad of ecclesiastics, educators and administrators, professionals and many intellectuals" acted as a sacred class.[15] Bogotá, like other Latin American cities, was the privileged center for the literati. As a *ciudad letrada,* Bogotá had several distinctive features compared to other Latin American cities. First, the proportion of people living in the capital (forty thousand people in 1871), compared with the total population of the country (2.9 million), was the lowest of any urban center within the Latin American region.[16] Second, Bogotá was the only city within the region whose population had declined since the beginning of the century (the capital had 2.9 percent of its total population in 1808). Third, Colombia was the only country in the region with no single center of power concentrated in the capital. Eight additional cities had more than ten thousand people (Medellín, Cali, Pasto, Socorro, San Gil, Soatá, Vélez, and Barranquilla). One of the characteristics of the nineteenth century was the fragmentation of the dominant class among local centers of power. It is in light of this fragmentation of power in relation to the total population and the competition of other centers of power that the power of the literati must be understood. This fragmentation provides the specific context of the political struggle (regional distribution of power) and partly explains the lack of a hegemonizing elite.[17]

The weakness the literati accrued from the geographical context as reflected in the distribution of "lettered cities" was in part compensated by the almost monopolistic position they possessed in civilizing capital.[18] Compared with the total population, there were two literati for every one thousand people. In order of priority, priests, educators, and lawyers were the groups involved in the civilizing mission. This explains, in part, the disputes between the Liberals and the Conservatives with regard to the presence of priests in politics and the arguments about religious freedom in the schools. Political power was restricted to a similarly narrow sample of the population. The low number corresponds to the requisites of citizenship established in the constitution of 1843: to be a citizen one had to be at least twenty-one years of age, male, an owner of land valued at at least $300 (or producing a yearly rent of $150), had to know how to read and write, and had to pay taxes.[19] The proportion is even more revealing in a context where most of the population was illiterate. The power that accrued to the male literati was enhanced by the low rate of school attendance of women. Of the thirty thousand students in basic education in 1847, fewer than five thousand, or one in six, were girls.[20]

THE LITERATI AND POWER

The nineteenth century was a time of government by grammarians. Novelists, grammarians, and university professors occupied the highest political positions. The literati's field of influence ranged from novels to constitutions and presidential decrees. This was the case of Jorge Isaacs, the author of *María,* considered the most popular nineteenth-century novel in Latin America, who was also deputy and president of the provinces of Cauca and Antioquia. *María* belongs to the foundational fictions that, in Doris Sommer's words, used erotic passions to transmit republican desires.[21]

Literati member and former president of Colombia José Manuel Marroquín authored *Tratado de Ortología y Ortografía Castellana,* which has been republished several times and is still in print; it has been used by several generations to learn spelling.[22] Miguel Antonio Caro and Rufino Cuervo were both authors of *Latin Grammar,* which went through several editions. Caro's work has been compiled in eight volumes. Miguel Antonio Caro was a fierce critic of utilitarianism and of laissez-faire liberalism on the grounds that they had a pernicious effect on morality and contradicted Catholic principles. Caro coauthored, with Rafael Núñez, the constitution of 1886, which dominated Colombian political life for 105 years. Caro also occupied the presidency of Colombia.

Mid-nineteenth-century philosophical work was less known than contributions to literature and grammar, but nonetheless played an important role for the literati. The creole literati were open to the influence of Spanish, French, and English philosophers such as Feijoo, Jovellanos, Montesquieu, Rousseau, and Bentham. For example, Bentham exchanged correspondence with Bolívar, Miranda, and Santander.[23] At the center of the philosophical controversy was the introduction of utilitarianism, which was considered to be at odds with the principles of the Catholic religion. Ezequiel Rojas, who was considered "the most conspicuous exponent of utilitarianism,"[24] met personally with Jean Baptiste Say in France and Bentham in England. Rojas had a definitive influence on the liberalism of the mid–nineteenth century. For forty years he taught law, morality, and political economy in the law department at San Bartolomé, where most of the literati received their education. Ezequiel Rojas's views on utilitarianism were also reflected in the document that was considered the first platform of the Liberal Party. In *What Does the Liberal Party Want?* he envisioned the republic he would welcome in the future, which embodied the principles he defended in the university classroom. In 1849 Rojas was named minister of the treasury, in 1862 he wrote the Constitution of the Province of Cundinamarca, and in 1863 he participated in the elaboration of the Constitución de Rionegro.

Political economy and sociology were other keystones of literati thought. The brothers Miguel and José María Samper, both students of Ezequiel Rojas, are considered the most distinguished representatives of laissez-faire principles in Colombia; both were also convinced of the superiority of British culture and were critical of Spanish institutions, which they saw as barriers on the road to progress.[25] Miguel Samper is considered the father of political economy, a well-known defender of free trade, and a successful merchant. As an individual, he was considered the archetype of the Englishman.[26] Miguel Samper not only wrote about political economy, but also wrote laws that ended slavery, state monopolies, and *patronato*.[27] He opposed the economic measures of Rafael Nuñez during the period of *La Regeneración* and became a candidate for the presidency of Colombia in 1897. As a journalist José María Samper advocated the reexpulsion of the Jesuits and, as a legislator he presented to congress several projects concerning constitutional reform. Florentino González, Aníbal Galindo, and Manuel Murillo Toro revolutionized the economic system that had been inherited from the colonial period and introduced important reforms in the communications and railroad systems.

THE STRUGGLE AROUND THE CIRCULATION OF WORDS

The tracing of a political economy centered on the will to civilization allows us to understand why wealth was not the source for the exercise of power in nineteenth-century Colombia, but rather the "surplus of vision" of the literati, which resulted from their being the owners of civilization in the middle of an illiterate society. Grammar conferred on the literati the capacity not only to write the rules of grammar, political economy, and constitutional law, but also to impose their vision from the highest levels of political power. A further issue that needs to be addressed is how the civilizing capital became politically useful and how techniques of linguistic differentiation were translated into mechanisms of social exclusion. Words cannot be separated from the power position of the speaker. Therefore, not all words are granted the same capacity to provide meanings. This was the case of native languages whose value was lost once the battle to generalize the use of the Spanish language was considered won:

> Some time elapsed before Spanish became a generalized language; but in the end it achieved victory, and became the unique, sovereign, and dominant language *(lenguaje dominador)*. The conquered languages were not strong enough to leave even a trace; there was only the provincial use of some native words to designate Indian objects.[28]

With the battle for the generalization of the Spanish language won, the battle turned to the mechanisms that granted the empowerment of some words and not others. The contest over the power to circulate, generate, and legitimate words became the most important contest between the Liberals and the Conservatives. This struggle was embedded in the often contradictory aim of spreading civilization while guaranteeing a privileged place to those possessing the art of circulating words. Contradictory positions over the monopoly of knowledge exemplified this tension. In 1850 the Liberals, in their urge to abolish monopolies, decreed freedom of instruction and removed the requirement of a university degree for all professions. Later this decree was overturned and the importance of keeping a small number of professionals was acknowledged. As Miguel Samper stated:

> The scientist, chemist, and engineer have access to education in order to exercise domination over nature; priests and lawyers go to the university to exercise a dominion over people. If both professions are contained within the limits established by the satisfaction of certain needs, they are both useful to society; but in excess number, they become oppressive and detrimental.[29]

Liberals and Conservatives struggled verbally at length over the extent of the freedom and privilege to be accorded to the circulation of the printed word. They held different positions as to the relationship between freedom of the press and civilization. The advent of the Liberals in 1849 was celebrated as introducing the "all-powerful era of the leaflet."[30] The Liberals exalted the written word, irrespective of content, style, or form. In 1850 they proposed that congress legislate freedom of the press. The secretary of the government, Zaldúa, used as his main arguments the benefits that the press had brought to the world; the fact that the offenses occasioned by the use of a printed

paper do not cause damage, because a printed paper can be responded to with another printed paper; and the difficulty of qualifying this
offense without running the risk that the press would be subjected to
arbitrariness. Before Congress he argued:

> A free press is the universal feature of the political body, the true
> democracy of thought. . . . Nothing must impede its illimitable do-
> minion, because the press is the light and life of a republican society.
> Everything related to happiness or unhappiness of the social belongs
> to [the press]'s dominion. To the press belongs the criticism and the
> praise of habits, laws, institutions. To the press must be accountable
> the exercise of power, political debates, the decision of tribunals, citi-
> zens' claims, the requirements of an era, people's problems, programs
> of political parties, and religious feelings.[31]

Samper's project was rejected in the senate when the Conservatives
unanimously voted against it.[32] In 1851, however, a decree guaranteeing freedom of the press was introduced. The constitution of 1853
endorsed the reform of 1851. The constitution of 1863 guaranteed
absolute freedom of the press by declaring, in the sixth article, "la
libertad absoluta de imprenta y circulación de impresos" (the absolute freedom of press and press circulation) and in the seventh, "la
libertad de expresar sus pensamientos de palabra o por escrito sin
limitación alguna" (the freedom to express thoughts using oral or
printed words without any limitation).

The Liberals came to power in the name of freedom of the press
and in the name of popular tribunes. At the beginning of the Liberal
revolution, José María Samper praised them as follows:

> The press and popular tribunals are going to appropriate the moment
> in order to inaugurate the kingdom of rationality and free intelli-
> gence. The power of the pamphlet will be established, and the con-
> structive storm of popular participation and electoral cycles will
> begin. Politics, preparing the future, will prepare the field where legis-
> lation will make real the revolution of ideas and popular life.[33]

According to Samper, popular tribunals and writers "were the owners
of the moment because they were the interpreters" for the masses.[34]

The Conservatives, on the contrary, were distrustful of the free circulation of words as a means by which to foster civilization.[35] They
equated "absolute freedom" of the press with "absolute freedom and
irresponsibility." Conservative J. E. Caro summarized the attempt by
the Liberals to establish freedom of the press as follows:

> By the year 1849 [when the Liberals gained the presidency,] . . . in-
> stead of asking for more morality, more order, more efficacy in the in-
> tervention of authority regarding the press and elsewhere, [the Lib-
> erals] began to implore loudly as a satisfaction of all that was needed,
> as a supreme good, more freedom in everything, and with a special
> eagerness more and more freedom of the press![36]

Caro considered Zaldúa's arguments in favor of freedom of the
press to be a barbarism not proper for rational men. He believed that
freedom of the press acted as an engine of revolutions.[37] In Caro's
view, a free press could be a source of crime committed in not small,
but large, proportions. On many occasions, Caro said that words are
as dangerous as arms. In an article published in 1888, he referred to
the story of one of the "several victims" of the 1863 constitution: a
priest "who died as a consequence of a defamation, made on the
basis of two false witnesses, who later died in the hospital of a despicable illness, after having confessed their false testimony."[38] Caro
looked with terror at the Russian example, where public libraries
were loaded with dangerous books. He saw the Russians' nihilistic
tendencies as a result of the practice of reading, since all publications
were allowed and were read equally by men and women:

> It is in this country where communist and materialist theories are
> going to occasion more damage. . . . Public libraries, filled with all
> kinds of dangerous novelties, are visited by all kinds of male readers,
> and especially *female readers*. There, in the reading allowed and en-
> couraged by the government, lies the main source of nihilism, nour-
> ished by erudite men and women.[39]

GRAMMAR AND EDUCATION: WORDS AS THE WAY
TO BRING POWER INTO BEING

Words were pivotal elements in the power strategy deployed by the
mid-nineteenth-century literati in the disputes over civilization. With
regard to the circulation of words, their origin, and the best strategy
for disseminating words, the Conservatives and the Liberals diverged.
The former emphasized the correct use of language (grammar) and
religion, whereas the Liberals emphasized the spread of enlightenment through universal education.

"Speaking well" (el bien hablar) was one strategy deployed by the
Conservatives to consolidate their power. Speaking well was an element of establishing hierarchical differences among racial and social

groups. Speaking well was, like the color of one's skin, something inherited at birth. As Rufino Cuervo wrote, "Speaking well is like good breeding. Those who had sucked from the mother's milk and had enriched its use with their contact with polished people (gente fina), know how to obey the rules of language even in the most difficult circumstances."[40]

The art of grammar was an exclusionist quality dividing rulers and the ruled: "Obviously, the oddness of ordinary people who write, compelled by their need, is easier to forgive, but it is not easy to be tolerant in this regard with those who pretend to order the world."[41] The art of grammar was meant for those who ruled. Cuervo introduced his treatise on grammar with the following statement:

> Speaking well is one of the clearest signs of cultivation and good birth, and an indispensable condition of those who wish to use, in favor of their equals, through speech or through writing, the talents which nature has given them: this is the reason for the insistence with which people recommend the study of grammar.[42]

Grammar was seen as a quality to be defended if the rulers were to maintain their differences, endangered by contemporary events, as grammarian Cuervo reveals:

> No one doubts that, as a matter of principle, the crowd cannot claim preeminence over the educated; all the same, something of the crowd can penetrate their sphere, in certain places and under special circumstances. Therefore, isolation from other brother peoples, which is the cause of forgetting many pure locutions and of the consequent inequality of language, rubbing shoulders with uncouth people, as for example children do with servants, and the disorders and dislocations of the social strata caused by revolutionary uprisings, which raise even to the highest posts ignorant and uncivil people, can vulgarize (aplebeyar) the language, bringing into general use antigrammatical terms and low words.[43]

Grammar was not the sole quality deployed as power; education served this objective as well. The passage of Colombia from a barbarian to a civilized country became one of the central concerns of Liberals as well as their Conservative opponents. Liberals and Conservatives agreed that education was the port of entry through which to reach civilization. They agreed that only education could transform the brutalized masses into thoughtful, productive people.[44] This consensus did not extend to the role of religion in educational curricula.

On the contrary, the battle over education was as fierce as the contest for the constitutions.

The priority given to education was evident as early as 1821, when the Congress of Cúcuta issued the first general education law under the presidency of Santander. Public primary education was seen as necessary for Colombians to learn the "sacred obligations imposed upon them by religion and Christian morality . . . [and] the rights and duties of man in social life."[45] In 1826 the government of Santander issued the *Plan de Estudios,* which established that every parish in the country, no matter what size, was to have a primary school. The plan also made compulsory the use of Bentham's principles for law students and introduced the study of English and French in high schools. These reforms were seen as being in contradiction to the principles of the Catholic religion. The controversy was centered on the use of Bentham's principles and on the "Protestant" orientation of several books recommended in the *Plan de Estudios.*[46] A priest in Bogotá asked the parents of his parish not to send their children to San Bartolomé, where Bentham's principles were taught. Vicente Azuero, a politician and one of the literati, undertook Bentham's defense, arguing that if his texts were considered harmful because they were written by a Protestant, the Colombian Constitution and laws should also be banned because they followed the constitutions of England, France, and the United States, countries where most of the people were "heretics."[47]

The debate on education continued in the following decades. The sponsoring of a German pedagogical mission and the Organization of the General Directorate of Public Instruction aggravated this debate. The Organic Decree of 1870 defined education as a function of the federal government (article 1), and at the same time prohibited the government from intervening in religious education (article 36). As a result of Liberal policies, there was an increase in the school enrollment, a school census was implemented, and more attention was paid to educational methodology. The Liberal government incorporated the German pedagogical mission, which was the subject of a strong controversy with the Catholic Church.[48] As a result of German assistance, twenty centers for teacher training *(Escuelas Normales)* were created that followed a methodology close to that used in the Prussian schools. The knowledge that several members of the German mission were Protestants renewed the opposition to the Liberal reform. The educational reform entered into contradiction not only with the indigenous culture, but also with the colonial past inherited from Spanish Catholic tradition. Although Neo-Granadins embraced the modern ideas coming from England, Germany, or France, they rejected their connection with Protestantism. The controversy over Bentham appeared on several occasions, and the tension between Liberals and the church persisted during the time when the Liberals were in power. The Organic Decree so heightened the disagreements between the two parties that the Conservatives decided to go to war in 1876. In this war the Conservatives were defeated.

A main issue at stake in this contest was the Liberals' attempt to undermine the church's privileged role in the definition and diffusion of truth. The position of the Conservatives regarding the linkages between civilization and religion appear in these excerpts from a public letter written by Rufino Cuervo:

> We support the [Catholic religion] because it is the only and most powerful element of morality and civilization for our ignorant and heterogeneous popular masses, dispersed in vast and harsh regions; we support [the Catholic religion] because it is the true principle to conserve social order, seriously threatened by the divisions and sectors in the struggle for power in our beloved country. To exert, conserve, and defend our magnificent religion is more than a right, it is a faculty, like thinking; and it is even more than a faculty, it is a duty, a sacred duty. . . . If we are wrong in our beliefs and decisions, our mistake will be common to *two hundred and fifty million* Catholics scattered in *the civilized world* in which we live. . . . The Christian religion is only distant from those countries captured by tyrannical governments or by the licentiousness of the masses when the corruption of habits, vices, crimes, and the forgetfulness of religious duties foretell the transition or the reversal of the social to the savage life. Religion emigrates, carrying with it the *true civilization,* its undetached companion [emphasis in the original].[49]

For the Liberals, what was at stake in the contest with the Conservatives was precisely the right to govern. As was succinctly stated by Liberal Camacho Roldán, "On the part of the government, it is a question of 'to be or not to be.' "[50] In his view, the dominance of religion should end so that governors would be able to perform their functions. He summarized, as follows, the Liberal position:

The Catholic priests want to exert an absolute dominance over all aspects of human thought, to draw limits to the unlimited activity of the human mind, and to be the only repository of truth and the only force in charge of spreading [the truth] to the people. From the *Index,* in Rome, whose pretension is to declare which are the only books permissible to be read, and on whose criteria very few would have been admitted, to the remotest priest that condemns every day the most simple scientific thought, Catholic religion has always been in antagonism and open struggle with freedom of thought and belief.[51]

The debate on the educational reform divided the elite between the *Instruccionistas* (Instructionists) and the *Ignorantistas* (Ignorants).[52] The divide between those who opposed and those who favored public instructions was mainly moral and political. According to *Ignorantistas,* mainly Conservatives, education should be moral and religious and should be based on Colombian manners and customs. They opposed the obligatory character of public instruction, arguing individual freedom to remain ignorant and therefore without obligation to receive instruction.[53] The *Ignorantistas* also rejected the secular character of education, arguing that only religion could control the bad habits of the poor; without religion, Colombians would be corrupted and crime would increase.

A strong resistance was organized against the implementation of the 1870 Organic Decree. The bishops of Popayán and Pasto announced that those parents who were sending their children to public schools were sinning and would be excommunicated and asked Catholic priests to boycott schools. Another priest condemned the Educational Census ordered in the decree and asked parents to hide their children to keep them from being counted.[54]

CONCLUSION

The Colombian elite, which emerged after the independence, was small and relatively poor when compared with the elites of other Latin American countries and was generally dispersed over a vast expanse of territory. Notwithstanding their limited economic power, this small proportion of the population (six thousand out of three million inhabitants) authored a regime of representation that allowed them to establish strong boundaries with respect to the rest of the population: they were literati in a country where 90 percent of the population was illiterate; they were creoles, descendents of Spanish parents, where the majority of the people were mestizos, Indians, and blacks; most of them were male, as the educational and legal systems were largely restricted to men.

In mid-nineteenth-century Colombia, political economy was not centered on the accumulation of wealth; it was centered on the accumulation of words and civilizing capital. Power was concentrated in those who possessed Western civilization's secrets: the male Creole literati. They reserved their own place in the regime of representation as the ones knowledgeable enough to direct the new republic on the proper road. They reserved their place by holding the highest positions in civilized society: the literati became prestigious politicians, and politics enjoyed high status. The literati were the architects of civilization, and their power stemmed from their capacity to produce, circulate, and value their most precious commodity: words.

How free the circulation of words should be, what was the veritable source of words' legitimacy, who were the most authorized voices, and from where their power was to be exerted, were contentious issues among the mid-nineteenth-century literati. The most important constitutional battles and the civil wars between the Liberals and the Conservatives were fought around the issue of how words were to be employed to forge the civilizing mission.

4

The Subalterns' Voices

Monologism denies that there exists outside of it another consciousness, with the same rights, and capable of responding on an equal footing, another and equal I (thou). For a monological outlook (in its extreme or pure form) the other remains entirely and only an object of consciousness. No response capable of altering everything in the world of my consciousness is expected of this other. The monologue is accomplished and deaf to the other's response. . . . Monologue makes do without the other.

MIKHAIL M. BAKHTIN, *PROBLEMS OF DOSTOYEVSKY'S POETICS* (1984)

The will to civilization as a regime of representation not only was built in a process of exchange between a backward Latin America and a civilized Europe, but emerged, as well, from the process of exchange between dominating and subaltern voices. Subalterns were not passive recipients of what was said by male creole literati voices. As participants in the dialogue, they collaborated in or even resisted certain actions. Subalterns, who were located in the lower ranks of civilization—Indians, artisans, women, and blacks—had voices and a view from which they contested the monological representation of the world. Therefore, the main task of my inquiry in this chapter is to recover these subalterns' voices.

This endeavor is problematic given the predominant narratives of "history" and "civilization." History has been told as the universal history of white male Western civilization in which all other histories culminate. The universalization of history encompasses the narrative of capitalism's development as well. Therefore, those outside Western civilization as well as subsistence-level peasants, indigenous communities, and women are left "without a history." Generally these groups embody all the characteristics that place them outside history by representing everything that is backward and primitive.

It is not surprising that the homogenization of history has been complemented by the representation of those "outside history" as potentially disruptive.[1] The effects of this double move are, on the one hand, the naturalization of concepts such as laissez-faire capitalism, civilization, and development. Because these concepts are presented as independent of their context, the power relations supporting them are obscured. These concepts, as Arturo Escobar remarks, are "historical contingencies" whose histories must be traced and their mechanisms of truth and power revealed.[2] On the other hand, as Edward D. Said has illustrated, the homogenization of histories into a universal (Western) history culminating in Europe or the West is part of the practice of imperialism.[3] The strangeness of the Third World forms the base for the authority of imperialistic practices. The invention of the Orient by Europe was the instrument that allowed the Orient's acquisition by Europe. Imperialism, in Said's view, encompasses not only the accumulation of territories and populations and the control of economies, but also the incorporation and universalization of histories.

To retrieve the subalterns' histories is therefore to take as objects of analysis both the discourses that enable practices of domination and those resisting authoritarian pretensions. Ranaji Guha and the Subaltern Studies group have pointed out the political implications of a project aimed at retrieving history. In Guha's view, the rebel has had no place in history as the subject of rebellion.[4] Rebels are seen as spontaneously responding to physical suffering or as a "contingent element in another history with another subject." Guha's conclusion is that both liberal and leftist historiography exclude the rebel as a "conscious subject of his own history." He proposes a history that recovers peasant or subaltern consciousness, independent of the dominant groups that have monopolized historiography.[5]

The recovery of the past, its actors, and their interpretations is a problematic endeavor, especially in the case of those who have been left "outside history." Gayatri Spivak, for example, has pointed out the difficulty of "retrieving" the subalterns' consciousness. In her view, as long as the subaltern is defined as different, that is, as deviating from an ideal, the subaltern "has no history and cannot speak." To be outside history means to be deprived of a voice and of a space from which to talk.[6] Spivak makes her case by pointing out the situation of the subaltern female, who is silenced by imperialism and patriarchy. Spivak's solution is not to abstain from representation. The historian's task is rather to measure silences, the things that a text cannot say.

RESISTING THE HISTORICAL MONOLOGUE

The retrieval of the subalterns' voices requires overcoming the monologism frequently found in the understanding of the positions of the self and the Other. We find different types of monologism even in those intellectuals whose aim is to uncover the effects on power of the Western system of knowledge about the Other. One consists in unifying in the name of the self, as is the case of Edward Said's *Orientalism,* where the Orient is seen as a construction of Western consciousness.[7] The last word about the Orient is the one pronounced by the West. A second type of monologism, which Spivak names "nativism," consists in turning the Other into a self.[8] In Spivak's view, this is not possible because the project of imperialism has already refracted the Other into a domesticated Other that consolidates the imperialist self. To guard against the temptation of "succumbing to a nostalgia for lost origins," she recommends turning "to the archives of imperial governance."[9] A third monological reading, named "maniquean" by Néstor García Canclini, consists in understanding the hegemonic and subaltern positions only in terms of confrontation or opposition. Such understanding ignores the compromises between those positions, since their interactions are not only "scenarios of struggle, but also the place where one and the other perform the experiences of otherness and self-recognition."[10] The way out of this monological thinking is to abandon a vision where each side is in opposition, as is the case with hegemon and subaltern or civilizer and barbarian, and is depicted as outside and exterior in respect to the other. As Fernando Coronil reminds us, subalternity and dominance are relational characterizations defining a state of being.[11]

Bakhtin's concept of hybridization illustrates the intersubjective character of identity.[12] The two consciousnesses are always present, that of the represented and the one doing the representation, even if the two belong to different language systems.[13] Therefore, the subaltern has the capacity to contest, as opposed to only passively reproducing, the dominant language system. According to Bakhtin, the unmasking of another's speech is accomplished through double-voice construction; the same word belongs to a single speaker, but contains "mixed within it two utterances, two speech manners, two styles, two 'languages,' two semantic and axiological belief systems."[14]

Bakhtin believes that the author defines Others' places and also assigns himself or herself a place. The position from which the author speaks, its temporal and spatial point of view, affects how the author looks upon events and constructs the meanings of these events. Therefore, it is crucial to understand who is speaking and the power position from which the author speaks. Two equally misleading positions are encountered when posing the relationship between the position occupied by the author and his or her worldview: one is to assume that there are not points of reference in which to ground the process of endowing things with meanings; the author's imagination will be free from constraints. A second is to assume that the author's worldview reproduces his or her position in either its productive or its cultural structures. Bakhtin solves this problem by positing a dialogical relationship between the author and his or her context: the represented world does not reproduce the real world, nor are authors absolutely free to construct their own views.[15] The process of endowing phenomena with meaning is also a process of incorporating phenomena into spatial and temporal existence. The process of assigning value to a phenomenon ensues from the incorporation of that phenomenon into time and space. We have seen that this was the case for Indians, blacks, and women who were distanced in time and space by assigning them to a distant past (Indians), to a wild territory (blacks), or to the domestic realm (women).

The author also establishes a relationship with the represented world that could be monological or dialogical.[16] In the former case, the author represents the world from his or her own perspective. Only the author's voice is presented, and the field of vision of the author is unified and confers meaning to others; others do not have an independent perspective. The privileged position the author enjoys is linked to the self-imposed capacity to "author" others because of the higher position assigned to him or her. Those in higher places enjoy a "surplus of vision" relative to others' positions. Under monological conditions, only the vision of those enjoying privileged positions is recognized. This privilege grants the power of finalization (governing).

THE DOMINANT VISION

One way to recognize the Other is by looking at how the self sees himself or herself through "the eyes of the Other," since how one defines oneself is not independent of the Other's gaze. To name the self civilized is to assign the Other an uncivilized character. The violence of representation designates this exclusionary character in processes of identity formation. Spivak calls epistemic violence "the construction of a self-immolating colonial subject for the glorification of the social mission of the colonizer."[17]

Medardo Rivas's *Workers in the Hot Lowlands* offers an opportunity to recover the subaltern from the dominant vision. It also provides an example of the violence implicit in the sacrifice of the Other, in this case the laboring poor, in the name of the civilizing mission of the *hacendados*. This text presents the perspective of the *hacendado* who was a member of the literati. Rivas was a lawyer from the National University, as well as a politician, representative to the congress, journalist, and literati member. The author explicitly stated that his aim was to tell the history of the "titanic men who brought civilization, wealth, and farming to the land covered by primitive jungle, and whose memory should remain forever."[18] His narrative is about those wealthy *hacendados* who moved to the hot lowlands during the tobacco and quinine boom. Only they were provided with proper names and a place from which to talk. The life of the poor laborers was structured through the eyes of the heroic virtues of the *hacendados*. The latter were the ones who were given the name of "workers." Poor laborers were robbed of a space from which to talk.

Rivas's depiction of *hacendados* as heroes is justified by the representation of both the land and poor laborers as wild and in need of *hacendados'* work to acquire a proper form. According to Rivas, "To own a property in hot lowlands was equivalent to having no property to the eyes of people from Bogotá. . . . The only value of hot lowlands was that of the crops of sugar cane in the small *trapiches* (sugar mills)."[19] The author, a *hacendado* himself, described a *trapiche* as primitive and female, and he reduced poor laborers to things whose worth was equivalent to the work done by animals. This representation legitimizes the penetration and possession of a land by the heroic workers from the city: "The *Trapiche* is a primitive machine invented to obtain the juice of the sugar cane. The wheel in the middle has a stick, which is continuously pulled by two mules, chased by a filthy young boy, half-nude and dirty." The sugar mill was not only primitive, but female as well, since it looked "like those poor abandoned women after serving tirelessly during their youthfulness, abandoned later by their lover, crying about their past and struggling against a wretched future."[20]

The work in the *trapiches* was not only gendered, but racialized as well. Rivas valued the *trapiches* according to the price of the container, generally made of copper, plus the value of the slaves doing the work and the mules. In his view, the Law of Abolition of Slavery (1851) annulled the value of slaves and was devastating for the hacienda economy; as he stated, after abolition "property without blacks was worthless."[21]

The hybrid character of language is revealed in the description of the working conditions in the *trapiche*. Rivas, the author, looked at the institutions he represented (civilization, democracy, and republic) through the eyes of the laboring Other: "This job is carried out by men whose cruelty is an indictment against the established republican and democratic government, against the country's religion, whose civilizing mission has been abandoned, and against any feeling of philanthropy which is supposed to reign in our society. Manly women, who have lost the proper charm of their gender, and live in the most humiliating situation, held by the physical necessity to earn pay, work there."[22] In the previous description there are two consciousnesses: the author, as observer, looks through the eyes of the observed. Nevertheless, the representation of difference implies both a relationship of power and a process of concealment. In Homi Bhabha's words, it was "a discourse at the crossroads of what is known and permissible and that which though known must be kept concealed; a discourse uttered between the lines and as such both against the rules and within them."[23] Although the situation of the poor laborer was rejected, a power relationship was implied in the representation of the Other as not civilized and therefore subject to the civilizing power of wealthy *hacendados*. Furthermore, there was an absence of linkages between the situation of poor laborers and that of *hacenda-*

dos, making possible the concealment of any connection between their respective situations. This was done by erasing the identification between the Other and the self. Therefore, women working in the sugar mill were not like women; they were "manly women," and laborers were closer to animals than to men: "In one extreme of the hut, like the devil's boiler where the condemned are cooked, the boiled syrup is stirred by a half-naked, dirty man, closer to a monster than to a human being. . . . Like Satan he walks in the deep, covered in smoke and standing on the burning ashes."[24]

Rivas's text also insinuated traces of the Other's voice. He could not stand completely outside the effect that these voices produced in his own consciousness: "Sitting on each side of the *trapiche,* two women crush the sugar cane between the two wheels, and they sing something sad, monotonous, and gloomy, producing sadness in the heart."[25] What was the song about? Rivas was deaf to the content of the song; therefore, we cannot hear the Others' voices.

THE SUBALTERNS' VOICES

Fortunately, literature is a good ally for recovering the Others' voices, as in the collection by José María Vergara, where he quotes the song entitled "El Trapiche" (The sugar mill) as an example of popular poetry.[26] According to him, before the struggles for independence poetry was not popular, given the isolation of the ethnic groups. The struggle for independence had as one of its effects the "unification of memories, and there was a fatherland and a common history."[27] This unification of memories, in his view, would give birth to "popular poetry," which he defined as an exchange between the dominant and the dominated.

In the poem the subaltern's voice reproduces both the gaze of the Other upon the self and her own voice. The black woman looks through the eyes of her owners: "My lady does not love me / My lord can't stand me." These words reflect the owner's feelings of hostility toward the slave. She knows the small value the owner places on her: "She is going to sell me / For the price of a ripe banana / And a cup of honey." The words of the owner are known by the community of slaves and are reflected in a third voice: "Your owner wants to sell you!" The "double voice" of the black woman is manifested in the poem's expression of rejection and collaboration: although the black woman experiences hate from her owners, she prefers to learn what she is expected to learn than to be sold for a very low price to another owner: "Although I knew nothing / I will learn, / And if I don't / You can sell me." The subaltern knows the owner's violence toward her; therefore, she does what is expected of her. But because fear is the reason for her compliance, she is rejecting the owner's framing of her own consciousness; hence the circularity of the chorus's voice: "Grind at midnight / Grind at dawn."

Canto del Trapiche

Mi señora no me quiere
Mi amo no me puede vé;
Mi señora, la chiquita,
Dice que me ha de vendé
Por un plátano maduro
y una totumita é mié.

—Mi señora, la chiquita,
No me venda sumecé (bis)
Fracica!
—Señó
—Tu amo te quiere vendé!
—Po qué? Po qué?
—Poque no sabé molé.

—Man que nunca sepa
Yo aprenderé,
Y si no aprendiere
Véndame uté.

Molé, mole!
Molé, trapiche, molé!
Molé la caña pasada,
Moléla a la medianoche,
Moléla á la madrugada

The Sugar Mill Song

My lady does not love me
My lord can't stand me;
My little lady says
She is going to sell me
For the price of a ripe banana
And a cup of honey.

—My little lady,
Don't sell me gentlewoman (twice)
Fracica!
—Sir
Your owner wants to sell you
Why? Why?
—Because you do not know how to grind.

—Although I knew nothing
I will learn,
And if I don't
You can sell me.

Grind, grind!
Grind, sugar mill, grind!
Grind the passing cane,
Grind at midnight,
Grind at dawn.[28]

Vergara's attribution of this poem to black authors was profoundly contested in a polemic by the literary historian J. M. Restrepo. He alleged that it was impossible for blacks to have their own voice:

Unmixed blacks, hunted as animals by slave traffickers . . . could bring their dance and maybe their own tunes; but only when they learned Castilian were they able to sing what they heard, that is, the songs of the learned tongue. The *Canto del Trapiche*, attributed by Vergara to blacks as something peculiar to them, and whose song we can still hear in Antioquia, has nothing exclusive to blacks *(hijos de Cam)*, because of their ignorance, and given the difficulty of passing from their own native dialects to the Castilian voices, soft and docile, pronounced by their owners, which were spoiled with cruelty, [the Castilian language] is even spoiled by cultivated blacks, despite the fact of living for several generations and during long periods of time among white and civilized people. . . . Before, what kind of songs, tunes, or poetry could ever be chanted by those wretched, oppressed by work and maintained under the foreman's whip submerged in the dark silence of their slave's prison?[29]

Contrary to Restrepo's opinion, popular songs and poetry constituted the space where subalterns played the drama of recognition as an interlacing of submissions and resistances, challenges and complicities.[30]

A BLACK MEMBER OF THE LITERATI: CANDELARIO OBESO

The work and life of Candelario Obeso expressed, more than anything else, the struggle for recognition of black literati living in a world dominated by creoles' imitation of the civilized world.[31] Obeso was born in Mompox in 1849, the year proclaimed by José María Samper as the beginning of the "pamphlet revolution." Obeso attended school in Mompox, which was distant from the center of power, but midway between the capital and the outside world. In 1866 he went to Bogotá, where he gained a scholarship in the military school founded by Colonel Tomás Cipriano de Mosquera. On the occasion of the coup of 1867, the school was closed and he went to the National University, where he studied language, literature, and law. Obeso, like most creole literati, was a student of Ezequiel Rojas, a prominent lawyer and the intellectual author of the Liberal program.

The work of Obeso provides a unique opportunity to explore the dialectic of recognition present in the processes of overcoming otherness and gaining self-recognition. As has been remarked by Laurence E. Prescott, "As a man of color and learning, living in nineteenth century Colombia, where the national literature and culture were largely considered to be the province and patrimony of the citizens of Hispanic or European descent, Obeso was not merely a rarity but an anomaly."[32] Obeso's language reflects the conflict of living on the boundary between the world of literati men and blacks. He struggled to liberate white men and women from racial prejudices, as well as to unmask the limits of white discourse about what was considered civilized and valued. When Obeso published his book *Cantos Populares de mi Tierra* in 1877, he saw popular literature as the way to build a true literature instead of imitating European letters. In his view, "The cultivation [of popular literature] is the only road to the founding of a true and positive literature. . . . I hope that our younger generations, lovers of our country's progress, will work in the building of a civilized country. And by doing so, will end the sadness of imitation, which delayed the growth of Hispanic-American letters."[33] According to Prescott, Obeso's *Cantos Populares* "celebrates and even vindicates the black population of the Coast, modest and hardworking, whose values, virtues and habits are extolled in front of the major white society, which did not look at them with sympathy or respect."[34] In this book Obeso used "authentic black talk," which he considered the "true, positive literature" of Colombia.[35]

Through his poems Obeso unmasked whites' desires with regard to blacks. He saw the nineteenth-century wars as a battle between creole literati, for whose ends black people were used in the struggle for civilization. Blacks were depicted as a stepladder in the *cachaco* battle.[36] In his poem "Serenata" he made clear that in this war he preferred not to fight:

Serenata

Ricen que hay guerra
con los cachacos,
Y a mí me chocan
Los Zambapalo
　　[. . .]
Cuando los goros
Sí fuí sordao
Pocque efendía
Mi humilde rancho
　　[. . .]
Si acguno quiere,
Trepacse en arto
Buque ejcalera
Por otro Lao
　　[. . .]
Ya pasó er tiempo
Re loj eclavos:
Somo hoy tan libre
Como lo branco
　　[. . .]
Quieren la guerra
Con los cachacos?
Yo no me muevo
Re aquí e mi rancho
　　[. . .]

Serenade

They say we are in war
With cachacos,
And I dislike
Fighters
　　[. . .]
When Conservative
I was a soldier

Because I defended
My poor hut
    [. . .]
If someone attempts
To go up,
Look for a ladder,
In another place!
The time of slavery
Is over.
I am free
As white men
    [. . .]
Do they want war
With the cachacos?
I will not move
From my hut
    [. . .]37

In this poem he expresses his feeling of equality with whites and their capacity for collaboration (if the struggle favors their own interests) or resistance (remaining at home). In his view, blacks are not step-ladders for the accomplishment of white desires.

Contrary to creoles who praised European civilization, Obeso defended local knowledge as opposed to European rationality. His poems are a continuous questioning of the rationality brought from the European world and of its status as the privileged entry to the world of knowledge. *Cantos Populares* opens with a poem entitled "The Pigeons" in which he advanced the notion that the conduct of these animals could be a source of knowledge. The author confessed that, although pigeons are poor animals, he had learned more from them than he had learned in school:

Los Palomos

Siendo probe alimanes lo palomos,
A la jente a sé jente noj enseñan;
E su conduct la mejó cactilla;
Hai en us moros ejertiva cencia
Siendo probe alimales lo palomos,
Se aprende en ello má que en la j'ecuela;
Yo, poc lo meno, en su cocto libro
Eturio re la vira la maneras
    [. . .]

The Pigeons

Even though pigeons are poor animals
They teach humans how to be more humane.
Their conduct is the best manual;
there is, in their habits, useful knowledge.
Even though pigeons are just poor animals
One can learn more from them,
more than at school.
I, for one, in their learned book,
Study the ways of life
      [. . .][38]

In Obeso's poems we can also distinguish the presence of desire that results from the lack of knowledge of whites' intentions toward blacks. This gap is reflected in Lacan's question "What do you really want?" Obeso depicted the ambivalence that characterized the situation of two different desire systems in the poem "Epropiación re Uno Córigos" (Expropriation of certain legal codes), which is about the friendship between a white man and a black man. In the poem the white man misunderstands the black's desire for support as motivated by hunger. Any attempt to clarify the situation results in misunderstanding. The ambivalence is reflected in the title of the poem and the emphasis on the word *expropriation,* which meant the taking away of property with compensation in order to accomplish a public good. The irony was that what was being expropriated was law (codes) in order to fulfil the need for shelter: the man decides to sell the code and buy materials with which to fix his hut. He compares the two value systems: the legal codes as seen from the white man's perspective and from the black man's perspective. In the poem the codes are valued according to the amount of material he is able to buy, in this case, half a pound of glue.[39]

Obeso had contradictory feelings regarding the postindependence milieu. In his poem "Espresión re mi amitá" (Expression of friendship) Obeso stood up for the democratic system and for the freedom granted to blacks and Indians. He can give up a bit of freedom for a friend, "but never by force, because I own myself."[40] At the same time, he complained about whites' disregard for local culture and the inability of whites to understand black culture. He expressed the hope that someday a white man would visit a black locale; then he would realize that black women also have "good manners."

Ojalá que arguna vé
Le mire a uté entre lo mío,
Verá bien cuanto mi negra
Tiene tratamiento fino
         [. . .]

I wish that some day
I might see you among my people,
Then you would realize that my black woman
Has good manners too
         [. . .][41]

Obeso expressed his belief that blacks, unlike whites, are able to differentiate the Other:

Cuando soi un probe negro
Sin más ciencia que mi oficio,
No ignoro quién merece
Actún repeto i cariño
         [. . .]

Although I am a poor black
Without more knowledge than my work,
I do not ignore those who earn
Respect and friendship by their actions.[42]

At the same time, Obeso expressed the oppressive character of the postcolonial state for blacks. In his poem "Canto rel Montara" (Song of the wild man) he praised the freedom of those living outside civilization: "Here [in the wilderness] no one oppresses me. / The Governor and the army live far away." In the wilderness he could control the fierce animals, while in the towns "There is no antidote / Against government. / Therefore, I do not change / What I have For the things others have / In the city."[43]

Obeso's poem "Struggle and Conquest" illustrates blacks' conflict with regard to recognition as seen in their desires for both equality and difference. This drama is represented in the conquest of a white woman. Obeso displays a double-pronged strategy for gaining recognition: one is to conceal differences. He asks the woman to ignore the color of his skin and to look at him as an equal. His soul is as white as hers. In a second situation, he contemplates the possibility of keeping both colors, black and white, one illuminating the other. The idea of sameness gives way to that of difference. Whitening disappears as a strategy to conquer the Other. Therefore, Obeso over-comes the idea of fusing the self with the Other, defended by white male literati. On the contrary, if he keeps both whiteness and black-ness, one can illuminate the other.

Lucha y Conquijta

Oh branca, branca hermosa,
Pocqué me trata asina?
    [. . .]
¿Pocaue me ve la cuti
Re la coló e la tinta
Acaso cré que é negra
Tamién er arma mía? . . .
En eso te equivoca;
La piedra máj bonita
En er cacbón, a vece,
se jallan ejcondías! . . .

¡Oh branca! . . . Tú lo sabe
    [. . .]
(Acécate tranquila);
Ar nacdo güeleroso
Qué fló lo revaliza?
    [. . .]
Acéccate y no tema)
Si engürto en er se mira
Un lazo bien lustroso
Re mi coló . . . espresiva?
    [. . .]
Tú te parece ar nacdo;
Mi brazo son re endrina,
Réjalos que a tu talle
Se enrollen como cinta
    [. . .]

Struggle and Conquest

Oh beautiful white woman,
What explains your disdain?
    [. . .]
Because you see my skin
as black as ink
Do you think that my soul

Is also black?
You are mistaken;
The most beautiful stones
Are, most of the times,
Hidden in charcoal!
        [. . .]

Oh white woman! . . . You know
        [. . .]
(Come closer, calm down);
Who will compete
With the white nard?
        [. . .]
Come closer, without fear)
If a nard is wrapped
In a bright ribbon
Of my color . . . expressive?
        [. . .]
You are the nard;
My arm is a wild plum,
Let my arm embrace your waist
Like a ribbon
        [. . .]⁴⁴

In this poem Obeso's self-recognition is linked to that of the white woman's consciousness of him, as reflected in the question "Do you think that my soul / Is also black?" Obeso looks at himself through her eyes, but at the same time he has his own consciousness, expressed in the statement "You are mistaken." The dialogic orientation of Obeso's language contrasts with Medardo Rivas's monologism. Although the latter does not expect a response of the Other, in Obeso's poem every word anticipates a response and is aimed at provoking an answer: "Come closer, without fear.)" The lack of a parenthesis at the beginning of the sentence also reflects his openness to the Other's response.

In 1882, two years before his death at the age of thirty-six, Obeso published a long poem "La Lucha de la Vida" (The struggle for being), a biographical drama about the ambivalence surrounding the life of a black poet living on the boundary between the world of civilization and popular existence. The poet's life is the product of a struggle between two alien consciousnesses that dictate what he is to be or not to be. The voice of these consciousnesses appear under the figures of a chorus of angels and one of devils:

Coro de Ángeles

Feliz allá en la tierra
Todo el que se resigna
A cumplir la misión que le fue dada!
           [. . .]
Desgraciado el que loco
Desgarrar imagina
El velo impenetrable en que se oculta
La esencia de la vida.

Coro de Demonios

Feliz allá en la Tierra
El que jamás se humilla
A cumplir la misión que le fue dada!
           [. . .]
Desgraciado el que necio
No alza la frente altiva
Y desgarrar intenta el frágil velo
Que oculta la esencia de la vida.

Angels' Chorus

Fortunate on Earth
Are those who will accomplish
The mission assigned to them!
           [. . .]
Unfortunate the insane
Imagining tearing
The impenetrable veil hiding
Life's mysteries.

Devils' Chorus

Fortunate on Earth
Is the one who does not know humility
In accomplishing the assigned mission!
           [. . .]
Unfortunate the silly
Who does not hold his head high
And tear the delicate veil
hiding life's mysteries.[45]

One voice, which is linked to moral consciousness, urges him to accept his own identity. The second voice, the devil's, invites him to dispense with his own identity and to become like the Other. The poet is not deaf to the voices of those inviting him to join his two selves:

Mis amigos,
Sin comprender mi mal, dicen airosos
Que de mi porvenir mis propias manos
La tumba caban; que aspirar debiera
De una ilustre familia a ser acepto,
¡Ay! pero olvidan mi atezado rostro
Y mi pobreza y dignidad;
        [. . .]

My friends,
Without understanding my misfortune, have the grace
To say that I am digging my own grave;
That I should aspire to be accepted by a good family,
Oh! They forget my black face
And my poverty and dignity
        [. . .][46]

Toward the end of his life, Obeso balanced his desire for progress, his yearning for his childhood years, and the waste of his life, which could be a model for his own people:

Hijo del siglo, como él, rodando
Corrí el facil camino de la vida
Me encenagué en el vicio, en el deleite
Batí las alas delirante. En vano.
Los ojos convertir pretendo al cielo:
De la niñez sencilla amedrentadas
Todas huyeron tímidas mis creencias.

¡Ay! del progreso el ideal sublime,
Que hoy a la humanidad la mente ofusca,
Será funesto como al genio el ánsia
De conocer lo ignoto.

Son of this Century, like him, running
I travel along the road of life;
Wallowing in mud, delighted
I flap my wings. Vainly.

I turn my eyes to heaven:
From my innocent childhood
Frightened, my beliefs ran away.

Oh! The noble ideal of progress,
Today source of confusion for the intellect,
It is unfortunate, the desire
To know the unknown.[47]

On July 3, 1884, the poet died from a gunshot. According to his friend Juan de Dios Uribe, "Candelario Obeso took death in his own hands instead of calmly waiting for her."[48]

A WOMAN MEMBER OF THE LITERATI: SOLEDAD ACOSTA DE SAMPER

The experience of Soledad Acosta de Samper, a creole woman member of the literati, differed from that of Candelario Obeso. Her voice, as that of a white woman, lay on the border between creole men, non-creole women, and subaltern men. Her writing reflects the dilemmas and ambiguities of being subordinated within a process of nation building from which women were excluded.

Acosta de Samper's education placed her in a better position than that of the average literate man. She received her early education in Halifax, Canada, while living with her English grandmother and completed her education in Paris, thus becoming fluent in English and French. Soledad Acosta is considered one of the most prolific writers of the nineteenth century, competing with writers such as José María Samper, her husband. She published forty-eight short stories and twenty-one novels.[49] Acosta's perspective is a creole woman's standpoint. In 1878, she founded the biweekly journal *La Mujer* (Woman), which was written by women on women's subjects. In this journal she published her own historical essays "The Role of Woman in Civilization" (La mujer en la civilización), "French Women Writers" (Literatas Francesas), "Gallery of Virtuous Women" (Galería de Mujeres Virtuosas), and "Aurora's Misfortunes" (Las desdichas de Aurora).

An analysis of Soledad Acosta de Samper's biography allows us to grasp the tensions between gender and authoring. Her first publication, *Novelas y Cuadros de la Vida Suramericana*, appeared in 1869 in Belgium. It is a collection of essays written in the previous years, generally in the form of leaflets, and in them she used a pseudonym. The disempowered character of the female writer is evident not only in the use of another's name, but also in the presence of a mediator between her writings and their readers. José María Samper presented Soledad Acosta's collection of essays. In his prologue to Acosta's book, he qualified her writings and then designated a "proper" place from which the reader should engage them with these words: "For my part, it was my will that my wife make a contribution with her efforts, even as modest as they are, to the common construction of the literature developing in our young Republic."[50]

Samper's self-imposed duties included assigning a subordinate place and a boundary to his wife's influence as a member of the literati. Soledad Acosta was presented as daughter, wife, and mother. She was the daughter of an eminent historian and general who had fought in the battle for independence. She must honor his name not from a public place, but from the private realm of her home as a mother as a condition of being a daughter of Colombia:

> Daughter of one of the most productive and prominent men, general Joaquín Acosta, well known in Colombia as a soldier and statesman, learned writer and professor, my wife's strong desire is to honor as much as possible the name she had, not only as mother of a family, but also as daughter of Colombia's fatherland. Since her sex does not allow her to serve the country in a different manner, she has found in literary activity, for more than fourteen years, a means of cooperation and action.[51]

Soledad Acosta transgressed the realms that men assigned to women's lives by relying on women's own spatial and temporal categories. While acknowledging that politics is a man's space, she rejected the idea that it is the only space for doing things political. She saw the private space as the place where the most "important and fundamental things happen":

> A big mistake with deep roots among us, is the belief that women must be outside politics. . . . Perhaps men are in charge of the material and visible side of public business; what is left, if women want, is the more noble part, [that of providing] the moral influence in society's important and fundamental issues. . . . But she must know and understand what parties want and desire. . . . The lack of influence of women in politics comes from their own ignorance of these matters, forgetting that their mission is moral.[52]

A woman's consciousness is not the product of the place assigned to her. Women perform roles assigned to them, but at the same time they subvert these roles; they overturn imposed, even natural, categories and are themselves. Soledad Acosta described a woman's heart as a mixture of contradictory forces leading to pain and happiness; the heart of a woman follows a natural pattern, but also transgresses this pattern:

> [A woman] has four different stages in her life: the child lives instinctively and suffers; the adolescent dreams and suffers; the young loves and suffers; the old understands and suffers. The life of a woman is a daily unhappiness. But this suffering is balanced during childhood by the candor that leads to forgiveness; during adolescence, by poetry which makes everything more beautiful. A young person balances suffering with love; a mature person, with resignation. But it can also happen that the laws of nature are transgressed, and girls are able to understand, adolescents able to love, youth able to live instinctively; and mature women to dream.[53]

In Soledad Acosta's account, women also live according to their own sense of time: "A man feels sorrow and understands love. The heart of a woman anticipates before understanding love."[54] A woman's strength relies on the capacity to foretell before understanding. Soledad Acosta denounced the changes in women's experience of time and space that accompanied the will to civilization. In her short essay "The Nun," she presented the consequences for women of the law, which closed the convents in the name of civilization.[55] Irrespective of their religious content, convents were women's spaces, where they could go in search of protection and relief of pain. Acosta introduced to the reader several stories of women who had arrived at convents for different reasons. Acosta's conclusion was that each case

> shows clearly that to seize from these miserable women the convents, to which *ambition, vocation, remorse, sorrow, disgrace, need, or faith* had compelled them to go in search of asylum, is the greatest cruelty ever done. Yet, the expulsion of the nuns from their convents has been done in the name of civilization, that is, in the name of humanity, and in the name of progress, that is, [in the name] of individual freedom![56]

The contradictory encounter between freedom and oppression, between the present condition and the past, as it pertains to the situation of women in the postindependence world, appears clearly in Soledad Acosta's essay entitled "Un Chistoso de Aldea" (The city's joker). The subtitle of the essay is "Novel-like Passages of the Fatherland's History." As the title suggests, history and fiction mix together to denounce the gendered character of the struggle for independence. This essay depicts the sense of contradiction and the ambiguity of women's experience in relation to the concept of the *patria* (fatherland). On the one hand, there is a feeling shared by most creoles against Spanish domination. On the other, there is women's experience of male domination.

To give expression to this contradictory experience, Soledad Acosta uses the figure of the carnival. Bakhtin has stressed the significance of using carnival figures. For him, "The rogue, the clown and the fool create around themselves their own spatial little world, their own chronotope. . . . Essential to these three figures is a distinctive feature that is as well a privilege—the 'right' to be the Other in this world, the right not to make common cause with any single one of the existing categories quite suits them, they see the underside and the falseness of every situation. Therefore, they can exploit any position they choose, but only as a mask."[57] Like Bakhtin's fool, Acosta's hero is a man who transgresses the behavior of ordinary men as a juggler. Named Justo, the Spanish equivalent of Justice, he is the son of a poor woman nicknamed *la guacharaca* and lives in a small city during the independence period.[58] Justo is the main figure in the town's carnival. Politically, Justo is a patriot, a fighter for independence, but his main cause is to protect women. The part of his life chosen by Soledad Acosta is Justo's intervention to protect the life of the Spanish vice-queen, who was threatened the day independence was achieved. This act was interpreted as favoring the Spaniards, called *Chapetones*. To the accusation of patriot creoles, Justo replied: "Am I a patriot? Yes, I am, and I am a strong enemy of the *chapetones*, but I cannot stand bad behavior against women. This is my way of being, and I cannot proceed otherwise."[59]

From Acosta de Samper's perspective, the battle for independence was fought against Spanish domination, but not against women's oppression. The figure of Justo was employed by Soledad Acosta to resist violence against women. Not protected by the law or by justice, Justo uses a devil's costume to scare men abusing women. Through the juxtaposition of violence and laughter, she demonstrates how laughter is used as a tool of the weak to resist and unmask the violence of the strong.

Soledad Acosta's "psychological essays" are also about violence, not physical, but the one exercised by the assignment of women's desires to specific realms. According to Soledad Acosta in the "heart of a woman there is an unknown world where lies the germ of empty ideals, dreams, and deluded visions surrounding her." Once in confrontation with reality, she is annihilated:

> Women with poetic spirits are embedded in an ideal world, and when they cultivate their own feelings, reality comes and discourages and annihilates them. Don't ask the cause of the sorrow, bitterness, or shame experienced by them: they have fallen from the ideal world, and reality has destroyed their illusions, leaving them in a moral void.[60]

The short essay "Matilde" is a narrative of the solitude and unhappiness of a woman succumbing to a man whose stronger will is imposed upon her. In Acosta's account, the counterpart of men's power is women's desire to be admired by them: "Oh! The desire to be admired is the main reason of a woman's unhappiness."[61] The psychological destruction of a woman's life is reflected in her body. Matilde's body disappears under her paleness and frailty: "In the first moment we only saw the brightness of her dark eyes as two stars in a dark sky."[62] Her husband silences her voice: "In his presence Matilde did not take the chance to pronounce her own opinion, and, if he entered into the room while she was talking, she became silent."[63]

In Soledad Acosta's collection of essays she attempted to give voice to the lives of these women. Nevertheless, we must not forget, as Spivak reminds us, that very often feminists articulate their goals in "shifting relationship to what is at stake." So "The 'native female' as such is excluded from any share in this emerging norm."[64] This ambiguity for a creole woman like Soledad Acosta is reflected in this passage:

> How curious! Despite the fact that liberals offer freedom and privileges not recognized by conservatives . . . most women, and not only from the upper class, but also from popular classes, are monarchical and imperialistic. How to explain this situation? Because of women's tendency to grandness and also their love for beautiful and noble things; for them, democracy is contrary to their nature.[65]

Hence, Acosta de Samper's ambiguous complicity with creole women and her tendency toward unification, in the name of the self, of the voices of subaltern women and the lower class. For example, the essay "Mercedes" is about the loss of power of a creole woman who took the Spanish side during the struggle for independence.[66] As a creole woman, Mercedes was in a position of power: "I was raised in a wealthy environment . . . and my caprices were like law."[67] Because of her loyalty to the Spanish Crown, she loses power over her patriotic male friends, and also loses her beauty, because a large scar disfigures her. After independence is won, her family is found in poverty. Poor, Mercedes has to accept work and to marry a mulatto who inherited land from his landlord. Love between the black and white races is seen as a nondesirable consequence of independence. Moved by the desire to save her family economically, she agrees to marry the mulatto "despite the horror he could inspire before."[68] Mercedes' desire for money is presented as a moral issue superior to the mulatto's desire for recognition: "Naturally, Santiago did not get married moved by her desire to share his money, but for the desire of an upper-class white woman and his desire for revenge against those who despised him before."[69] When Mercedes is asked by an old friend why "a wealthy, proud, and beautiful woman . . . is married to a despicable mulatto" she replies: "Poverty." From Acosta's perspective, a mulatto's desire for independence is seen as an occasion to dominate women, as reflected in Santiago's words to Mercedes: "As daughter of a gentleman, you must be the servant. . . . This is the main purpose of the Independence war."[70] In fact, the proclamation of independence meant that there was a need to surrender to an equality that from a creole's perspective meant inferiority.

5

The Will to Civilization and Its Encounter with Laissez-Faire

The political doctrine of laissez-faire is absurd, mistaken, and utopian. . . .
Absolute tolerance, laissez-faire, is utopian nonsense.

MIGUEL ANTONIO CARO, CONSERVATIVE (1869)

The selfish and regrettable doctrine praised by Jean Baptiste Say and his
school synthesized in the formulation laissez-faire *allows robbery, allows*
oppression, and allows the wolf to eat the lamb.

MANUEL MURILLO TORO, LIBERAL (1853)

Contrary to Mr. Murillo's opinion, capital accumulation, far from being evil,
is precisely a source of wealth, and one of the most powerful elements of
civilization.

RICARDO VANEGAS, LIBERAL PARLIAMENTARIAN (1853)

Scholars have turned to nineteenth-century Latin America in search of answers to the riddles of development. In the nineteenth century, Latin America opened up to external markets and the region adopted laissez-faire principles. This makes it a relatively recent real-world experiment whose results can be used to inform the liberal theory and liberal policies that are currently fashionable. The challenge for both liberals and their critics is to discover why in Latin America, after 150 years of linkage with the world economy and the introduction of capitalist property relations—ample time for the "logic of capitalism" to unfold—laissez-faire policies did not reverse the initial international division of labor. Even today precapitalist and capitalist elements still coexist, and the use of force is still a regular part of the process of capitalist expansion.

Colombia, like most of Latin America, lowered tariffs and adopted other policies said to favor free trade. Colombians anticipated a future in which the country would produce agricultural commodities and European manufactured goods would yield mutual benefits. Colombia's exports of tropical products were to pay for the importation of goods from Europe. Merchant and literati (but not necessarily wealthy) visionaries from the main cities moved to the inhospitable lowlands to cultivate first tobacco, then quinine and indigo. The power of the state was reduced and estranged from production.

Violence was implicated in the failures as well as the progress of Colombia's economy. Export activity, with the interesting exception of hats manufactured by women, was characterized by the direct exercise of violence in the process of surplus extraction. A study of tobacco production depicts the regions dedicated to the crop as "lands of brigandage and fear," due to the presence of private armed guards whose role was to force "vagrants" to work on the haciendas.[1] The methods used for quinine extraction were even more violent.[2] Commercialization was implemented by private companies (national and international) that bought the product from *cascarilleros*—Indians exploiting their communal lands or working on public lands on concession. Private armies used violence to control production and exchange; they fought each other, and they provoked violent resistance on the part of the suppliers. The failure of the export sector is related to violence in the relations of production and to the violent forms of exploiting nature. The decline in tobacco exports was linked to a decrease in the international price of Colombian tobacco, the latter precipitated by a decrease in the quality of tobacco. The violent methods of production were an obstacle to the exercise of any kind of quality control of tobacco exports and also contributed to overexploitation of the land.[3] Quinine production led to brief booms followed by a decline that coincided with the exhaustion of the forest. Once the jungles of Pitayo (Cauca) were depleted, the production shifted to San Sebastián (Huila). After this source dried up, extraction began in Santander. The cities nearest to the extraction centers "experienced an ephemeral golden age, to be forgotten a few years later."[4]

Therefore, economic growth and the rapid accumulation of capital did not materialize in mid-nineteenth-century Colombia despite the country's openness to external markets and the growth of exports to levels previously unknown. Instead, the agricultural exports that initially positioned the country among the main suppliers of the world market disappeared as a consequence of land depletion and poor quality control. Moreover, despite the adoption of laissez-faire principles, coercive use of labor continued in the system known as *la hacienda*. Not surprisingly, by the end of the century imported textiles had replaced national production, and the country was immersed in poverty and civil war. An explanation is required.

INTERPRETING POLITICAL ECONOMY

In liberal analyses laissez-faire is generally defined as a policy prescription that seeks to free economic activity from all constraints on the market and to promote the international division of labor.[5] The questions asked have to do with why laissez-faire failed and why its principles did not apply. To answer these questions, economic historians provide laissez-faire with a positive, fixed meaning from which reality is interpreted. Once a privileged position is adopted to interpret a reality that is complex, unknown, and most of the time contradictory, it is easy to conclude that the hostile context is the most likely explanation for its failure.

This is the path chosen in William Paul McGreevey. He asks why the adoption of laissez-faire principles in mid-nineteenth-century Colombia had a negative effect on the growth of the national economy, contradicting the predictions of liberal economic theory. The answer, he concludes, is grounded in the "different" working conditions of economic liberalism in West European countries from those of most of Latin America. The failure of economic liberalism was the result of an elite "trying to apply solutions appropriate to a homogeneous country [such as the countries of the North Atlantic,] without an indigenous population, to an environment formed by distinct societies."[6] McGreevey's explanation illustrates the monologism implicit in the tendency to interpret reality from a single, exterior position. The concept of laissez-faire is not submitted to scrutiny so as to inquire about the conditions under which it is possible. The use of the "differential" character of the surrounding environment allows him to save the theoretical "truism" of economic liberalism: when applied in the proper context, economic liberalism produces the intended effects. To fall back on "anomaly" as an explanatory mechanism is a violent interpretation, an "epistemic violence" of the sort described in the previous chapter.

A second explanation focuses on the kinds and conditions of products exchanged between the center and the periphery. José A. Ocampo proposes this pattern. He attributes failures in the process of development to linkages with the external market resulting from the location of the country as a "secondary periphery" in the world economy. In a secondary periphery, the extraction of economic surplus takes the form of "production-financial speculation," where the intention is to profit to the maximum from the opportunities offered by an unbalanced world market. An interest in long-term investment or the establishment of an export sector with some stability is absent. The need to appropriate extraordinary profits explains the "savage" character of capitalism. The violence associated with certain forms of production necessarily results from the priority placed on the speedy extraction of profits from the export opportunities. This form of "production-financial speculation" is a "rational" option, according to Ocampo, given the articulation of Colombia's economy with the world economy.[7]

Ocampo's economic history of the nineteenth century offers rich insights into the linkages between the development of the Colombian national economy and the opportunities offered by the international market. He offers a good illustration of the instability of the world market for peripheral countries: the tobacco boom lasted less than four decades, that for quinine less than three. Ocampo's explanation is flawed by his reliance on external market conditions as an explanation for the violent behavior of mid-nineteenth-century elites. It is difficult to deduce from this external linkage either the form adopted nationally in order to fulfil the external demand or the change toward a "less speculative," less violent, and more capitalistic form of exploitation. External determinants are unable to explain the diversity of internal processes, as is discussed in the following chapter. A diversity of forms of production, rather than uniformity, characterized the linkage with the external market. The problem becomes more complex if we consider that violence did not characterize all exports. For example, the exportation of *jipijapa* hats, made by women artisans, seems to have been largely free from physical violence. Ocampo's analysis is silent about how gender relations affect exchange relations. His comments on the process of coffee expansion seem to suggest that the answer lies in a change in the internal process of production and not in the external world economy. He signals changes in the internal structure of property relations in the regions of Antioquia and Caldas, which used *parcelaria* production (sharecropping):

> The *parcelaria* production had several advantages from the point of view of capitalist development. On the one hand, it abolished monetary investment in coffee production on the part of the entrepreneurs, and the problems of lack of discipline of the traditional hacienda. On the other, it allowed the inclusion of lands otherwise unused in the agriculture of *roza y quema* (slash and burn).[8]

According to this passage, internal rather than external considerations are more likely explanations for changes in the social organization of production.[9] The questions not answered are related to how the problem of the "lack of discipline" was related to the elite's perceptions of workers as being in need of control, why in some regions this problem did not appear, and what effect this difference had on the development of capitalism in these regions.

A third explanation common throughout Latin America was the feudalist character of the rural society. Salomón Kalmanovitz, for example, states that in the nineteenth century Colombia was in a superior stage of the social development of feudalism.[10] Opening to the external market constituted not the transformation to capitalism, but rather an involution toward feudal structures, a process called *enfeudamiento* (feudalization). In the hacienda system the labor process uses coercive practices:

> Relations of force in addition to juridical and ideological relations restricted a peasant's freedom. Arbitrary indebtedness of the *arrendatario* and his family to the landowner was reinforced by the presence of judges, public officials, private or public armies at the disposition of the proprietor. . . . The true legal status of the peasant was the same as [that of] an insane person or a child: he could not seek employment with another landlord, was unable to sell, buy, or rent or to perform any operation like those within the *private* sphere of bourgeois society. Even more, in some regions the *arrendatarios* had to offer their daughters to the sexual appetite of the owner and their sons were drafted into the *patron*'s army.[11]

The mode of production is, then, a "hybrid" between feudalism and capitalism, where the relationship between peasant and landowner is servile.[12] This violence encourages other violence: "Violence awakened in the peasants 'slyness, fraud, and all human possibilities' to avoid the landlord's exploitation, and in addition gave rise to violence on the part of the oppressed."[13]

Answering the question as to why there was a return to feudalism, Kalmanovitz argues that the conditions of the external market encouraged cost reductions and the desire to maximize profits, but not enough to move capitalists toward the use of free labor and the "scientific" organization of jobs. In his view, the use of forced labor "would not change until the breakdown of the social structure by the mobilization of the oppressed and until the general conditions of capital accumulation would create the social environment for the freedom of labor from its 'obligation' to landowners."[14] Kalmanovitz acknowledges that the external market was unable to change the conditions of production.

Despite the rich insights of his analysis, the use of categories from which history is deduced leads Kalmanovitz into interpreting reality from the laws of development of capital accumulation. Nonetheless, certain passages suggest a different dynamic, as in the analysis of Antioquia, which industrialized first:

> [In] Antioquia the population was more white, homogeneous, and *free* than in the rest of the country. Those were key factors in the formation of a society of small units of production (miners and peasants) with mercantile linkages, side by side with haciendas with sharecropping or with cattle raising with waged labor. . . . In addition they did not have an aversion to physical work, independent of the status of the individual, that is, each one had a broad capacity of *self-determination* [emphasis in original]. . . . Also, within the Antioqueño society appeared a heterogeneous population, which included capitalist classes and had pronounced individualization. . . . In the highlands there was a primacy of moral order and accumulation, while in the lowlands the predominant element was licentious behavior and accumulation was in few hands (owners of cattle and gold intermediaries), that is, people abandoned themselves to an underdeveloped destiny.[15]

To accept an explanation of capitalist development based on the racial character of its population is to fall into an ethnocentric explanation whose roots come from the nineteenth century. Had Kalmanovitz factored in processes of identity formation, the Antioqueño phenomena could have enriched his discussion of the dynamics of capitalism by considering the importance of conceptions of the self in the process of capitalist expansion.

Therefore, those adducing that a poor economic structure or an adverse environment is necessary for laissez-faire to work and explanations adducing the persistence of old forms of production all failed to address pivotal questions: "Why did the mid-nineteenth-century upper class not improve production in the direction of greater efficiency and competitiveness? Why did they not extend the agreement about free trade to labor relations as well? Why was technology not bettered? Why was land exhausted, and why were resources depleted?

A Dialogical Political Economy

The main argument of this chapter is that a proper explanation must broaden the study of political economy from an exclusive concern with production and circulation of things to the production and circulation of meanings. The concept of political economy that I propose includes those forms of production, circulation, and exchange embedded within broader forms of signification. This approach reinstates the space where struggles for representation take place. To reinstate this space means to acknowledge the presence of other interpretations and different desires that did not emanate solely from one single foundation, such as the ownership of the means of production as invoked by Marxists, and whose motivations could diverge from the pursuit of egotistic rational interest, as invoked by liberal economists.

A dialogical political economy accounts for local meanings that accompany forms of accumulation. It allows for the incorporation of other voices that have the effect of denaturalizing those practices that otherwise would be taken for granted. Traditional political economy has long silenced those arguments and taken for granted the voices of the supporters of rational self-interest. The incorporation of the Other's voice also has the effect of showing the relationship between economic practices and the construction of desires linked to them. The representation of gender, race, and class identities was central to the generalization of wage and labor relations and to the manufacturing process. The struggle surrounding the winning over of each economic practice is visible only in the encounter that took place between distinct contenders.

A dialogical political economy also supposes the presence of actors with different points of view. These points of view result from the different position of the actors involved and the capacity of certain actors to impose or to give salience to certain views over contending ones. Meanings attributed to events, the salience of certain representations, and the silence surrounding others are the results of the interplay of unequal relations of power.

The proposed approach allows one to make a detailed examination of concepts such as laissez-faire and to explore the ways in which concepts are subject to reinterpretation. Words, as Bakhtin acknowledges, "enter a dialogically agitated and tension-filled environment of alien words, value judgements and accents, weaves in and out of complex interrelationships, merges with some, recoils from others, intersects with yet a third group."[16] The way in which laissez-faire was conceived was complicated by its interaction with the religious, political, and disciplining desires on the part of the mid-nineteenth-century elite. Borrowing Roberto Schwarz's expression, laissez-faire ideas were "misplaced."[17] This expression does not refer to truth or falsehood, since in its European as well as its Third World meaning laissez-faire is accompanied by a simultaneous play of true and false. As Schwarz argues, "Free labor, equality before the law and, more generally, universalism were also an ideology in Europe; but there they corresponded to appearances and hid the essential—the exploitation of labor. Among us, the same ideas would be false in a different sense, so to speak, in an original way."[18] In mid-nineteenth-century Colombia this originality refers to the laissez-faire encounter with the regime of representation based on the will to civilization.

A dialogical political economy acknowledges temporal, spatial, and ideological encounters. Therefore, spatial exchanges between representations coming from Europe and North America, as well as local representations coming from the recently independent countries, are considered. This approach accounts for exchanges taking place between groups of individuals endowed with different capacities to impose their representations. There was not a single source explaining the endowment of diverse capacities. They have to be brought into the light of the meanings attributed by the local actors. In order to incorporate the voice of the Other, this approach calls for the use of alternative texts. Texts about political economy are but one of the spaces where meanings are produced and exchanged. As a general rule, however, political economy texts have already won at least one decisive battle: they adhere to the space defined as legitimate by the discipline's supporters. In order to incorporate other voices, in this chapter I use texts outside the mainstream discipline: novels, poems, popular songs, and drawings. In addition to being alternative sources, these texts provide, on most occasions, battlefields where struggles for representation were fought.

As appears in the following sections, in nineteenth-century Colombia the will to civilization preceded, and in most of the cases contradicted, the main principles of laissez-faire. A dialogical method allows us to examine the exchanges that took place between diverse representations. In the middle of the nineteenth century, the will to civilization encountered laissez-faire and the latter was subordinated to the former. Because political economy was founded upon the desire to civilize classes, races, and genders, the prerequisites for laissez-faire could not be achieved. Arguments about local artisanship, the causes of poverty, and the international division of labor were embedded in distinctions between things local and European: supposedly ignorant artisans were contrasted with English workers, theory was preferred to reality, and coarse textiles were compared to imported ones. Negative representations of female and Indian dress increased the desire for imported textiles, which in turn led to the displacement of local manufactures in favor of European ones. In those nations seen as deprived of civilization, the idea of a self-regulatory principle did not prosper. In Colombia, the formation of gender, class, and racial identities within the will-to-civilization regime of representation arrested the formation of a free labor market. A free labor market presumes the presence of an "undifferentiated" labor force.[19] The economy was not perceived as a sphere separate from politics, but, on the contrary, the former was subordinated to the latter. The fact that the accumulation process was centered on the will to civilize hindered the expansion of productivity.

The Encounter with Laissez-Faire

Creoles in Nueva Granada had been familiar with laissez-faire principles since the early postcolonial period. In 1825, thirteen years after independence, political economy was included in the law curriculum at the Colegio San Bartolomé, using Jean Baptiste Say's book as the prescribed text. The importance attributed to this event merited special comment in the *Gaceta Oficial:* "From the moment of Conquest to the present, the words political economy, values, and productive and non-productive capital have not even been heard in our universities."[20] Santander, then president of the country, issued a decree ordering that the law was to be taught according to Bentham's utilitarian principles. These principles were also part of his educational reform *(Plan de Estudios).*

From that point, Bentham's utilitarianism became the center of an important debate.[21] Bentham's moral doctrine was considered to be opposed to the Catholic religion and was thought to incite mischief in the young. When Simón Bolívar regained power in 1828, he issued a decree that banned Bentham's books from schools and universities. The controversy attained such importance that an attempt against Bolívar's life in September 1828, which included the participation of some students of San Bartolomé, was attributed to the pernicious influence of Bentham's principles. After the attempt against Bolívar's life, J. M. Restrepo, one of the authors of Santander's plan, reconsidered the benevolence of Bentham's doctrine in the following terms:

> An examination of the philosophy of educational reform brings me to the conclusion that the origin of the wrong behavior lies in the political science taught to students by professors without enough judgment to modify the principles according to each nation's circumstances. The wrong behavior increases when certain authors are chosen for the study of the law, such as those of Bentham, et al., since besides enlightened principles, their doctrine contains principles opposed to people's religion, morality, and peace.[22]

From this moment on, the debate surrounding Bentham's doctrine took a partisan form: Liberals took Bentham's side, whereas Conservatives became Bentham's main opponents.[23] In 1842, José Eusebio Caro, who in 1848 would author the Conservative Party's ideological program, published a series of antiutilitarianism articles in the newspaper *El Neo-Granadino.* The same year, Mariano Ospina Rodríguez, minister of the interior, issued another educational reform. The main emphasis of his plan was the attainment of science, morality, and discipline.[24] Ospina again forbad the use of Bentham's principles in universities.

From 1848 onward, the Liberal Party, in power, intensified its open commitment to free trade principles. Free trade was defined in the Conservative program as "legal freedom of movement, import and export, without prohibitions and without other rights than [those dictated by] fiscal needs."[25] The Liberals stated that "laws should guarantee freedom and security and should not obstruct the production and the circulation of property for any reason; private individuals will do the rest, because the will for wealth does not need inspiration."[26]

THE ENCOUNTER BETWEEN LAISSEZ-FAIRE AND
THE WILL TO CIVILIZATION

The contradictory encounter between laissez-faire and the will to civilization appears clearly in the main polemic between Liberals and Conservatives, as well as in the debates between Liberals and artisans. In 1849, the year that the Liberal Party assumed power, the Conservatives published a newspaper entitled *La Civilización*. Conservatives Mariano Ospina Rodríguez and José Eusebio Caro edited the newspaper. According to the editors, the newspaper's aim was "to promote and defend civilization in Nueva Granada and in Spanish America."[27] The editorial in the first issue, entitled "La Civilización Se Define" (The meaning of civilization), defined civilization as the accumulation of the means to reach perfection: in their respective order they were enlightenment, morality, and wealth. Security was identified as the reason for the creation of civilization and violence as the main reason for the destruction of civilization. What is important is that behind both security and violence, according to the author, there is another cause, namely a good or a bad doctrine: "A belief, idea, doctrine can pull [men] out from barbarism, and guide them along the road to civilization: a belief, idea, or doctrine is able also to detain or reverse the march of civilization."[28]

According to Ospina, a doctrine proclaiming interest as its main principle destroys civilization and causes barbarism:

> A doctrine that humiliates men by comparing them to beasts whose only function is to eat, enjoy pleasure, and then to perish; which establishes interest as the point of departure of all actions, makes egoism the regulation of all actions, and dries all the seeds of virtue; [a doctrine] where justice and law have as their only foundation selfish

rational calculation, never right, deprives property and security of their base; as a consequence [property and security] are left either to the mercy of the free will of a mass without a restraining force or in the hands of a tyrant, equally unrestrained and volatile; in other words, violence becomes a substitute for justice, and force replaces reason. This doctrine ruins intelligence, isolates and divides men, destroys the principles of property and welfare, and destroys morality: all this is the same as saying that this doctrine barbarizes men.[29]

For Conservatives, what was at stake through the adoption of a bad doctrine (laissez-faire) was the future of civilization. The principles of "interest" and "rational calculation" were linked to violence, force, and barbarism. This conception is opposite to the one sustained in early arguments favoring liberalism.

Laissez-Faire as a Form of Government of Individuals

Laissez-faire was not represented as applying to an isolated realm, the economy, or to the independent realm of the exchange of things, as had been the case in early arguments about capitalism. Liberals and Conservatives held a view of laissez-faire as it applied to all aspects of social life, well beyond exchange in the market. What becomes clear from the most important debates held on the improvement of the species, the manumission of slaves, the search for the causes of poverty, and even free trade is that laissez-faire was applied to the conduct (sexual, moral, political) of individuals and not to an independent sphere of the government of things.

The need to improve the human species was used as an argument against laissez-faire in an article published by Conservative José Eusebio Caro entitled "The Falsity of Laissez-faire." Caro, for whom society was not the individual, but the species, contended that in matters related to the species, laissez-faire was not applicable; it was inapplicable to the institution of marriage and sexual relations: "Laissez-faire will lead to marriage among the immature, bigamy, polygamy, and concubinage."[30] It also was not applicable to those acts that lead to the destruction of the species, such as consumption of alcohol, gambling, bullfights, hunting, and deforestation.

The debate on the freedom of slaves was raised in the context of relations of property. The debate was not argued along partisan lines. Rather, factions of both parties supported or opposed the manumission of slaves. The discussion centered on human freedom as contrary to property. The abolition of slavery was seen by some as an assault on property rights. José María Samper, who favored abolition, summarized the two positions as follows:

> It has been argued on the part of those opposing the law of manumission of slaves, that their freedom will be an attack on property. Why must property be respected when it is an attack on freedom? Answer this question. The property of the slave-owner is an assault on freedom, and the freedom of the slave is an assault on property. Which one is more violent, more harmful and inexcusable, the one that moves more social interests? The first one without any doubt. The Liberal Party is divided on this question, and one side supports the most important right, while another faction favors the less important one.[31]

The abolition of slavery in 1851 was the culmination of a long crisis manifested in phenomena such as cimarronism and rebellions by black populations. At the moment of the formal recognition of their freedom, 1851, there were approximately 16,468 slaves as compared with 53,788 at the end of the eighteenth century.[32] Nevertheless, the Conservatives went to war to protest the decree, but were defeated by their Liberal opponents.

Despite the Liberals' support of laissez-faire principles, the debates among Liberal factions also reveal the use of the concept in a sense not restricted to exchange in the market or to property relations. The opposition of Liberal Manuel Murillo Toro to the reforms inspired by laissez-faire principles is enlightening. Murillo Toro, considered the most radical Liberal, opposed the adoption of laissez-faire because he saw in its principles a political and not an economic agenda.[33] In a letter to Liberal economist Miguel Samper, he denounced laissez-faire *(dejad hacer)* as a selfish and pernicious doctrine. According to him, laissez-faire signified a rule of conduct that "allows robbery, allows oppression, allows the wolf to eat the lambs."[34] In his eyes, the Liberal reforms were political reforms and destined to failure if they were not accompanied by economic reforms. The doctrine of laissez-faire was unable to achieve what he conceived the two most important goals: the first was to be an "agricultural nation *(pueblo)* and nothing else." This aim, in his view, required ownership of the land; the second goal was the "desire to live in democracy"; this mission required "freedom of standing as a precondition of freedom of character."[35] *Dejad hacer,* according to him, provided neither.

Miguel Samper, the addressee of Murillo's letter, was considered a fervent advocate of laissez-faire and the most prestigious Colombian political economist.[36] If Murillo's ideal country was one without government, Samper's ideal was one without trade barriers. In his opposition to the protectionist measures demanded by the artisans, Samper suggested that a better solution "would be to assign to each artisan a payment of one thousand pesos each year."[37] Despite Miguel Samper's commitment to economic liberalism, his major theoretical works also point to his lack of belief in the self-regulatory capacity of the market. His well-known study "Poverty in Bogotá" is a clear indication of this tendency. The causes of poverty, he said, are moral, social, and political.[38] Superseding these causes, though, is a precondition of peace and progress. In Samper's view, morality was the precondition for liberty: "To maintain that a nation is free when it can do whatever it wants and avoid what is unpleasant, is an incomplete assertion. If habits are immoral, beliefs are mistaken or superstitious, desires are immoderate, the freedom of this nation will be similar to the freedom of cannibals."[39]

When the government attempted to introduce protectionist measures, Miguel Samper became its fiercest opponent. His solution to the problem of an imbalance in trade (the country's imports exceeding its exports) was of a moral nature:

> The problem that we have at hand is not economic, but moral. To establish the equilibrium between appetites and their satisfaction is more urgent than the problem of reaching equilibrium between what we buy and what we sell in the external market. Unfortunately, the social facts are subject to laws whose action is too complex and hard to fight. Priests, parents, and schools are the most suitable to counter these kinds of bad habits.[40]

Samper attributed the backward situation of Latin American republics to the lack of political order. The series of articles he published on freedom and order was written in an attempt to discern the causes of political disorder. "The day," he said, "when we lay the foundations of a political order that results in the establishment of peace, the solution of the remaining problems will be easy."[41] The basis of Samper's thought was the belief that the spirit of freedom was lacking in the Latin American republics. Political institutions clashed with a tradition in which there were no moral habits: "Independence took us by surprise without freedom emanating from the social condition, at the same time that the authority used to impose obedience was collapsing."[42] He compared this situation to the one in the United States, where there was already an orderly freedom and the institutions did not clash with the people. Samper did not see in laissez-faire the principle of order; he expounded against the dangers of laissez-faire in both the economic and the political realms: "In the political a literal application of this principle [laissez-faire] would be the refusal of order, and in the economic, it would be the negation of the good things that a community can provide under the leadership and the action of government."[43]

From the previously mentioned debates emerged the importance of isolating the notion of the "economy" in order for laissez-faire principles to become the guiding representation. Liberal and Conservative alike thought of laissez-faire as a principle governing the relations among individuals. This explains why there was a consensus about lessening trade barriers between the Liberals and the Conservatives, although at the same time there was paradoxically strong opposition to laissez-faire doctrines.

Laissez-Faire and the Partisan Divide

In postindependence Nueva Granada, both parties agreed on the need for civilization. The argument between the Liberals and the Conservatives was about "how to foster civilization." The Liberals claimed that the best means to achieve civilization was to make each individual free, but the Conservatives believed that the best way was to work through governance and morality.

Liberal thought is well expressed in José María Samper's writings about Colombian history.[44] For him, what the revolution for independence and the Liberal revolution of 1849 had in common was that both were part of a social revolution aimed at installing the individual as sovereign. He defined the spirit of civilization as "the search for the individual as sovereign as the ultimate goal of the political and philosophical spirit."[45] Individual sovereignty became the condition for political freedom: "Political freedom is possible only when everyone is free."[46] Samper regarded the revolution of March 7, 1849, the day the Liberal Party gained power, as having brought about a transformation in the government of individuals. He defined the revolution as a profound change in ideas and political habits and as the end of the oligarchic system based on clericalism, authoritarianism, and state monopolies. People, science, and freedom replaced oligarchy, sophistry, and immobility.

However, good government was central to the Conservatives' plan for civilization. In their opinion, laissez-faire implied that there was no need for a government to accomplish the civilizing task. Conservative José Eusebio Caro asked the following question: "How is it possible to *educate* and to *civilize* men without an excess in government? Those individuals, families, and nations who attained civilization were submitted in an intense manner to the influence of a civilizing power" [emphasis Caro's].[47] Morality and knowledge are cited as prerequisites to the accumulation of wealth: "What comes first, *morality, instruction,* or *wealth*? Is it possible that the attainment of one guarantees the rest? The answer is in the New Testament: 'Look first to God's kingdom and justice, and everything else will be provided.' . . . Instruction and wealth alone do not form civilization. The true character of civilization appears only in *morality*" [emphasis Caro's].[48]

Miguel Antonio Caro, José Eusebio's son, also voiced what he saw as the open contradiction between laissez-faire and governance: it was "entirely at odds with the mission of government."[49] He saw laissez-faire as "absolute permissiveness" resulting in either anarchy or despotism. Despotism occurs when the sovereign applies the principle of pleasure to himself; anarchy occurs when the governed apply the principle to themselves.[50] The roots of both anarchism and despotism, according to Caro, are laissez-faire based on utilitarianism.[51]

Miguel Antonio Caro was opposed to the utilitarian principle of interest because, in his view, interest contradicted the Christian principle of charity: "Interest, the utilitarian feeling, has moved people to enslave other people in the search for wealth. Interest has traded human beings, and this reiterates what freedom can expect from interest, or from the utilitarian principle, which are the same."[52] The utilitarian principle is depicted by Caro as a Satanic principle, opposed to Catholicism: "There are only two masters: Satan and Jesus . . . Satan who tells us *'Be like god,'* and Jesus who tells us *'Be like children.'* The school of Satan here and everywhere else is entitled *utilitarianism*. The school of Christ is named here as everywhere else *Catholicism*. Those are the concepts, the true formulation of the moral question as debated in the world" [emphasis Caro's].[53]

THE ENCOUNTER BETWEEN CIVILIZERS AND ARTISANS

The production of textiles, the heart of the English industrial revolution, declined drastically in postindependence Colombia.[54] This situation has traditionally been explained by productivity increases in the textile industries of the more advanced countries and by the lack of local innovation:

> [In Colombia] production took place in the family, using mainly women and children. Women performed all domestic labor. There was no division of labor: the production units performed all the labor of spinning, tinting, weaving, and marketing. The production was oriented to ordinary textiles. . . . The production technology was primitive and did not experience any important transformation during the nineteenth century.[55]

There is no doubt that the decrease in international prices played an important role in increasing the demand for imported textiles. The gap in technology, however, is not enough to explain the lack of innovation. In the case of textile production, the gap between Europe and postcolonial Colombia was not very profound at that time.[56] Furthermore, the lack of technological innovation is the key issue that needs to be explained: why was the drive to transform production, to become more efficient and competitive, absent from the minds of mid-nineteenth-century Colombian entrepreneurs?

The answer to this question is related to the "uncivilized" character attributed to those engaged in textile and manual production: mestizos, Indians, blacks, and women. Their identities were defined in terms of "passionate" attributes, which precluded a channeling of resources that would increase their productive capacities. They were perceived as "barbarians" in need of civilization before they could be incorporated into the productive world. In nineteenth-century Colombia, interests and civilization were perceived as European characteristics that deserved to be adopted locally. The international division of labor, wherein Europe and North America specialized in manufacturing and Nueva Granada in agriculture, furthered the belief in the "uncivilized" local character of Neo-Granadins. Florentino González, a leading figure in the Liberal reforms, asserted:

> Granadins cannot compete in manufacturing with Europeans and Americans. Any directive aimed to increase manufacturing, despising the resources of agriculture, has no place in a Government inclined

toward the well-being of the nation of which it is in charge. Europe, with an intelligent population, possessing steam technology, already skillful in the art of manufacturing, achieves the mission of transforming raw materials within the industrial world. We must accomplish our mission, and we cannot have doubts about it, when we look at the prodigality of natural resources with which Providence has endowed our land.[57]

This polemic at the time illustrates the self-defeating character of this regime of representation. The decline of manufacturing was justified by the absence of "interest" on the part of "ignorant" male and female artisans. The accumulation process was centered primarily in the will to civilize them. The abandonment of manufacturing as a pattern of development was more the result of the will to civilize than of any other force: the will to civilize hindered any will to increase efficiency and hence productivity.

As the following passage illustrates, Colombian followers of laissez-faire doctrines were aware of the importance of "interests" in the process of accumulation and civilization, but contradictions ensued from the identification of these characteristics with Europeans and the considered need to create those same characteristics at home. In a letter from Europe, Florentino González, wrote:

> The best way to guarantee peace is through the creation of general interests. Big commercial companies are natural allies of government because interests cannot be maintained without order and public security, and [interests] halt foolish political projects given the influence of the social position of its members, always in harmony with the general interest. We can say that Rothschild, Parning, and all European bankers are the ones in charge of European peace; they are the guarantee of freedom and individual security. Because the government needs them for public credit and finance, [the bankers] exert surveillance to avoid measures that could cause revolts that would lead to financial paralysis. [The bankers] also let the governments know that their resources would not be available in the case of senseless wars. . . . In this way, interests have solved the problem of peace and social guarantees. Proletarian classes could protest but they are limited in their protest since their subsistence depends on the jobs provided by the proprietor classes; [proletarians] cannot be involved in risky initiatives leaving the secure though poor position provided by big interests.[58]

Therefore, interests in Nueva Granada were not universalized; they were particularized to certain nations (Western Europe and North America) and to those who knew the secrets of civilization: enlightened creoles. Property by itself, however, was not enough to provide a guide to run the nation; property had to be accompanied by enlightenment. According to the creole literati, the world of artisans embodied a lack of enlightenment: their world was represented as guided by ignorance and passions. The main debate between the Liberals and the artisans centered on the polemic between "enlightened" political economists and "ignorant" artisans.[59] José María Samper narrates the political economist's side of the debate:

> One day there was an extraordinary session in the democratic society whose aim was to decide on the signature of a petition to Congress asking for a strong increase in their rights. I attended. There were more than 300 members at the meeting, and I suddenly realized that the artisans were guided by their emotions and did not understand a word about the whole subject. I asked permission to address the auditorium, then I went to the gallery, and very clearly lectured about the reciprocity linking the production and consumption of wealth. I made them see that each individual produces just one thing and consumes a lot of them and that on some occasions the individuals are subject to the inevitable law of competence. I proved that given the existence of several manufactured products, such as blankets, cloths, *ruanas*, and other fabrics, hats, tanned skins, alcoholic beverages, etc., it would be extraordinarily unjust not to extend to everyone the protection asked by the petition regarding simple "devices," such as shoes, dresses, saddles, carpentry, and iron works. I finally proved that in order to protect everyone, according to equal justice, all consumption articles under protection would necessarily increase their price. The result would be an artificial increase in price for everyone, and the artisans formerly favored in their profits would lose all their profits and even more, as a result of the increase in price of all consumption.
>
> But how can these economic and ethical arguments have any effect on the spirit of the artisans, who although good men and loyal to the country, were almost all of them ignorant, especially in scientific matters? Instead of being grateful for my interest in the well-being of artisans, almost all of them were angry with my reasoning, and one of them—an iron worker, Miguel León, well known for his harangues about "tiranibería"—asked me to step down from the gallery.[60]

This "dialogue" is illustrative of the encounter that took place between the two contending representations: political economists represented the artisans' world as guided by emotions, in contrast to their world of rationality. The contest between the artisans and the Liberals was a contest between parties who were unequal on the basis of possession of knowledge: artisans' words were worthless and were given the connotation of "harangues" (peroratas). Samper describes himself, on the contrary, as a speaker whose authority comes from the knowledge of the scientific principles of the laissez-faire doctrine. The artisan's barbarian character is exposed in Samper's mockery of León's improper use of language. According to Samper, "tiranibería" was a noun invented by León and used instead of the correct expression, "tyranny": "The poor man had heard the expression *Tirana Iberia* (Iberian Tyranny), and created a strange noun to refer to tyranny in general."[61]

The encounter between artisans and laissez-faire, represented by political economists as an opposition between enlightenment and ignorance, was perceived by artisans as an encounter between "theory and reality."[62] In a leaflet entitled "La Teoría i la Realidad" artisan Cruz Ballesteros branded Liberals "speechmakers." Ballesteros foresaw this art as a political economy of discourse. Speechmaking, according to him, is the "most economical of all systems; a speech does not cost anything and benefits the orator, who possessing a frugal table is the more interested in the promotion of lust."[63]

Leaflets, letters, and street protests were not the only testimonies of the struggle for representation among different world visions. Poems, novels, and drama became part of the contest. The opposition between "theory and reality" is the main argument of Candelario Obeso's drama *Secundino, the Shoemaker,* which tells the story of an artisan who despises his occupation and ventures into the world of theory and politics. He is impoverished in the process, and his wife, Marta (representing reality), tries to convince him to go back to shoemaking:

> Doña Marta: Go back to your molds
> and forget about elections
> and this showy life.
> Nothing remains of our scarce property.
>
> Don Secundino: How silly!
> It is evident that you have not read

Tracey and Bentham's works . . .
Power of knowledge! . . .[64]

Secundino attributes the stupidity of his wife to her ignorance of the main political economists, Bentham and Tracey. He identifies the knowledge of political economy as "the power of knowledge." The drama ends when Secundino, abandoned by politicians because of his artisan's status, is about to lose his house to the local authorities. Marta's savings and the money of Félix, a hardworking and honest artisan in love with Secundino's daughter, guarantee Secundino's debts, thereby preventing the family's ruin.

The debate between José María Samper's brother, Miguel, and the artisan J. Leocadio Camacho is even more interesting, since it allows one to appreciate the struggle between "theory" and "reality." Miguel Samper's study of poverty in Bogotá had identified artisans as one of the causes of poverty.[65] Artisans were depicted as assistants of insecurity who were moved by passions, not by interests. In Samper's view, the hatred artisans felt toward the rich hindered progress: "If the rich person feels threatened by hatred or resentment of the poor, he restricts consumption and hides or exports his capital. . . . Rich men's consumption is the fuel of the poor's industry."[66] The artisans' laziness, passions, gambling, drinking, and political disputes were seen as the main causes of poverty and misery.

José Leocadio Camacho, an artisan from Bogotá, replied to Samper's study.[67] Artisans, according to Camacho, were far from being the cause of poverty:

> For some time we have noticed with sorrow a decay in the guilds of artisans: some workshops that before had 14 artisans, today employ only four. The owners were not gamblers, nor drunks, nor did sensual passions exert a noxious influence on them; none of them had been *guerrilleros* because they did not belong to those engaged in small wars. Notwithstanding their struggle against poverty, it is poverty that was victorious. We can conclude that the cause of poverty is elsewhere.[68]

Like Camacho, other artisans had voiced their resistance to laissez-faire principles. In the artisans' petition to Congress in 1850, laissez-faire ideas were called "the *vanity* of theoreticians and the *greed* of speculators" [emphasis in original].[69] Artisans felt that "manual labor was seen as a despicable occupation." Contrary to the political economists' picture, artisans thought that hatred for manual work was at odds with civilization. They asked:

> How is an advancement of civilization possible in a country where manual occupations are dishonored? . . . the hatred for manual work would only lead to those who are less able doing manual work, and in these circumstances the craft industry will not benefit from human intelligence. The result will be barbarism and generalized poverty, a tendency to laziness, massive greed. . . .[70]

Samper's study also criticized the inefficiency of artisans: "In Bogotá, workshops are too small and use foreign raw materials. The lower quality of the materials results in inferior products. The amount bought is too small and the price too high." Contrary to Samper, Camacho imputes these problems not to the artisans, but to political economists:

> The best instrument against foreign competence is to establish workshops and factories with the capacity to supply raw materials of good quality. But answer my question, who is in a position to establish these factories you mentioned? Are the poor artisans, whose income only covers their daily maintenance? Or are the capitalists, who instead of using the money for imports . . . should use their money to build the factories we need? . . .
>
> Did you remember the glass, paper, and cloth factories? Why have these factories declined? The reason lies in the predilection for foreign products and the hatred of national products, like the scorn you have manifested for ponchos and shoddy shawls (manto chileno de frisa y la levita de manta). If France had the same hatred for its infant products, it would have become a *political* country, like ours, slave of England or the United States.
>
> You have argued that the protection of national industry is socialism's daughter. I do not oppose your ideas because I do not know about economics; but what I know is that twenty gentlemen, using political economy concepts, and with government support, have little by little been the cause of poverty, whose cause has been the origin of your own research.[71]

Camacho was most likely referring to Samper's argument against protectionism based on a disdain for domestic textiles compared to those imported from Europe:

Maybe this action [protectionism] has a nationalistic character, but we must agree that the result would not be at odds with good taste. A coarse poncho? A shoddy shawl? Tailors will be the first to be upset. And what about the feelings of carpenters, not hurt by foreign houses or doors, but harmed by protectionism since they would be deprived of wearing a calico shirt, and their wife or daughter will be deprived of wearing a scarf made of silk or cotton?[72]

The opposition between "theory" and "reality," the struggle between civilizers and artisans, also took place around the representation of the body. It was a struggle embodied in dress habits and ways of looking. The difference in appearance between the literati and the lower classes is illustrated in a watercolor (figure 2) by Manuel María Paz (1855). The scene is a picnic near Bogotá. The Bogotanos are wearing English-style suits and, according to the painter's description "the *tiple, bandola* (musical instruments), poetry books, and good food were required elements in picnics."[73] In the background are lower-class people wearing *ruanas* (Colombian ponchos) and shawls. Dress habits divided the followers of the Liberal Party into *guaches* (a derisive expression denoting artisans wearing *ruanas*) and *cachacos* (a term applied to Liberals wearing the European-style coat). According to an artisan's description,

In this corner of Spanish America, the man wearing a *ruana* is named *democrático.* . . . Proletarians, that is, the people of *ruanas* and *alpargates*, are a majority. There are 2 million *ruanas* and a few thousand *casacas*. The presidency, provincial assemblies, governorships, treasury boards are reserved for those wearing *casacas*. For those wearing *ruana* there are bullets, lances, nakedness, hunger, and death.[74]

Antonio José Restrepo described how dress habits, which differentiated poor from rich, were enforced—the infringement of these distinctions was subject to public sanction in the form of offensive nicknames, popular songs, or even physical punishment.[75] This was the case of a miner in Antioquia nicknamed the "cachaco de las vetas" because he abandoned the *ruana* for the American jacket. Restrepo also told the story of a lawsuit in the city of Cali as to whether the head of a family was allowed to wear the Spanish coat *(capa)*. Although the individual won the dispute, he could not afford the coat because he was impoverished after the lawsuit. Restrepo

Figure 2. Paseo de una Familia a los Alrededores de Bogotá *(A family outing to the Bogotá countryside)*, by Manuel María Paz, *1855*. Watercolor. Courtesy of Biblioteca Nacional de Colombia.

also referred to the story of an artisan elected to the municipal assembly in Medellín. Following the rules, the artisan attended the meeting wearing a frock coat. Not only was the artisan humiliated during the meeting, but also he was beaten badly at night and given notice that he would be beaten again if he did not wear his *ruana*.

One point of contention concerning dress habits involved the opposition between local and foreign textiles. Here women were subject to control both as producers of textiles and as the place of encounter with the desire of male creoles. The following passage illustrates the latter position as represented by José María Samper:

> The Indian man is always ugly and his features are rough and abject; but rarely we find in the other sex graceful and even pretty young Indians, with rosy and round cheeks, lovely and well-formed bodies. Nonetheless, what diminishes their gracefulness is the ugly dress they wear, made of an ordinary straw hat, a black blanket made of ordinary wool . . . and a poor shirt of local cloth. . . . In some places, distant from Bogotá, the Indians use a repulsive skirt called a *chircate* (considered an opprobrious form of dress); it is a black rag of wool,

of a gloomy color, covering the whole body. The female Indian looks like a walking mummy.[76]

Samper's depiction of the Indian dress contradicts the gracefulness of the female figure drawn by Edward Mark (figure 3).[77] Male Indians, for their part, were happy with their own dress practices and were distrustful of Indian women's changing their fashions to the creole style. The importance of local clothes appears in the following two songs of the Boyacá region. The first, entitled "Song of the Happy City" (Canción de la ciudad regocijada) narrates the dress habits during a religious festival in the city of Chiquinquirá. The quotation marks around the compliments show that the poet probably was a creole:

Los indios están muy "majos,"
y muy "lujosas" las indias;
ellos estrenando ruana,
y ellas, enagua y mantilla.
Todos, sombrero, alpargatas,
"rabuegallos" y camisa.

Male Indians are "good-looking,"
and women Indians very "elegant";
males with a new poncho,
women with skirts and shawls.
All with hats, *alpargatas,*
rabuegallos, and shirts.[78]

The other song, probably by an Indian, is "Song to the Female Lover Who Will End Badly" (Canción a la amada que va a tener mal fin). It refers to the negative consequences for a woman who has changed her dress habits:

Eran una maravilla
tu pantorrilla y tu pié;
pero ahora, con los zapatos
nadita de eso se vé.
Ya no te vistes como antes,
con carolina y olán;
ni te pones alpargates
ni quimbas de cordobán.

Ya no te llamas María,
sino Maruja, ay de mi!

Figure 3. Atuendo Campesino, Bogotá Febrero 1847 *(Peasant attire), by Edward Walhouse Mark, 1847. Watercolor. Courtesy of Biblioteca Nacional de Colombia.*

No decís "pa vos" como antes;
hora decís: "para tí."

Sabes más cosas ahora
que cuando eras querubín;
tanto sabes, Marujita,
que vas a tener mal fin.

They were marvelous
your feet and ankles;
but now with these shoes
they cannot be seen any more.
You don't dress like before,
with *carolina* and *olán;*
neither do you wear *alpargates*
nor *quimbas* of *cordobán.*

Your name is not María any more,
but Maruja, oh poor me.
You do not say "For you" like before;
now you say "For thou."

You have more knowledge
than when you were a little girl;
you know so much, Marujita,
that you will end badly.[79]

These passages suggest the complex process of exchange that took place between laissez- faire political economists and artisans and between theory and reality. Different systems of exchange (based on gender, prestige, and trade) accompanied the regime of representation. Women embodied the production of textiles, as artisans and as textile users, so that the representation of women and women's bodies supported the import of textiles and the displacement of local manufacturing in favor of European.

CONCLUSION

In Colombia laissez-faire principles, which were based on premises that equated economic activities and interest, entered into contradiction with the will to civilization as the predominant regime of representation. The former was subordinated to the latter. The uneven development of capitalism that occurred in mid-nineteenth-century

Colombia was the result of the contradictory encounter between the will to civilization and laissez-faire capitalism as conceived in Europe. In this encounter a contradictory exchange of representations took place: the Colombians, mostly passionate and ignorant artisans, were contrasted with English workers; morality was compared with rationality; theory was preferred to reality; coarse textiles were compared with imported ones; and the representation of female bodies supported the desirability of imported textiles. In nineteenth-century Colombia those representations voiced in the name of civilization and enlightenment silenced local claims. The violence of representation in the construction of identities along the continuum from civilization to barbarism was an important factor in the displacement of local manufactures in favor of European ones. The construction of hierarchical identities also explained the absence of a regime of representation in which the economy could "go alone" and interests were universalized. Not only were blacks, Indians, and local artisans seen as barbarians needing the employment of force, but also the pursuit of self-interest was seen as contrary to the principles of morality and civilization.

6

Representation, Violence, and the Uneven Development of Capitalism

*Each social group obeys the laws of its own physiology and geography;
[each group] develops according to their own point of departure and con-
curs in the work of Colombian civilization according to its own aptitude.*
JOSÉ MARÍA SAMPER, *ENSAYO SOBRE LAS
REVOLUCIONES POLÍTICAS I LA CONDICIÓN SOCIAL DE
LAS REPÚBLICAS COLOMBIANAS* (1861)

Throughout this book I have put forward the hypothesis that the relationship between the development of capitalism and violence is better
understood if we factor in the formation of meanings that have
accompanied the expansion of capitalism, particularly meanings related to differences, identities, civilization, and violence. In preceding
chapters I have conducted a critique of a political economy removed
from the world of meanings. Similarly, I have rejected approaches that
reduce violence to a phenomenal event or elevate violence to an inexorable law. I have argued that the strategies of understanding must incorporate the analysis of discourses. Furthermore, I firmly believe that
it is analysis of the processes of making meanings that reveals the
violence associated with the uneven development of capitalism. This
violence, as I have argued before, encompasses as well a violence of
representation: practices of resistance are rewritten in a way that both
obscures the transgression on the part of the dominating people and
endures the consent of the dominated. Santiago-Valles summarizes

117

this double move well: "Subjects are recognized as not just subordinate but also in need of policing and, synchronously, in need of policing precisely because they are subordinate subjects."[1]

In this chapter I demonstrate that the viability of capitalism is related to its capacity to provide a solution in representation to the contradiction of a regime of representation whereby hierarchies of civilization and barbarism mediated the relationships between elites and subalterns. I demonstrate that the development of capitalism was influenced by its ability to provide a solution to the contradictory encounter between the regime of representation known as the will to civilization and the homogenizing tendencies of capitalism. This contradiction was reflected in diverse ideological struggles around education, grammar, religion, and law that were seen as appropriate strategies of civilization. Different processes of resignification mediated between local practices of domination and resistance and the universalizing tendency toward capitalist expansion. Therefore, meanings related to gender, class, or race were articulated in diverse manners, with meanings related to what is proper and legitimate and who is and is not transgressing a given conception of order.

I concentrate on the problem of the persistence of the use of forced labor, which has been posed as the main obstacle to the expansion of capitalism in the Third World in general and in Colombia in particular.[2] Not long ago, this problem was analyzed as if capitalism or feudalism was the most appropriate mode of production on the periphery. Although the defenders of one or the other side differed in their theoretical and political positions, they had in common the tendency to read reality from theoretical constructions.[3] What I want to emphasize is that the "freeing" of the peasants from their land did not immediately place them into a "wage-labor" relationship. Labor relations—and, more specifically, what was known in the nineteenth century as "el problema de falta de brazos" (the problem of lack of workers)—was mediated by struggles over identities that involved issues such as discipline, morality, and work habits. Employers decided issues such as whom to hire, how much to pay, and which system of surveillance to employ based on gender, race, and class distinctions. I develop this argument by comparing four regions in nineteenth-century Colombia: Cauca in southern Colombia, Bogotá and Ambalema in the center, Santander in the east, and Antioquia in the northwestern part of Colombia.[4] I propose the existence of regional regimes of representation. This analysis allows one to conclude that only Antioquia succeeded in providing a solution in representation to the contradictory encounter between local and global struggles for recognition.[5]

COMPARING REGIONAL REGIMES OF REPRESENTATION

The argument is facilitated by the presence of regions that in the nineteenth century were relatively isolated and highly differentiated. Geography was a main factor in the regional differentiation of Colombia's population. Three branches of the Andean Mountains—the Western, Central, and Eastern Cordilleras—divide the territory into regions (see figure 4), which in the nineteenth century had no communication except by mule or river.

Two additional factors favoring a regional comparison are that in the nineteenth century individuals tended to identify themselves with the region rather than the nation[6] and that in Colombia regions were clearly structured around racial, religious, and partisan identities. This complexity of factors that intervened in the formation of the region is suggested in the following description by Camacho Roldán:

> The Antioqueño, a settler of the mountains, miner, or metal trader, with a tendency to banking, must be different from the inhabitant of Bolívar and Magdalena, where huge plains and cattle raising are predominant. The peaceful Boyacense peasant, coming from the Indian race disciplined by the iron yoke of the Spanish *encomendero* . . . cannot be similar to the African-Spanish mestizo raised under the tender protection of the owner, [working] in cattle raising and [living] amidst a natural environment which calls for freedom. The farmer from Santander, perhaps a descendent of proud Catalans whose lands were freed from feudalism and *encomiendas,* resulting in a more equitable distribution of property, has few things in common with the polite Cundinamarqués of the capital, and even less in common with descendants of the Chibchas, mixed with Spanish blood, who were ruled in the semi-feudal hacienda by an arrogant, unkind, and nondemocratic owner.[7]

This historical construct of identities and forms of production embedded in the "invention" of the Colombian regions also supports a nonessentialist understanding of race, gender, and political economy. The historical and contested character of racial construction has been stated by Peter Wade: "In Colombia, history gave race a regional

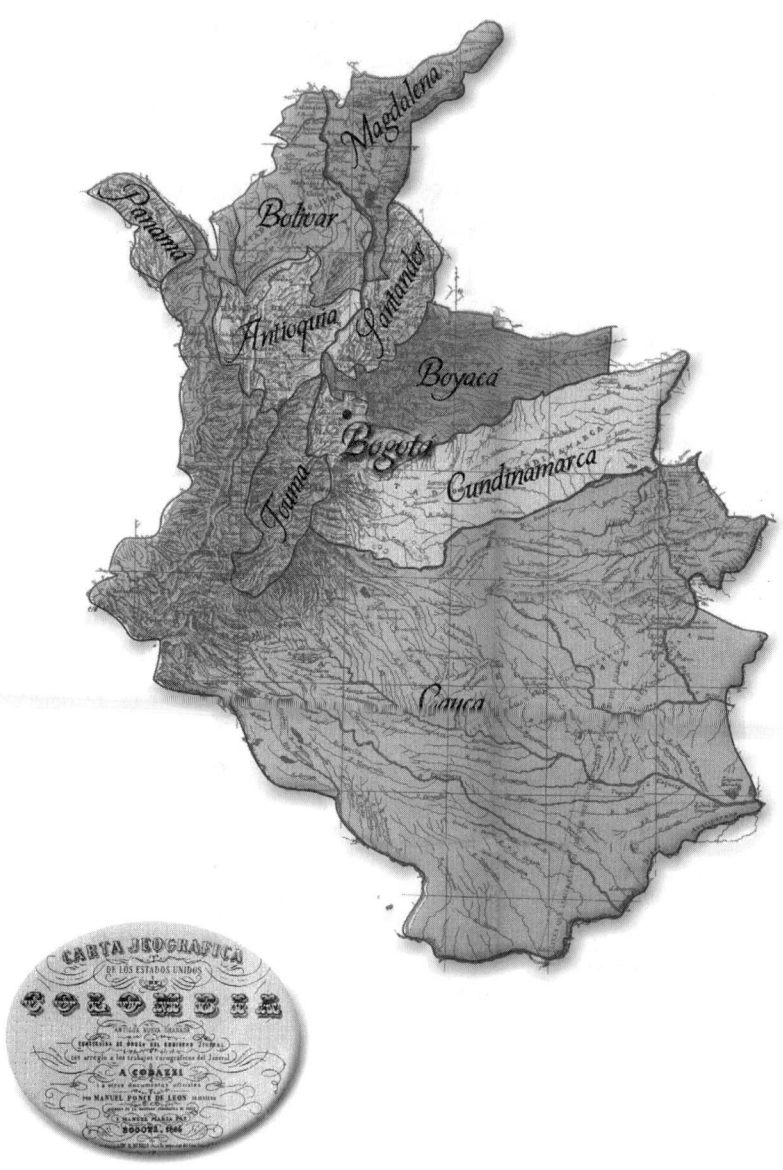

Figure 4. The United States of Colombia, 1864. From Atlas de Mapas Antiguas de Colombia, Siglos XVI a XIX *(Bogotá: Instituto Geográfico Agustín Codazzi, 1967), 24.*

structure such that race cannot be properly understood simply as a social construction around phenotype, but must also be seen as a social construction around region."[8] Some regions were imagined to be more homogeneous and civilized than others. These images were shaped along with the racial identity of their populations. This formation of the image of a region as predominantly white, black, or Indian was not grounded in physical differences or the ethnic origins of their inhabitants. The "invented" character of the Colombian regions is clear in the case of Antioquia, which was considered white and descending from Jews. This is also the case of Santander, which was considered to be predominantly composed of whites and the descendants of immigrants. In both Antioquia and Santander, the representation related to "whiteness" or ethnic origin was a myth that had little to do with the physical differences of the population. ·

The regions were also structured by their political affiliation with the Liberal and Conservative Parties. Both parties reinforced their distinctions by furthering identifications with religious beliefs, race, and class. In Cauca, the Conservatives were predominant in the election of 1848, in which the Liberal Party gained control of the country's presidency. The Conservatives opposed abolition and forged alliances with the Catholic Church. The partisan divide between Liberals and Conservatives was formed along racial and class distinctions.[9] In the election of 1848, the Liberals won in those places that had predominantly black populations. As blacks and mulattos were more likely to be enrolled in the Liberal Party, the Liberals were equated with the black movement. The province of Santander was considered the bastion of Colombian Liberalism. In the elections of 1848 and 1856, the Liberals won by a large majority.[10] Antioquia has been identified as the "most staunchly Conservative state in Colombia."[11] It was also considered a bastion of Catholicism.

It is also possible to relate the diversity of disciplinary methods and the social organization of production in each region with the uneven development of capitalism, as well as the viability of the diverse forms of capitalism in each region.[12] A hierarchical conception of differences had an effect on relations of production through the implementation of disciplinary practices and methods of surveillance. The use of force was not a remnant of a feudal past, but resulted from the interaction of practices of domination and resistance, which found expression in political struggles for representation. Therefore, economic prosperity and the social organization of production varied between regions. Cauca, the main gold producer of Colombia and the most important region during the colonial period, declined in importance toward the middle of the nineteenth century. During the tobacco and quinine booms, Santander had the economic predominance that Cauca had enjoyed before. Toward the end of the century, Antioquia became the main gold producer and also a major coffee exporter. The state of Antioquia experienced prosperity in the nineteenth century. During the second half of that century Antioqueños ruled the tobacco industry, controlled commerce, and were considered the most important moneylenders in the country.[13] Antioquia not only surpassed Cauca in gold exports, but also became the main exporter of coffee, passing Santander, the pioneering region for the cultivation of coffee beans. In the twentieth century Antioquia also became a leading region industrially. Both Cauca and the central regions were characterized by hierarchical distinctions. In Santander and Antioquia, contractual relations were prevalent, whereas in Cauca the use of force predominated. Table 1 summarizes the main characteristics of the four regions included in my comparison.

Table 1. Comparison of Colombian Regions

Region	Main Economic Activity	Concentration of Land	Racial Cleavages	Labor Relations	Level of Violence in Labor Relations	Economic Growth
Cauca	Mining (gold)	High	Yes (whites and blacks)	*Terrajes* and *concertado*	High	No
Santander	Agriculture (tobacco)	Low	No	*Aparcería*	Low	No
Central regions (Cundinamarca and Ambalema)	Agriculture (tobacco)	High	Yes (whites and mestizos)	Mutual contract	High	No
Antioquia	Mining (gold)	Low	No	Sharecropping	Low	Yes

Adapted from Marco Palacios, *El Café en Colombia, 1850–1970* (Mexico City: El Colegio de México/ El Áncora Editores, 1983), 190.

THE CAUCA REGION

Cauca's gold-based economy made it the most important region during Colonial times, although it was second in population. Mining extraction made the region the center and breadbasket of the slavocracy (see table 2).[14] Popayán, the capital of the province, was a major administrative center during the Spanish regime. The elite in Popayán has been considered a local aristocracy of Spanish origin; this aristocracy intermarried with Spanish immigrants who were absorbed into the elite. Slaves were part of the economic and social power of Cauca's elites, who had many women slaves working in domestic activities.[15] From the eighteenth century the agrarian sector was dominated by large estates; Cauca's haciendas were concentrated in the production of cereals, cattle, and sugar. Sugar production, the most profitable economic activity, also used slave labor. Cauca has been depicted as characterized by a paternalistic and authoritarian colonial system whose economic and political life was controlled by few families.[16] Nineteenth-century reforms with regard to freeing of slaves, abolition of *resguardos*, and public lands affected the foundations supporting this authoritative order in a definitive way.

Table 2. Ethnic Distribution in New Granada, 1778–80: Cauca Region

Ethnicity	Population	Percentage
Whites	9,768	15.15
Indians	11,363	17.63
Freemen of all colors	29,949	46.46
Slaves	13,380	20.76
Total	64,460	100.00

Source: Anthony McFarlane, *Colombia before Independence* (Cambridge: Cambridge University Press, 1993), 353.

Racial tensions were common in the Cauca region. As has been noted by McFarlane, the threat of a black attack on white society was very small because of the geographical dispersion of slaves and because they were outnumbered by whites and free people.[17] Nonetheless, the region was marked by a "culture of terror" in which the control of the population developed around the cultural elaboration of fear.[18] From the sixteenth century a "negro code" allowed the owners of slaves to control their social conduct: slaves could not move around the territory without proper identification, and every black person without an owner was considered a criminal and returned to the presumed owner. Infringement of this code resulted in severe corporal punishment.[19]

The spatial distribution of populations was the result of practices of resistance among members of the black population. A common practice of resistance among slaves was to run away from their masters

and to form black communities, *palenques;* this practice was preferred to open rebellion. According to Catherine LeGrand's description, from the eighteenth century runaway slaves sought refuge in
inaccessible *baldío* forests, forming *palenques* or armed agrarian colonies.[20] Other blacks who won legal manumission also withdrew to
public lands and away from white society. A law of June 22, 1843, entitled Repressive Measures against Insurrectionary Movements on
the Part of Slaves, made it legal to export slaves or to send them to develop new areas under the guise of protecting public peace. There
was also a strong debate around the possible renewal of a law of
1836 that had created a new criminal category, "vagrants," for the
manumitted *(libertos).* Vagrants were defined as "all those without a
job or rent, or those whose rent comes from gambling or prostitution."[21] According to this law *(Recopilación Granadina),* a vagrant
was subject to punishment, ranging from an arrangement *(concierto)*
with a private individual or public establishment for a term of two to
six years to military service or colonization of empty lands. The Conservative literatus and politician J. E. Caro thought that the best way
to deal with the problem was military service, as established in article
6 of the law of June 22, 1843.[22] The provisions for the army recruitment of *libertos* and vagrants addressed the problem of disciplining
the new *libertos* to conform to the economic system and also allowed
recruitment to be used as a form of punishment for disobedience. In
Caro's view, the "legislation does not assign the *libertos* to the army
only for being *libertos,* but [applies] to the *libertos* that *degenerate*
into vagabonds, that is, the ones destined for the army since they are
vagrants, not *libertos* as such."[23] Using this logic, there could be no
ambiguity in the application of the law, since it was thought that the
"difficulty of proving [nonvagrancy] . . . for those experiencing difficulty is, by itself, an indication of vagabondage."[24]

After the abolition of slavery in 1851, the movement of blacks and
mulattos toward public lands increased. Augmenting the physical
distance of the workplace or exclusion from national territory were
the strategies most commonly employed by *hacendados* to keep
blacks away. Running away into communities was not the only practice of resistance among blacks. Michael T. Taussig's study of Cauca's
African-American peasants also underlines the importance of the
struggle for meanings as a way to resist capitalist expansion and
bondage.[25] Peasants used to believe that men employed as wage work-

ers on sugarcane plantations entered into secret contracts with the devil. These contracts had negative consequences for both capitalism and the peasants; no more cane would sprout if a cane cutter had entered a contract with the devil. The peasant, invariably a man, would also invariably die prematurely and in pain. According to Taussig's interpretation, the devil was the mediator between a precapitalist and a capitalist system of production. In the latter system there was a split and subordination of persons to things; in contrast, in precapitalist societies products and creators were seen as intermeshed.[26] Taussig concludes that in peasants' eyes capitalism is "contrary to the laws of nature, evil, and ultimately destructive of the conditions of objective existence."[27] The gender issue was also manifest in the fact that only men were seen as entering into contracts with the devil.

Indian groups were not indifferent to the capitalist expansion in the Cauca region. Joanne Rappaport has documented these changes, as well as the resistance of an Indian group, the Páez, who live in the northeastern corner of Cauca.[28] In the nineteenth century, while legislation sought to destroy or weaken the *resguardo* system, Indians were recruited into the army in the elite's contest for power, the quinine economy targeted Indian land, and the haciendas were in the process of expansion into land occupied by Indian communities. According to Rappaport's analysis, the Páez encoded their history of struggle in sacred geography: moral links with the past supported the achievement of political goals. For example, in the nineteenth century the Páez revitalized their memory of the eighteenth-century chiefs, or *caciques,* who had created the *reguardos.* Furthermore, although Indians collaborated with the Colombian army as carriers, spies, messengers, and trailblazers, "they were never respected as disciplined soldiers, capable of carrying out the orders of non-Indian officers."[29] The Páez also used the pretext of civil war to attack neighboring non-Indians.

Contradictions existed not only between the elite and subalterns, but also among the Cauca's elite. Class, race, regional affiliations, and religious beliefs formed some of the partisan division between Liberals and Conservatives. As has been noted by Francisco Gutiérrez Sanín, the relationship between the Liberal elite and the black movement in Cauca was characterized by ambiguity.[30] In 1841 slaves were banned from the army, despite the "blacks' hope for joining in." The reason was that it was thought that the army would give a black "disrespect for and rebellion against the owner and a lack of love for work (desamor al trabajo)." That same year, as part of a different discourse, slaves joining the army were granted their liberty. In a speech to the black population of Timbio, the army commander stated: "You are going to fight for the country and your own freedom . . . brave and faithful Timbianos: the troubled freedom has found some hope within you."[31] Most of the time, blacks were interpellated as a "wretched horde of barbarians."

The period between the 1840s and the 1850s was characterized by the *hacendados'* desire to restore the old order. In 1851 former slaveowners resisted the manumission laws and went to war in the name of the Conservative Party.[32] Liberals formed *sociedades democráticas,* which gained the adherence of the black population, while Conservatives reciprocated with the formation of the society *amigos del pueblo.* The whip was the symbol of authority over the slave, and on several occasions the use of this instrument was recommended. According to Ramón Mercado, in the newspaper *La Civilización* there was an article that asserted that the pseudo-nobility of Cali was saying that the "wretched *democrática* should be controlled by the whip, using this instrument to threaten artisans and peasants."[33] The whip became a symbol of resistance to those who were called *hordas de salvajes.* The popular resistance was known as the "whip regime" (régimen del perrero o zurriago), which was a reversal of the slave-owner relationship: blacks entered the haciendas and lashed the owners. The aim of these "punitive expeditions" was not to expropriate the owners, but rather to scare the *hacendados.*"[34] Women, who were the main victims of the expropriation policy, as well as peasants and members of the *democrática,* took part in the "whip regime."

In 1859 the president of Cauca, Tomás Cipriano de Mosquera, led the Liberal Party to revolt against the Conservative Party, which was in power, claiming that the Conservative president intended to strengthen the executive's control over the provincial governments.[35] Mosquera interpreted the president's proposal of these laws as a declaration of war against the provinces and announced that the province "would no longer consider itself part of the Confederation if the Congress refused to repeal the law."[36] For President Mariano Ospina, on the other hand, the Cauca rebellion was a struggle of the dispossessed against property owners, of "criminals" against "justice," and a struggle of "corruption and barbarism against morality and civilization."[37] A racial fear appeared as well in the mobilization against the Cauca rebels:

> Do you believe that the ignorant black from Cauca, the outlaw, the criminals from the villages, that those men enrolled in the rebels' armies are interested in a metaphysical question about the form of government? No, that is a silly belief. The mob's motives are not different from an appetite for your property and hatred against your race, fed by the outrage and humiliation of their families.[38]

Production relations were affected by this contest among the elite and by its effects on the subordinated. Racial and gender beliefs were reflected in the organization of production, which employed a diversity of hiring practices in accordance with surveillance and policing needs. For example, when faced with legislation freeing slaves, landowners sought methods that would allow them to continue exerting control over the black population.[39] Some opted for a *concertado* system: in return for a small plot of a few hectares, blacks worked a certain number of days on the hacienda. A refinement of this system was the *terrajes:* virgin forest was divided among former slaves who had to clear the jungle. Land was provided to them for cultivation and for the hacienda. Their task was to clear the jungle and pay off their rent dues *(terrajes)* by giving five to ten days' labor each month to the hacienda. A further variation of this system was the establishment of contracts and subcontracts; in this system "honest white peones" from central Colombia were allowed to work on the hacienda. The owner maintained all rights to buildings, and no recognition was given for land improvement. Tenants were not allowed to work for anyone else. Control was exercised by the establishment of a "hierarchy of latent status differences" and by "informal, underground controls."[40] The outcome could not have been more discouraging: soil exhaustion, a capital infrastructure that remained the same as under the old hacienda system, and, according to the owners, anarchy so great that due to the "horror that permeated those woods, nobody would enter to claim *terrajes.*"[41]

The centralization of control exercised on the hacienda at the time of slavery was replaced by a dispersion of power relations characterized by a "series of concentric spheres of authority, with a great variety of distinct but overlapping relationships to the central power. Large cattlemen who rented land, white peons, free contract workers, cash-paying tenants, and labor-paying tenants found themselves in a gridwork of opposition to one another."[42]

Labor practices differed for white men, blacks, and women. Taussig illustrates this in the case of the Arboleda hacienda:

> [Arboleda] established a laboring elite of whites. In his instruction to the state manager in 1857 he said that the blacks worked too slowly in the mill and ruined the animals; only whites were to be employed there. He instructed that these whites have a three-year contract on a regular salary and be given a plot to cultivate and to build a hut. . . . Arboleda stressed that the working day of the blacks should be organized by piecework rates, never by time, and that it was better to leave work undone than to owe money. In the planting and harvesting of readily edible crops, like rice, only male peons from far outside the hacienda were to be hired, [but the manager was told to] do this without people understanding that you do it intentionally.[43]

The problem of labor was seen as a problem of discipline. According to a local authority of Palmira, the problem was not "lack of hands" (carencia de brazos), but "lack of workers," which insinuated the lack of "disciplined" workers. His proposed solution was to use "faster, more efficient, and safer methods of coercion."[44] As a consequence, the organization of production increased the system of surveillance over workers via private armed guards and diverse systems of punishment, as described by Harrison for the locality of Palmira:

> The governor of Cauca, in 1858, ordered the police of the tobacco-growing community of Palmira to keep an up-to-date list of all day laborers and people claiming to have sedentary occupations and to see to it that the employers of vagrants made use of the authorized punishments. The police were to encourage good and patriotic citizens to denounce those who fell into the various classes of vagrants and to volunteer their services as comisarios de policía.[45]

An analysis of social relations in the Cauca Valley suggests that the generalized labor exchange was poorly developed. The collapse of the slave system was accompanied by the construction of a regime of representation regulated by race and gender distinctions. Rather than relations of exchange among equals, racial distinctions fostered a system based on fear. Fear regulated the spatial and temporal relations of production; fear also regulated partisan relationships among Liberals and Conservatives. The consequence was economic ruin for the haciendas and relations based on distrust: "These haciendas now produce nothing. . . . The only hope is with the *terrajeros,* but they refuse to pay. And the plantains! You have to place a guard beneath each tree so they aren't stolen."[46]

THE SANTANDER REGION

An analysis of the eastern region, in particular the province of Santander, offers interesting challenges for the study of capitalist development. Indeed, Santander offered the best conditions for the progression of capitalism. The region was characterized by an important tradition in the manufacturing of fabrics, clothing, and hats. During the early nineteenth century, Santander dominated the internal demand for textiles, and in the second half of the century, it exported hats to the Caribbean. Santander adopted the most important principles of laissez-faire: free trade and a profound skepticism about government intervention. For example, the Santander Constitution of 1858 sought to make the province a model for the abolition of government. In the words of the region's most prominent leader, Murillo Toro, "The Constitution of Santander has abolished the government, as it was supposed to."[47] Nevertheless, Santander, like Cauca, was struck by a severe crisis toward the end of the century. This crisis was related to the contradictory visions of capitalism put forward by the region's elite and the resistance by those affected by capitalist expansion. On the one hand, they sought to combine a comunitarian vision of rural peasants with equal access to property by means of laissez-faire utilitarian principles. On the other hand, the vision of a society of white merchants importing goods from foreign markets collided with Santander's artisan production centered on women's labor and rooted in an indigenous and neglected past.

The eastern Cordillera was an important Indian settlement. When the Europeans arrived, the region had more than one million Indians, one-third of the Indian population at that time. Tunja used to be the most densely settled Indian province. In 1564 the Indian population of Tunja was 168,440; by 1635 it had declined to 42,334, and by 1755 to 22,543.[48] Physical annihilation played an important part in the destruction of Indian communities. Still, erasing the Indian's history was a mechanism as destructive as physical annihilation. For example, the colonial policy during the eighteenth century was to assimilate Indians into mestizos to solve the land problem of the white and mestizo populations. In 1770 the protector of the Indian, Moreno y Escandón, undertook a census in order to reduce the number of Indian villages, which were auctioned among white settlers. Their populations were sent to other villages. The legislation established certain "privileges" for the Indians who lost their land: they were exempted from the payment of tribute for one year, and they were to receive land in the new villages. In practice, most of them became landless.[49] Once in the assigned villages, they became *arrendatarios* (renters) who had to pay rent for the land. Those who resisted remained in their own villages, without a right to land, and were called *agregados* (added) because they did not belong to *resguardos*. In the words of one of the representatives of the colonial order who visited the eastern region: "Your Majesty will not lose anything, but on the contrary will gain, if the Indians will become Spaniards *(se españolizasen)* and the memory of the tribute will disappear with their caste."[50] As documented by Phelan, "Where formerly there had been sixty villages, now there were twenty seven. The suppressed Indian villages became "Spanish parishes.""[51] Despite the process of annihilation, toward the end of the eighteenth century Tunja still had 32,107 Indians, 20 percent of its population (see table 3).

Regardless of the numbers of Indians living there, the presence of Indians is ignored as part of the region's history. Nineteenth-century travelers usually depicted the region as having a white population. Manuel Ancízar, a member of the Comisión Corográfica, attributed whiteness to the rapid mixture between Indians and Spaniards. Regarding the province of Tunja, he observed:

> The indigenous race forms the smaller number of inhabitants, it being admirable how rapidly it has crossed with and been absorbed by Europeans, since half a century ago the province of Tunja presented a compact mass of Indians and very few Spanish families. Today one notes in the new generation the progressive improvement of the castes: the children are white, blond, of fine and intelligent features and better-built bodies than their elders.[52]

Ancízar initiated his pilgrimage to the Santander region by recalling the Indian resistance to Spanish domination in the year 1540:

> I pass the path where events occurred with veneration and respect in remembrance of those vanquished, defending fatherland and the freedom of their homes, already lost. . . . It was like hearing the clamor of

Table 3. Ethnic Distribution in New Granada, 1778–80: Santander Region

Ethnicity	Population	Percentage
	Tunja	
Whites	101,658	50.09
Indians	32,107	20.51
Freemen of all colors	97,897	26.59
Slaves	4,767	7.34
Total	236,429	100.00
	Giron	
Whites	1,470	21.02
Indians	126	1.80
Freemen of all colors	4,593	65.68
Slaves	804	11.50
Total	6,993	100.00
	Pamplona	
Whites	3,399	12.44
Indians	4,475	16.38
Freemen of all colors	17,980	65.80
Slaves	1,471	5.38
Total	27,325	100.00

Source: Anthony McFarlane, *Colombia before Independence* (Cambridge: Cambridge University Press, 1993), 353.

the combatants. . . . Destruction triumphed over the numerous, and solitude reigns where a town was before filled with the songs of innocent Indians and the happiness of their immolated sons. Today the descendants of these many martyrs travel through the Peñón de Tausa without knowing its meaning.[53]

The contradictory representation of an indigenous past appears clearly in this paragraph. On the one hand, like many nineteenth-century republicans, Ancízar deplored the situation of Indians that had resulted from the Spanish domination. On the other, he referred often to Indians as characterized by a lost memory of past history, which was another way of denying Indians their capacity to forge history on an equal footing with creoles. Indian resistance, exemplified during the important movement known as the Comunero Movement (1781), contradicted the creole view of the passive role played by Indians in history. As it will be shown later, this vision also contradicts the resistance of Indians, which influenced special legislation on the part of the Santander Assembly.

In Santander and Boyacá, the economy was based on agriculture. Indigenous traditions were embedded in agrarian, textile, and commercial practices. Land was more equally distributed than in the rest of the country. The prevalence of small landholdings gave an image of equality and homogeneity, as in the following description by Ancízar of the province of Vélez:

> The base of a happy population is formed, since it consists of small owners without the oppressive influence of big capitalists. This fortunate circumstance, common to the province, and the occupation of everybody in agriculture, plus a school of civic virtue, foretells that with time all of them would be equal in the society, as they are now equal in fortune.[54]

According to Fals Borda's study, in Boyacá the population distribution was in accord with the Indians' practice of living on isolated farms instead of in town. This practice survived despite the Spanish effort to concentrate Indians in *reducciones* that would make it easier to teach the Catholic religion and to control the payment of tribute.[55] Even social and labor arrangements, such as the *convite* and *compadrazgo*, were communitarian practices that survived from Indian culture.

Agriculture was supplemented by the manufacture of coarse cotton textiles and hats. The production of textiles was inherited from the Guane Indians. In 1660 the city of Socorro produced cotton fabrics, and in 1694 the *cabildo* of San Gil accepted the use of cotton as legal currency.[56] According to the statistics elaborated by Salvador Camacho Roldán for the year 1848, the cotton and wool fabrics produced in Tunja and Socorro were valued at 6 or 7 million pesos, and two-thirds of Colombia's population dressed in local textiles. Also, these fabrics were exported in small proportions to Ecuador and Venezuela. The value of hats manufactured in the region surpassed 1.5 million pesos, with half exported to the Caribbean.[57]

Women dominated the artisan sector: in both Santander and Tunja, there were 140,000 artisan women compared with 45,000 men. The proportion of the total Colombian employment made up of the artisan sector has been considered very high when compared with modern Colombia: in 1870, 11.6 percent of men and 63.2 percent of women were employed in the artisan sector. For the Santander region, the proportion was 10.3 percent and 88.3 percent, respectively.[58]

A census taken in 1890 reported 5,800 spinning establishments, 1,640 factories for the production of woolen and cotton textiles, and 300 establishments for the production of hats.[59] There was also production of *fique* sacks that were used as containers for coffee. In the province of Vélez, as in most of the provinces of the region, women worked in textiles and hat production. Ancízar described the working life of Zapatoca as follows:

> If a traveler arrives in Zapatoca on a laboring day, he may think that the city is empty since no one is in the windows or in the streets, except for some domestic workers going to the store or the man attentive to his business. All the rest are not visible. Peasants spend the week on their small farms taking care of the land. . . . Women are always inside the houses, weaving *nacuma* hats, with such industry and dexterity, that there is no foreign piece that intimidates them and they are not able to copy. They attempt everything and everything is well done. It is admirable the perseverance of these women when they work; they work from morning to night time, when 10 or 12 of them get together in a friend's house, together pay for an oil lamp, and sitting on the floor keep working part of the night.[60]

A more equal distribution of rural property linked to artisan production at home furthered the vision of the region as a place without violence. Unlike the *terrajes* in the Cauca province, in Santander labor relations were less violent. In Santander there was a system of "mutual contract" (contrato de compañía). According to Palacios, in the mutual contract estate owner and sharecropper agreed to share the proceeds of the harvest according to a form of contractual arrangement where land, work, resources, and expenses were shared.[61] Characteristics of this system were that there was no personal subjection of the sharecropper to the estate owner and that the contract was for a fixed, rather short, period of time.[62] In the artisan sector, the use of force was absent. As Ancízar wrote of the province of Vélez:

> There is a middle class, composed of female laborers occupied in commerce and in the fabrication of products for consumption, being an example of the contribution of work and economy to welfare. . . . They exert authority over the proletarians not with dominion but with a soft treatment like equals. . . . In this excellent daughter of the *pueblo*'s

heart there is no room for the haughtiness nor for the harshness which wealth produces in others.[63]

Ancízar also suggested a relationship between a lack of criminality and employment. He praised cities, like Barichara, for the absence of crime, as they had only small robberies, fights, and common injuries. This situation he attributed to the "absence of the two major causes of crime, idleness and misery,"[64] whereas in other towns, such as Socorro, he noted a higher rate of criminality and illegitimate children. According to the author, this situation could be prevented "if the rich neighbors of El Socorro would take an interest in the industrial education of poor women, if they had opened industrial shops and thought about the road to honest living."[65]

The high proportion of women participating in the activities of production was, perhaps, not independent of the fact that the province of Vélez recognized women as citizens as early as 1853.[66] This decision was not well received among the creole elite. Juan de Dios Restrepo, known as Emiro Kastos, published an article in 1855 asserting that the possibility of women's political participation was unthinkable. He preferred to think that the legislation "was inspired by an act of gallantry and not by a political thought. . . . We are sure," he continued, "that women would not use that right, and if they do, politics would not profit at all, and goods habits will lose a lot."[67]

The situation of Santander, a peasant economy with an equal distribution of property and an artisan sector with broad participation by women, was evidence of the contradictory characteristics of laissez-faire liberalism. First, the reality of women's artisan activities called into question the male and agricultural premises of the creole vision of capitalism. Women's work was rendered invisible, and the activities of those engaged in productive labor were romanticized and stripped of any economic connotation, "they [women] work with pleasure, although without great profit" (con gusto pero sin provecho). The production of hats was seen, in the best case, as redemptive, but not in a productive manner. Emiro Kastos expressed the following opinion: "[A woman is] able to live and work in a job appropriate to her weakness, beside her parents, under the protection of her family and under the shadow of her home. This industry would produce four times more than cooking, ironing, and washing; [a woman] could live a life less shameful, more honest and modest."[68]

Manuel Ancízar explicitly described the gendered character of women's work in the following passage. In his description, the market appeared as a scene where the main contenders were male merchants and female weavers. Women and men used body language as the carrier of market messages:

> Saturday is a day of almost no sales because the female weaver goes to explore the market, assess the demand, and foil the merchant's intention to pay only the minimum. The woman weaver is not fooled by her opponent's indifference: she knows that he must fill the order for hats demanded by the merchant in Cúcuta [the big city] and she counters the hilarious stoicism of the merchant with an infinity of feminine artifices. At a certain moment the merchant is nervous, he calls the weaver, smiles at her, whispers, and by Sunday the merchant has surrendered: he has forgotten the previous offer and takes as many hats as possible. Victorious, as always happens when it is in their interest, the daughters of Eve return to their homes with the *nacuma* needed to accomplish the next job, forming happy groups, walking around, and at night they begin the hats for the next week.[69]

This system of exchange also captured the attention of artist Carmelo Fernández (see figure 5).[70] His painting illustrates a racial

Figure 5. Tejedoras y Mercaderes de Sombreros Macuma, Bucaramanga *(Weavers and straw hat vendors in Bucaramanga), by Carmelo Fernández, 1850. Watercolor. Courtesy of Biblioteca Nacional de Colombia.*

mixture of whites, *zambos,* and mestizos and the defiant attitudes of males and females in the process of exchange.

Despite the preceding passage about the triumph of artisans when they fooled the merchant, toward the end of the century artisan-produced textiles disappeared from the market.[71] Today the decline is still attributed to the women's incapacity to transform the old forms of production. According to Frank Safford, "It is hard to see what the ladies engaged in cottage weaving have to do with the development of mechanical skills in the modern sector. Might these women, if through economic autarky somehow maintained in their late colonial prosperity, have been the progenitors of a new army of ironworkers and machinists? More likely they represented an economic dead-end and thus irrelevance to technological modernization."[72] Women's work was seen, at most, as a protection against misery, sexual oppression (mainly in the form of prostitution), and more oppressive forms of labor, such as domestic service.

A second contradiction emerged between the elite's vision of laissez-faire and the nature of a region formed by small peasants. The epitome of this contradiction is a prominent figure of liberalism, Manuel Murillo Toro, known by his enemies as a "communist" and "socialist." According to historian Gerardo Molina, Murillo certainly was acquainted with the theories of Sismondi, Saint-Simon, Fourier, and Proudhom.[73] For him, republican and socialist ideals were equivalent. In his view, socialism meant the increase of rural proprietors; he defended both land distribution and a system of progressive taxation. His opposition to laissez-faire in matters of property was found in an article addressed to Miguel Samper and published in the newspaper *El Neo-Granadino* in 1853.[74] In his view, economic reforms should go before political reforms, because the working of democracy presumes an independent economic position. Murillo Toro saw the wrongdoing in society as due to the unequal distribution of land. By allowing the wealthy to become wealthier and the poor poorer, laissez-faire "does not allow everybody's participation in the progress of civilization."[75] He envisioned a country of rural producers: "We must be a country of rural producers and nothing else."[76]

As president of Santander, Murillo Toro stated that crime did not have its origin in the individual, but was the result of political, religious, and economic causes. How could the government severely punish these faults?[77] Murillo also endorsed the right of individuals to defend themselves against the existence of a permanent army, to a government by the majority as opposed to the right of minorities to govern, and to geographical representation in elections.[78] Nevertheless, there was among the Liberal elite a firm belief in individual capacities, and in that sense a coincidence with laissez-faire's belief in the principle that interests govern the world. In a circular sent to all municipalities, the secretary of government summarized the philosophy of the Santander Assembly: no one knows better an individual's own interest than does the individual.[79] As a corollary to the principle of individual interests, the circular stated that individuals should bear the responsibility for building schools, bridges, and hospitals. The president recommended that individuals get together and finance these activities in a free association. He also stated that education, industry, and public works, including the construction of roads, should be an individual responsibility. The abolition of government was Murillo's ideal. According to Molina, Murillo epitomizes the ambivalence of a fraction of nineteenth century Liberalism that aimed to combine the principles of individualism and comunitarianism.[80] Murillo's liberalism exhibited a contradiction between two different messages, one the message of the French Revolution of 1789 centered on individualism, and the other the message of the European ideas of 1849, which gave voice to the victims of capitalism's harshness.

The ambivalence of the Liberals' message explains the conflictive political situation in Santander, which was characterized by strong opposition and open confrontation between Liberals and Conservatives. At the center of the debate was the type of laissez-faire reforms decreed by the provincial government. Conservatives interpreted these reforms as anarchical and closer to communism than individualism. The following was the position of the Society Estrella del Norte of San Gil with regard to the Liberals' conception of equality:

> The Society cherishes equality. . . . But in no way is it inclined to that kind of equality which, contradicting natural inequalities, confuses merit with ineptitude, probity with vice, and hard-working with laziness; since this equality is destructive of the social order. And by virtue of this the Society will conduct propaganda against the dissolving doctrines of communism.[81]

The opposition mounted by the Conservative newspaper *La Voz* revealed the uneasiness of Conservatives with what they saw as anarchy resulting from the reforms. Under the motto "Alliance of freedom and order," the newspaper called for laws that would take into consideration the wickedness and passions of individuals.[82] Conservatives rebelled against the provincial administration in 1859. Predominantly Conservative towns asked to be liberated from the Liberal government. According to them, this "freedom does not lead to progress. . . . We prefer to give up this freedom and to protest against these guarantees and these benefits. We prefer a different order of things."[83]

A third contradiction emerged between the vision of a "country of foreign merchants" and Santander's artisan tradition. This contradiction was reflected in the artisans' opposition to free trade, which in the case of Santander took the form of racial tension between German merchants and local artisans. German immigration began in Santander with the arrival of the Pedagogical Mission in 1871. The mission was engaged in the creation of a school for artisans and had its own newspaper, *El Pestalozziano,* inspired by the pedagogical thought of the Swedish educator Pestalozzi. The German educators also gave singing, violin, and piano lessons. This mission was followed by the immigration of almost one hundred young male Germans who settled in Bucaramanga, Cúcuta, Ocaña, and Socorro. By 1875, the Germans had a monopoly on imports and exports such as coffee, tobacco, and quinine that were exported to Hamburg and Bremen.[84] Some Germans, such as Geo von Lengerke, combined commerce with the construction of roads, following Santander's policy on private construction of public roads.[85] This policy increased the German influence on public affairs. The Germans had their own army during the period of road construction. Furthermore, the government provided prisoners for the construction of the roads, and often prisoners were freed without government intervention. According to one account, in Lengerke's house, "built and decorated as a German castle, he coined his own money to conduct internal transactions. On Sunday, the day of payment, the German flag was lifted and the German Anthem was intoned, at the same time that Lengerke fired a European gun-barrel."[86]

By 1879, Bucaramanga witnessed an open confrontation between its population and the Germans. Several groups voiced their resistance to German penetration.[87] A priest in Tunja criticized *El Pestalozziano* for its liberal, anticlerical, and atheistic ideas, and the newspaper was burned in a public meeting in front of the church. In El Socorro, a newspaper entitled *El Amigo del Pobre* (The friend of the poor) accused the Germans of precipitating the crisis in the manufacturing sector. In 1879 several conflicts developed in Bucaramanga between artisans and German immigrants who were involved in commercial activities. The opposition was voiced by the artisan democratic society called La Culebra Pico de Oro (The gold-mouthed snake). Two Germans were shot to death, and the German consulate as well as the houses of German citizens was painted with anti-German graffiti.[88] Two members of the society were accused of the assassination. In their written defense, the artisans accused the Germans of being disrespectful of good habits; of engaging in obscenity, concubinage, and orgies among men; and of "being Protestant and atheist."[89]

The private construction of roads was also a source of conflict between the regional government and the Indian population. In a letter to the Santander Assembly (1869), Lengerke reported a crime committed by an Indian on the Barrancabermeja road, and he asked the assembly to take steps to "reduce or to drive away the savage tribe of Chucurí . . . if [they] do not want barbarism to replace civilization, thanks to the construction of the Magdalena road."[90] Lengerke's text also evidences the racial construction of crime that obscures transgressions on the part of the dominating and depicts dominated as in need of policing. Narratives describing Indians as a threat to the white population were more common in the second half of the nineteenth century than in the first half. For example, in 1837 the government sent a mission of twenty-four armed men to the Carare Opon. The report to this mission describes the Indians as peaceful. A letter sent by the head of the mission to the governor of the Santander Province reads as follows:

> Certainly, after reading this letter, you must think that I am out of my mind, because I took the decision of being devoured by the animals, killed by the arrows of the savages, or to risk myself to hunger. Nothing like that happened, Mister Governor: there are tigers and lions, but they flee from humans; Indians have milliards of arrows, but only for hunting and fishing, and it is hard to find among humans people as pacific as they are.[91]

Aquileo Parra, governor of the Santander Province, mentioned that before 1853 the Indians "did not terrorize" the population, citing only one robbery that had been committed fifty years before. Parra took part in a government mission to the Carare Opon in 1855. The mission, formed by thirty men, encountered a group of only eight or ten Indian families in the Opon, who ran away when they saw the troops.[92]

Later on, the governor of Vélez presented the same mission in a different way; in his view, "the report proves that the tribes are even more dangerous than what people used to believe."[93] According to him, those who fell into the hands of Indians were shot with as many arrows as possible and died in horrible pain. The fantasy embedded in this text is reflected in the contradictory claims with regard to those "witnessing" the Indians' savage character: "None of those who had the bad luck of looking at the people of the jungle had the opportunity to 'tell their story.'"[94] Furthermore, some passages of the governor's version of the savage character of Indians cannot be distinguished from racist stories produced elsewhere. Reflecting on the muscular strength of the Indians, he concluded by saying, "The same happened on Sandwich Island and several other places where savages live, according to Spencer's observations in his book *Political Institutions*."[95]

In 1861 the Legislative Assembly of Santander issued a decree authorizing the president of the state to take the measures needed to civilize the Indian tribes. These measures included the use of Christian missions and administrative regulations between Indians and civilized populations, such as those regarding the formation of settlements, as a communication channel with the Indians. Prisoners condemned to more than two years of prison could be used in these settlements. Meanwhile, the decree allowed the use of a military expedition to drive Indians away from the Carare and Barrancabermeja road. In 1878 the *Cabildo* of Zapatoca fined Lengerke two thousand pesos for abandoning the construction of the road. Lengerke refused, complaining that he did not have the strength to contain the Indians and that the government would "neither annihilate nor domesticate them."[96]

In summary, conflicts became common in Santander and Boyacá. Economically, the region was in decay. Commerce between the towns almost disappeared due to the lack of well-connecting roads. By 1865 Santander had abandoned its radical laissez-faire position and begun a more regulatory system.[97] The region's economy did not prosper at the same pace. There was a crisis in the agricultural exports of tobacco, cinchona, and cotton. The traditional tobacco region of Girón, which had been known for the high quality of its tobacco, had ceased to be an export region by the 1870s as a result of soil exhaustion, poor quality in the packing process, and low international prices. Cinchona bark did no better; by 1880 exports had almost disappeared.

The crisis in the artisan sector was no less great than that in agricultural exports. National textiles, which had clothed the nation at the end of the Colonial period, supplied only 10 percent of national consumption in the 1870s, and less than that by 1890.[98] The crisis in this sector was reflected in the decrease in population of the main artisan centers. Toward the middle of the nineteenth century, 10 percent of the Colombian population inhabited the artisan centers of Santander; sixty years later, this percentage had diminished to 4 percent.[99]

THE CENTRAL REGION: BOGOTÁ AND AMBALEMA

During the tobacco boom, strong linkages developed between Bogotá and Ambalema. Creole literati dominated Bogotá, the capital and center of administrative power. Creoles were nicknamed *cachacos* (dandies) after the *casaca* (English coat) they wore. Ambalema was the most important economic center during the tobacco boom. Exports of tobacco from the Magdalena Valley grew from one thousand tons in 1835 to five thousand in 1856.[100] By mid-century, the region was the main tobacco exporter and had the biggest tobacco factory. All kinds of immigrants settled in the trading center of Ambalema.

There was a migration of literati and merchants from the capital to the lowlands, in search of fortune. Ambalema captured the imagination of nineteenth-century Colombians, as tobacco exports represented the dream of an economy based on agricultural exports. Ambalema's location near the capital serves to illustrate the linkages between *hacendados* and literati. During the tobacco boom, young Liberal lawyers and merchants from Bogotá went to Ambalema as *hacendados*. Among those literati who went to Ambalema were José María and Miguel Samper, defenders of laissez-faire and prominent literati; young lawyers such as Pedro Navas Azuero, members of *la escuela republicana*; the brothers Evaristo, Eustaquio, and Alejo de la Torre (Evaristo, as a law professor, established the economic and juridical bases of public credit); Salvador Camacho Roldán, a pioneer of sociology and successful businessman; and Aníbal Galindo, politician, governor of Cundinamarca, minister, and author of a book on economic history and one on national statistics.

In addition to illustrating the heterogeneity of class composition of the Colombian elite, the case of Ambalema enlightens the complexity of labor relations in mid-nineteenth-century Colombia. *Hacendados* were very often literati and merchants who combined their careers with agricultural export. Their knowledge of political economy and their adherence to laissez-faire did not ensure that they would play according to the rules of the market. The use of coercion in labor relations resembled what was called "liberal feudalism." Hiring practices and methods of surveillance were mediated by racial and gender considerations. The case of Ambalema illustrates both the desire of male creole literati to civilize the lowlands and peasants' resistance to creole domination.

The heterogeneity of the central region of Cundinamarca and Tolima and the changes that occurred in the region, first with tobacco and indigo and then with coffee, facilitate the argument for a relationship between identity and labor practices. A division between white *hacendados* and Indians prevailed in Cundinamarca, whereas in the Magdalena Valley the predominant divisions were between white *hacendados*, *zambos* (those with a mixture of black and Indian blood), and mulattos (table 4).

Before 1830, tobacco was produced mainly on small farms by *cosecheros,* who were free to sell what they produced directly to the tobacco factory.[101] During the tobacco boom, the big hacienda replaced the *cosechero* system. Production relations changed toward a system of *aparcería,* or toward a mixture of piecework contracting and *arrendamiento:* the *hacendado* rented the land and the peasants acquired a contractual obligation to sell the crop at a price agreed to in advance.[102] The peasant was indebted to the *hacendado* for his subsistence and that of his family.

This system of production was devastating to the tobacco industry. Soil exhaustion and a poor system of packaging and handling had a detrimental effect on the quality of the leaves. Colombian tobacco, which had been considered of high quality, deteriorated; by the end of the nineteenth century, Colombia was importing tobacco from Cuba and other countries.

Unlike in the Cauca region, where labor relations were centered around the threat presumably posed by blacks to the white popu-

Table 4. Ethnic Distribution in New Granada, 1778–80: Cundinamarca and Tolima Regions

Ethnicity	Population	Percentage
Santa Fe		
Whites	28,057	28.88
Indians	32,054	33.00
Freemen of all colors	35,573	36.62
Slaves	1,463	1.51
Total	97,147	100.00
Mariquita		
Whites	12,336	26.15
Indians	4,436	9.40
Freemen of all colors	26,313	55.79
Slaves	4,083	8.66
Total	47,168	100.00
Neiva		
Whites	5,908	22.33
Indians	3,850	14.55
Freemen of all colors	15,810	59.76
Slaves	888	3.36
Total	26,456	100.00

Source: Anthony McFarlane, *Colombia before Independence* (Cambridge: Cambridge University Press, 1993), 353.

lation, in the central region the problem of "lack of workers" (la falta de brazos) centered on the Indian, *zambo,* or mulatto peasant's presumed ignorance, lack of morality, and low capacity to work. A description of a Cundinamarca hacienda by Malcolm Deas points to discipline as crucial to the functioning of this system.[103] As the author noted, the predominant mode of bringing a hacienda into production was to parcel it out in lots to *arrendatarios.* The owner was an absentee, and the hacienda was administered by an administrator who identified totally with the interest and, in this case, puritan habits of the owner. The *arrendatarios* grew their own food crops, but not coffee; the latter was planted under the administrator's direction. One source of difficulty was the administrator's rule that obliged the *arrendatarios* to do unpaid work on the hacienda. Another source of difficulty was the fact that the *arrendatarios* were prohibited to plant coffee themselves. The administrator had to apply at his own discretion techniques of "reward and punishment" to enforce discipline on the hacienda. According to the administrator, "I have had to have an open struggle with the *arrendatarios*: they are so stupid that one has to make them earn their money by force."[104] The administrator often complained about the *arrendatarios*' laziness, which he attributed to the Indian character: "I'll never understand these people: they really are *indios*. Now they get a good day's wage in the harvest, but one still has to force them and mule-drive them just as if one was asking them to work for nothing."[105] From Deas' description we also know that the hacienda hired peones and female pickers, *cosecheras* or *cafeteras*. They were seasonal harvest workers who had come from Cundinamarca and Boyacá. The hacienda appointed a special *mayordomo de cafeteras,* or overseer of discipline, for *cosecheras*. Deas characterized this market as a "free labor market with some advantages on labor's side."[106] Workers could argue about conditions and even resist discipline, as in the case of workers who refused to work under a *mayordomo*'s direction. Evidence suggests that in the central region the advantages were not on labor's side. As has been illustrated by Michael Jiménez, the estate's management was hierarchical and arbitrary.[107] The use of peonant labor depended on arbitrary job regulation that included brutal beatings, whippings, evictions, and sexual abuse. This situation remained until the early twentieth century.

The spatial organization of production prevalent in the region contrasts with the one found in the Cauca region. The response on the part of the *hacendado* was not to increase distance, but to increase the system of surveillance and the control over the everyday lives of peasants and their families. The spatial distribution of elements of the hacienda and the village maximized the surveillance of the peasants, as is apparent from Camacho Roldán's description:

> In addition to the house of the *hacendado,* there are two *tambos,* huts with straw ceilings but without walls. The cane mill occupies one of the huts, and in the other is the shelter for the workers, men, women, and children, without distinction as to sex. . . . Nevertheless, each family of *arrendatarios* had its own room in a hut in the middle of the forest, and a small plot of land with corn, yuca, and plantain. This was located as far possible from the owner's house, whose surveillance the *arrendatarios* always want to avoid.

In contrast, the owner's house was located in an elevated place allowing the direct supervision of most of his land. The families of small properties used to live in the house since they could not afford to live in the capital or in a bigger house: the wealthiest *hacendados* used to live in the capital and visit the hacienda during summer time. . . .

The parish was formed by a few houses . . . governed by four main establishments: the church with the house for the priest annexed to it; the prison, whose main furniture was a stock for punishment . . . ; the cemetery . . . ; the host house and the place where provisions (food and liquor) were sold. . . . The prison was the symbol of authority and justice, a protective divinity in the leaders' imagination, but represented by a cell, a stock for punishment, and an inflexible jailer, to awaken ideas of terror and hatred.[108]

Two texts written during the tobacco boom serve to illustrate the struggles over meanings that took place around Ambalema's story. One is Medardo Rivas's *Los Trabajadores de Tierra Caliente* (Workers in the hot lowlands).[109] Rivas depicted the life of those "pioneers of capitalism" like himself who had become *hacendados* in the Ambalema region during the tobacco and quinine booms. The second text is Eugenio Díaz Castro's novel *Manuela*.[110] The author, a peasant, presented the rural resistance to the hacienda's labor conditions and the literati's civilizing mission. *Manuela* is a novel about violence. Unlike Rivas's description, which is organized around male heroes moving to the hot lowlands, Díaz's narrative centers on a female heroine, Manuela, nicknamed *la pacificadora* (the peacemaker), representing the oppressed people of Ambalema. Manuela, a poor black woman living near Ambalema, is both a site of resistance and an object of desire. The basic plot of *Manuela* revolves around the desire to exert control over her of four male characters: a lawyer and member of the literati, a public officer, a peasant, and the *hacendado*. *Manuela* is the story of the contradictory encounter between her desire for peace and the violence of both the *hacendados* and the Liberal literati who have immigrated to the lowlands. The novel ends with the destruction of the object of desire. Manuela dies the day she is going to marry her peasant bridegroom, July 20, the anniversary of Colombian independence.[111]

Rivas describes the life of at least 150 creole men who had property in Ambalema. One of the few references to blacks and women takes the form of a local story about the dangerous sexuality of blacks. It is the story of a runaway mulatto who abducts the daughter of a white *hacendado* the day of her marriage to a white man. Although the young lady is returned safely to her husband, as the story goes, her soul and mind are gone forever. The story suggests the relationship between desire and violence that haunted the nineteenth-century will to civilization. Creoles advanced the practice of miscegenation as the road to civilization. This process was located in women in terms of desire. Violence and desire became central to the construction of difference. As the story shows, creole men fear the loss of the object of desire, the beloved woman, through contact with black men. Therefore, a "double-bind" arises from two desires converging on the same object; the creoles' gain in the name of civilization is their loss of women's sexuality.

Also seen in Rivas's story is a naturalization of social relations and of the process of land appropriation. Owners and landscape are in perfect harmony. Rivas's hacienda, Guataquicito, was located in a beautiful valley at the edge of the Magdalena River in front of the village of Guataquí. In the past, the land had been owned communally by the Guataquí Indians. The Indians had "transferred" their rights during the previous fifty years, and, according to Rivas, only three hundred people had rights to the land, even though over three thousand had land claims. This situation caused a legal dispute, after which Rivas had legal rights over most of the land.[112] He described his great happiness as follows:

> I was happy with nature's light, with the Magdalena River's majesty as the border of my property, and with the feeling of being a landowner, since I was born poor. I enjoyed being an important person for all the people around me; I enjoyed being strong and able to work. I enjoyed collecting the tobacco from the *cosecheros* and counting my *cosecheros* by the hundreds as my protégés. I enjoyed knowing that I was increasing the national wealth. . . . I read a lot, wrote novels and poems. And I always had my mind fixed on the hundred thousand pesos that I would extract from this land, so that I did not feel the passage of time.[113]

Rivas's text also reveals the relationship between the conception of race and the strategies behind the hiring practices on the *hacienda*. Indians were not feared, but they were considered a problem due to their lack of initiative and their work habits. *Zambos* were considered lazy, and, unlike the submissive Indians, they were characterized as having a natural resistance to work. The image of the *zambo* was related to the wild environment and the lawless life:

> The evident inferiority of the original race (black African and copper indigenous) and the subsequent decay, increased by the presence of a fermenting climate . . . produced in the *zambo* a race of animals in whose figure humanity hesitates to find their image or a part of their being. . . . The *zambo* exhibits his ugliness in three different ways: in the *champan* or boat, on the beach dancing the *currulao,* and in his hut, near the river, enjoying the *dolcissimo far niente* of the savage.[114]

Both groups were considered opposites to the ideal of the good worker: "If we take a Magdalena boatman or an Indian from Cundinamarca and compare him with an educated Bostonian, we will have before us both our starting point and our goal."[115] In Ambalema hiring practices varied according to region, race, and gender. For example, those clearing the jungle or collecting tobacco leaves were not locals, but migrant workers brought from Antioquia. Rivas explains: "To turn Guataquicito into a meadow I ask for workers from Manizales; and suddenly I had two hundred Antioqueños with their wives, children, and dogs" (p. 224). They were a testimony to laboriousness and discipline: "A few days later they were installed, submissive, working and following my orders in the same manner as the Indians from la Sabana [de Bogotá]" (p. 245). The results were evident: "With knives they began the logging and the mountain was consumed ravenously as a mirage. . . . In three months the forest had disappeared; six months later, one thousand *cargas* of corn were harvested; one year later the land to settle 500 livestock was ready" (p. 245). Rather than contract these migrants directly, he hired a *capitán* (chief) who received pay for each acre cleared; *el capitán* directly commanded these groups of local migrants.

From Rivas's description it can also be concluded that despite the *hacendados'* knowledge of political economy and their adherence to laissez-faire, they did not play according to the rules of the market in contracting labor or in initiating a process of capital accumulation. Most of the *hacendados* returned to their homes ruined. Morally, the wage relationship was seen as inferior to the hacienda system. In the eyes of Rivas

> Coming to the Magdalena Valley, after traveling to Colombia's Capital and looking at their filthy population slave of a salary, is a pleasure,

because here we have the *cosechero,* surrounded by his family, in the middle of plenty, and relieved of the need to earn the bread from the sweat of his brow (p. 260).

To the question, "Does the *cosechero* have needs not fulfilled?" he responded:

He had work, prosperity, home, family, and future. Yes, he needs something else; a friendly voice who teaches morality to him; who changes his semibarbarian habits; who will make him sober and economic; who turns him on the road to civilization; and who, without depriving him of his children's work, inspires in him the desire of bettering his condition, making him a lover of virtue and showing him the pleasures and charm of social life (p. 264).

It is clear from Rivas's description that *hacendados* were familiar with the wage relationship. It is also clear that their decisions regarding the type of labor contract in which to engage were not based on economic considerations. Their arguments were of a moral nature, since they considered that a salary relation did not "civilize" the workers. They preferred practices such as the *cosecheros'* being indebted to the landlord and closer surveillance in order to ensure that the workers would fulfill their obligations. Furthermore, it could be concluded that these practices were not efficient even from a cost/ benefit perspective. Rivas mentions the case of those *cosecheros* who did not learn their lessons and fulfil their obligations to the landowner. Indebted to the landowner, they smuggled tobacco, and one day ran away to Ambalema searching for better land. According to Rivas, of those who went to Ambalema "most of them ended impoverished; others, unable to pay the capital borrowed at a high interest, had to turn over the haciendas to the moneylender; others during the crisis of the Ambalema tobacco, after many years of labor, returned to their homes, like war invalids, sick and poor" (p. 175). The fate of those engaged in the extraction of indigo was no better.[116] Those places where indigo was planted became "covered by yellow straw, symbol of the infertility and abandonment of the soil."[117] As a witness to the disastrous indigo production, Rivas quoted from a poem written by his partner, Francisco de la Torre. In "Farewell of a *Tanquero* to His Horses," a *hacendado* recites the frustrations of his struggle with both workers and nature, leading him to consider committing suicide (p. 309). Rivas, who had equated the ruin of tobacco to the ruin of the nation, attributed the misfortunes to destiny or chance.

Eugenio Díaz's *Manuela* also ends with the destruction of the nation, represented by Manuela. The reason for this destruction is attributed to the foreign presence in the region, which takes the form of law, religion, and capitalism. Demóstenes, the lawyer, is a literatus who arrives in Ambalema as a representative of the Liberal Party. His name represents the Liberal's view of law (*demos* = people; *sthenos* = strength). The source of his power is not wealth, but his enlightenment: "Books and clothes" are the only things in his suitcase. He reads "The Mystery of Paris" and praises printing: "Oh Gutenberg! Even here has arrived your marvelous discovery" (p. 10). His hobby of reading kept him away from the main events in the town, "buried in his books, he did not pay attention to the movement in the streets" (p. 13). Demóstenes' relation to Manuela is to be that of a protector and guardian: "She is under my protection and favor" (p. 170). The constitution and the law are his main instruments to gain Manuela's favor and to fight the one he considers Manuela's main enemy: Tadeo. The Liberal Demóstenes and the Conservative priest are allied in their civilizing mission, although pursuing opposite means: law and religion (pp. 24–25).

Tadeo is the town's Liberal *tinterillo* ("ink-spiller"), one of those practitioners of law, mainly in rural localities, who had not attended university. Ink-spillers do not derive their power from their enlightened nature; they derive it from their knowledge of the law and from knowing how to use it among illiterate people. Most of the writing in the nineteenth century refers to them as troublemakers and producers of violence. In Díaz's description, *tinterillos* are equated with ticks, blood-sucking insects that are almost impossible to eliminate (p. 8). In *Peregrinación de Alpha,* Manuel Ancízar referred to them as a plague whose presence occasioned conflict and division among the people. According to him, towns were destroyed by *tinterillos* in alliance with priests.

Tadeo's power comes from the control he can exercise by means of his interpretation of the law. His power is represented by his ownership of the town's memory, his understanding of laws, and his control over women's lives. As another character tells Demóstenes, when he came to the parish, he was in charge of delivering the citations:

> Then, he began writing documents; then he had the list of laborers and elections . . . ; then he became director of the judges and in this job he gained money by confusing the neighbours with allegations and

litigations; then he became director of the municipal *cabildo* and was in charge of all the things in the parish. Things did not stop there, he won everybody's dominion, either because they needed him to free them of their problems, or as an ally in their rogueries, or simply because they feared him; in the end he had everybody under his power. And the worst thing is that he is the only one who understands the *Recopilación Granadina*. He understands elections, lawsuits, contributions. . . . He intervenes in testaments, marriages, family fights, dances, everything. You must know, Don Demóstenes, that he wants to have the same control over men and over the young women. He desires that all of them, especially the most beautiful ones, be under his will (p. 153).

Tadeo's archive is depicted as a "photograph of the parish, taken by daguerreotype. All political fractions are there, civilization is there, the march of the Republic is there." Taking possession of Tadeo's archive is part of the people's struggle.

Hacendados exert control over the *arrendatarios* of the hacienda using the power they have derived from ownership of the land and their power over women. The following is a dialogue between two *hacendados,* Cosme and Damián:

—How is your situation with regard to peones? Cosme asked his friend.

—I have plenty of them, responded Don Blas.

—One day I was short of peones; I sent someone to destroy the hut of an *arrendatario* who was insolent, and they are obedient now. There is no chain as strong as the land. . . . They blindly obey my orders whatever they are. If we could rent the air, as we rent the land which gives peones their living, can you imagine how much respect we would receive from these animals? (p. 44).

Peones considered their situation close to slavery. As one says: "I am slave three times: slave of the *gamonal* because he releases my daughters from working and two times slave of the landowner." Asked if he considered his situation fair, his only answer was "Fear, friend, fear. Do not you believe that [fear] has a lot of resources to make damage?" (p. 248). The novel illustrates the contradictory principles of Liberals, ostensibly believers in laissez-faire, who use feudal practices. Díaz referred to *hacendados* as "liberal feudals" whose only laws were those that came from control over the land.

Women were doubly exploited, as peones and as women. They

were used to pay the foremen's *(mayordomos')* favors to the owner. Sexual coercion, as noted by Michael Jiménez, represented a powerful weapon at the disposal of planters in imposing their will on the workers. Forced intimacy was an integral part of the process of labor control.[118] As Manuela explains to her *arrendataria* friend:

> Poor women! They are forced to go to the peones [for sex] without considering their health, religion, or any other condition; and everything to make the landowners richer! Why care about spoiling their women *arrendatarias* if the cane mill produces more sugar? Poor *arrendatarias* who had to suffer their slave situation not only for themselves but for their daughters too![119]

The situation of factory workers in the tobacco factory of Ambalema, especially women, is compared to that of the *arrendatarios*. In Ambalema, Manuela meets a well-dressed former friend who seems affluent: "Her fingers, neck, and ears were shining with fine gold, and even her hair was ornamented with gold" (p. 258). In the street she notices that the women working in the tobacco factory all dress like her friend, Matea. At the same time, Manuela observes that Matea's room, which she shares with five women, has no ventilation, little furniture, and poor conditions, leading to the death of the working women. To Manuela's question about how it is possible to live there, Matea responds that in addition to having a daily salary, there is no one who oppresses her against her will. The view of a sick factory worker living in the streets increases Manuela's confusion. "With so many things, and so many landowners and merchants," she asked, "is there not one hospital for sick workers? . . . Is this the protection and caring you were talking about?" (p. 267). Manuela's perplexity increases with her visit to the tobacco factory:

> Manuela was astonished by the activity of the people, especially the women, who moved their fingers as fast as the hummingbirds move their wings. These women left their post with dissatisfaction when it was time, willing to make six or eight pesos a week, without fearing the hunger, thirst, heat, or tiredness. Honor to the man who installed the first factory (Don Francisco Montoya), which with his commercial habits, his remuneration for work, and his spirit of order maintained, in the interior of the Republic, a place of venture for rich and poor! . . . Manuela asked her friend where the landlord *(amo)* was:
> —Master? Answered Matea . . . Master? There is no need of master around here.

—Then, who is in charge of whipping?
—This is the whip which governs everything, said Matea, placing in front of her eyes three or four pesos (p. 271).

The factory workers, all women, came from the rural areas to escape oppression and the violence exerted on them. Women were exploited both in the factory and on the hacienda. In the former, "dull economic necessity" replaced the direct use of force.

Violence in labor relations, as described by Díaz, contributed to the contradictions on the *hacienda* and to the lack of economic viability of this system. By 1875, Ambalema had failed as a tobacco-exporting region. In 1871 the price of land was one-third of the 1856 value. The price of each kilo of tobacco went from forty cents in 1857 to twenty-five cents in 1868. A tobacco disease deepened the existing crisis caused by the low quality of tobacco and diminishing international prices. Ironically, the disease, which put an end to the area's dream of prosperity, was called mulattization.[120]

THE ANTIOQUIA REGION

Antioquia's economic growth during the nineteenth century has been seen as a puzzle by scholars interested in capitalist development. During the colonial period, Antioquia was one of the poorest regions of the country. According to the report of a Spanish visitor, Juan Antonio Mon y Velarde, the province was very poor, agriculture and commerce were stagnant, and government was corrupt and disorganized.[121] Poverty was linked to the high cost and scarcity of foodstuffs.[122] Another visitor reported that as a result of food scarcity many slaves died of hunger.[123] Yet in the second half of the nineteenth century, Antioquia became one of the most prosperous provinces.

The relatively successful capitalist development of the Antioquia region has been the object of a considerable debate among economic historians. The myth of the Jewish origin attributed to Antioqueños has been at the center of this discussion and was common among nineteenth-century scholars, as typified by José María Samper:

> The Antioqueño is a very interesting person, physically the best-looking and the strongest by his character and his influence in the federal government. . . . The old province of Antioquia[,] . . . conquered by Robledo y Heredia, attracted the first Spanish immigrants because of its gold mines and the good weather. Later, during the Spanish persecution of Jews, even those converted to Christianity by force, they or-

ganized an emigration of 200 families, converted to Catholicism, and settled in Antioquia. . . . Spaniards, Israelis, and creoles mixed and created the most beautiful and vigorous race known in Hispano-Colombia. Today the state of Antioquia has over 300,000 people, and at least 250,000 are the result of a mix with Jews.[124]

In an article published in 1926, Eduardo Zuleta still sustained the thesis of the Jewish origin of Antioqueños. Even among contemporary authors there is a tendency to present the population of Antioquia with a homogenous composition and to offer this characteristic as an explanation of its economic success. As becomes clear later, both the thesis of the homogeneous character of Antioquia's population and their Jewish origin have been dismissed. A comparison of table 2 with table 5 shows that proportions of white and slave populations in Antioquia and Cauca were very similar. The main difference is in the lower proportion of Indians in the former (4.3 percent) as compared to the latter (17.6 percent). In Antioquia blacks did the work elsewhere done by Indians, since by 1590 the Indian population was very small. In some localities, such as Santa Fé de Antioquia and Medellín, blacks and mulattos outnumbered whites. The proportion of mulattos was high in the mining areas.[125]

Table 5. Ethnic Distribution in New Granada, 1778–80: Antioquia Region

Ethnicity	Population	Percentage
Whites	7,866	16.97
Indians	2,034	4.39
Freemen of all colors	27,535	59.39
Slaves	8,931	19.26
Total	46,366	100.00

Source: Anthony McFarlane, *Colombia before Independence* (Cambridge: Cambridge University Press, 1993), 353.

Even as a legend without much base in empirical evidence, the representation of the ethnic homogeneity of Antioquia and its Jewish origin continues to puzzle scholars interested in economic development. The myth about Antioqueños' origins has been used to support the thesis of "need achievement" as a condition for economic development. Berkeley professor James Parsons began his doctoral dissertation on the Antioqueño colonization by reminding readers that Antioqueños named themselves the "yanquis de Sudamérica," signaling "energetic individualism" as one of the Antioqueños' most important qualities.[126] Parsons stressed poverty and the harsh conditions of the territory as the main factors forming this distinctive character. Antioqueños were also the center of attention in Everett Hagen's *Theory of Social Change*.[127] Hagen attributed Antioqueños' success to their psychological characteristics. In his view, the myth about the Jewish origins is a key contributing factor: he argued that because of this legend, those in the cultural centers despised the Antioqueños. In his view, the Antioqueños emphasized the acquisition of wealth to counter this disdain.

Historian Frank Safford entered the debate with an alternative interpretation: the legend about the Jewish roots of the Antioqueños was not the origin, but the result, of their economic success. Engagement in gold activities was the true explanation of the region's economic well-being. The legend, in his view, was the expression of a kind of "sour grapes" attitude to the region's success by the economically weak provinces.[128] But as Álvaro López has pointed out, it is difficult to say that the control of resources is enough to ensure financial control, business management, and social influence.[129] Until the middle of the nineteenth century, Cauca was not only a more prosperous region, but it also dominated political life in the postindependence years.[130] Yet it attracted neither the legendary quality of Antioquia nor its success with capitalism. Santander also experienced tobacco and quinine booms, but that region failed to establish a stable environment favoring the accumulation process.

I believe that a key factor needed to explain the process of development in Antioquia is its capacity to provide a solution, in representation, to the main contradictions of the predominant regime of representation. These contradictions had to do with, on the one hand, the hierarchical classification of individuals along racial and gender lines, and on the other, to the adoption of laissez-faire as the practice governing individuals. The Conservatives' religious beliefs contradicted a laissez-faire emphasis on utilitarianism, and the Liberals' distrust of government and religion were in deep contradiction to their desire for "civilization." The following elements contributed to a resolution of these contradictions in Antioquia: the first and most vital was a conception of "undifferentiated" individuals. As a result, in Antioquia the use of force in the relations of production was less marked than in the other regions. Second, the political affiliation of Antioquia as a Conservative state in the midst of a Liberal country shaped its strong sense of difference from the rest of the country, as well as a feeling of internal homogeneity. The Antioqueños' representation centered on the *raza Antioqueña* (Antioquia's race), where an inclusive rather than exclusive concept of identity prevailed. Third, the "Jewish identity" of Antioqueños allowed them to overcome the contradiction between their Catholic beliefs and their laissez-faire practices. And fourth, the Conservative affiliation also accounted for the support for government intervention and Catholicism.

Most of the descriptions concur in attributing to the province racial homogeneity, habits of hard work, and physical attractiveness. Unlike people of the other provinces, where a feeling of fear or frustration with laziness was expressed toward the lower class, the Antioqueños realized that they, too, had positive attributes: "The lower class (el bajo pueblo) Antioqueño, the most beautiful of the province and the Republic, is smart, hardworking and honest. . . . All the population is homogeneous and the accent is distinctive."[131] Antioquia, like the other regions, had racial diversity. This racial diversity appears clearly in Enrique Price's watercolor entitled *Types of the Medellín Province* (figure 6), where blacks and mestizos are predominant.

Figure 6. Tipos de la Provincia de Medellín *(Races characteristic of Medellín Province), by Enrique Price, 1852. Watercolor. Courtesy of Biblioteca Nacional de Colombia.*

It is important to notice also that the spatial distribution of individuals differs from that in most pictures by other artists of the period. To illustrate the point let us compare Price's image of the people of Medellín with Carmelo Fernández's picture of three women of Ocaña-Santander (figure 7).

In Price's picture, all the individuals, disregarding race or gender, are located on the same level. The black woman is placed at the center, captivating the attention of three of the four characters. However, in Fernández's watercolor, entitled *White Women,* not only is the black woman erased from the picture's name, but she is located at the back of the other women and is facing the opposite direction from the "representatives" of Ocaña's women.

The problem of labor was defined in a different manner in Antioquia than in Cauca or the Central region. According to Alejandro López, the modern history of Antioquia began at the end of the eighteenth century with the arrival of a member of the Spanish Crown, Mon y Velarde.[132] In the Spaniards' eyes, the problem in the province was the *desidia y abandono* (negligence and lethargy) of the population. In the words of Spanish Crown visitor Mon y Velarde:

> Using all kind of instruments I made all of them believe, from the oldest to the youngest, that they were born to work, and that we should see as delinquents those useless to their fatherland and those who do not employ their strength in gaining their own subsistence. . . . Once this idea was happily spread among the people, they awoke from their lethargy, and like those awakening from a deep dream, began to settle new towns.[133]

Mon y Velarde did not only spread ideas, however. He initiated political and fiscal reforms ensuing from his belief in the undifferentiated working habits of the population. His main reform was to grant free access to land to those who wished to found towns *(pueblos)* and agricultural villages. Alejandro López pointed to the enormous difference between these reforms and the process of colonization elsewhere. The mechanisms of social control differed from those mentioned in the case of *terrajeros* in Cauca, where fear became an important element of the power held by the white landowners. In Antioquia a different form of social organization emerged. As was stressed by Palacios:

> The dominant classes in Antioquia are not scared . . . of the "barbarism" of dances or cultural expressions of the people; on the contrary,

Figure 7. Mujeres Blancas de Ocaña *(White women of Ocaña), by Carmelo Fernández, 1850. Watercolor. Courtesy of Biblioteca Nacional de Colombia.*

they were able to recreate from peasant folkloric traditions a holistic vision of an Antioqueño world, with the vision of a free, proud, frugal, entrepreneur-peasant from the mountains *(montañero)* as the epitome of the *raza antioqueña*.[134]

Labor relations on the hacienda also differed from those developed in Cauca or Ambalema. The system is depicted as one of relatively free *aparcerías* (sharecropping) where the *aparceros* had more freedom to organize for market production.[135] They were also able to hire additional workers, and both products and expenses were shared with the landowner. The work system had important effects on productivity:

> The technical backwardness of haciendas using forced labor was a consequence of the negative and violent incentives of direct producers, while the relative freedom in the case of [Antioqueño] colonization and individual incentives acted as engines propelling an improvement in labor, discipline, responsibility, and initiative and in the technology of production.[136]

In the political arena, ballots did not guarantee power to the Conservatives in Antioquia; they took power by rebelling against the Liberal government in 1864. General Pedro J. Berrio, who led the revolt, became provisional governor. He was elected to a four-year term in 1865 and reelected in 1869. His first years in office were characterized by a fear that the Liberals, led by President Mosquera, would intervene in the region to depose the Conservatives. The tension was increased by Mosquera's reluctance to give federal recognition to Antioquia's government. The relationship between the radical-federal government and the Antioquia Conservatives was far from harmonious.[137] Antioquia adopted a strategy of "tactical isolation" that allowed it to remain at the margin of the conflicts in other regions and also forged the feeling of internal homogeneity among its population. Antioquia remained apart from the nation's civil wars for most of the second half of the nineteenth century. In 1865, the Conservatives discussed the possibility of a nationwide uprising, but were discouraged by the fear that because of the Antioqueños' "selfishness" they would not support the revolt.[138] In the meantime, as a result of the tensions of 1867, the Liberal newspaper *El Índice* published the poem "El Canto del Antioqueño" in recognition of its government.[139]

Literature contributed to the creation of regional distinctiveness. For example, a poem by Gutiérrez González highlights the regional attributes of Antioquia, especially its language, to the point of describing the Spanish used in Antioquia as a regional language:

> I will not underline the regional expressions
> That I often use in my writing.

Thus while I write only for Antioquia
I do not write Spanish but the Antioquian language.[140]

The entrepreneurial character of the Antioqueño elite was not linked to the laissez-faire school adhered to by Colombian Liberals. Laissez-faire principles collided with the religious beliefs of Antioqueños. It appears that the Jewish legend about the Antioqueños' origins may have allowed the population to harmonize their utilitarian tendencies with their religious beliefs. Therefore, in a local newspaper an article entitled "Israelis and Antioqueños," although recognizing that the legend was not founded in reality, used the legend to differentiate Jews from utilitarians. It argued that, whereas the latter were a threat to society, Jews "with their activity, work, and economy increase wealth and spread civilization."[141] This is precisely the compromise between civilization and capitalism that so often eluded Colombians.

Antioquia's regional representation allowed it not only to avoid the local turmoil of the other regions, but also to reach the point of separating from the nation in the pursuit of regional interests. The following selection from a letter written by Mariano Ospina Rodríguez is very illustrative: "The merchants of this province (Antioquia) had embraced with joy the idea of joining the Republic to the United States, as the only means to ensure security. . . . This step will entail some inconveniences, but is the only solution to stop the barbarism which menaces the destruction of this country."[142]

In Antioquia the regional administration had a more interventionist character than in Santander or Ambalema. The increases in primary education and road construction were important policies of Governor Pedro José Berrio. The same was the case at the municipal level. As has been pointed out by López Toro, local authorities depended on the power of the *hacendados,* but were elected by the community.[143] Another characteristic was the existence of collective effort in activities such as the selection of land for settlement, the preparation and financing of new expeditions, the clearing of land, and so on.[144]

CONCLUSION

An analysis of the four main regions of Colombia brings to light the linkage between the representation and manifestation of violence, on the one hand, and between these forms and capitalist development, on the other. In Cauca, representations were dominated by a culture of terror. The use of fear was a dominant element in both the organization of production and partisan alignment. Fear was related to the attempt by Cauca's elite to retain the control of labor before the abolition of slavery. Spatial and temporal distancing and relations of surveillance corresponded to the hierarchical differences between the creole landowners and newly manumitted blacks. Once a prosperous region during the colonial period, Cauca turned into a "land of brigandage and fear."

Indians and *zambos* were the majority in the central region (Cundinamarca-Boyacá-Tolima). Indians were said to be stupid, submissive, and to have a low capacity for work. *Zambos* were said to be lazy, negligent, and lawless. The Indians' image of submissiveness and the *zambos*' image of laziness did not create the same feeling of fear as in the Cauca region. However, control of their lives became a major concern on the haciendas. This control was related to the discipline of Indians and *zambos* to turn them into hard workers. The control exerted over them included everything from sexual coercion to strict regulations regarding planting, time allocation, and distribution of crops, not to mention rituals regarding threats and punishments. The hacienda system did not prove economically more successful than the *terrajes* of Cauca. Briefly successful ventures such as tobacco and tannin production failed within a few decades.

In contrast, Santander offered the appropriate environment for laissez-faire principles to prosper. Thought of as homogeneously white, the region became the bastion of Liberalism. Legislation was enacted to provide for the individualistic character of the region. Violence was almost absent from those locales where production by artisans and small holders prevailed. "Mutual contracts" between estate owners and sharecroppers reduced the extent of personal subjugation that characterized relations in the Cundinamarca-Boyacá region. Despite Santander's prosperity in manufacturing and later in tobacco production, the region's experience with laissez-faire ended in local revolts and economic crisis.

Antioquia, like Santander, was said to be a homogeneous region inhabited by a white population with strong work habits inherited from their Jewish origins. The myth surrounding the Antioqueños not only allowed the people to be represented with positive attributes related to habits of hard work, but also had an effect on the organization of production in the region. Labor was not seen as a problem as in Cauca or Cundinamarca, fear disappeared as the main element of control, and the population could concentrate on "conquering the land with axes."

These cases illustrate, on the one hand, the importance of the formation of meanings about gender, race, and class in elite-subaltern relationships and in the subsequent transformation of these relationships into wage-labor, free-market capitalism. Those places where identities were constructed negatively tended to employ coercive relations of production. This was the case of Cauca: the system set up after abolition had the effect of maintaining blacks within slavery-like restrictions on time, spatial distribution, and discipline. On the contrary, in places where the population was perceived as being homogeneous, independent of racial differences, as in Antioquia and Santander, contractual relations prevailed, although not necessarily in the form of wage labor.

These cases also illustrate the historical character of the construction of the category of "good" workers. The value of the work done by blacks, women, and Indians was evaluated differently, as was the perceived need for labor control and surveillance. In certain regions women's work was romanticized and rendered invisible, Indians were considered lazy, and blacks were seen as a threat to white privileges. The resistance of these groups was interpreted as transgressing the elite's conception of order. Therefore, violence was applied to them and the transgression of those dominating them remained invisible.

Conclusion
Civilizations—Clash or Desire?

Whatever fosters the growth of civilization works at the same time against war.

SIGMUND FREUD, "WHY WAR?" (1932)

For peoples seeking identity and reinventing ethnicity, enemies are essential, and the potentially most dangerous enmities occur across the fault lines between the world's major civilizations.

SAMUEL HUNTINGTON, THE CLASH OF CIVILIZATIONS (1996)

These epigraphs illustrate well the main paradox addressed in this book: the relationship between civilization and violence. Sigmund Freud's statement was a response to Albert Einstein's question "Why War?" which he formulated at the end of the First World War, and Huntington's was a proposal for a new paradigm for interpreting the evolution of global politics after the Cold War. Although Freud saw in civilization a solution to war, Huntington saw civilization as a source of war. According to the former, the evolution of civilization consists of a progressive displacement of instinctual aims and restriction of instinctual impulses. One way to displace destructive impulses is through identification. In Freud's view, "Anything that encourages the growth of emotional ties between men must operate against war."[1] Huntington, on the contrary, believes that communal identities are more likely to result in "identity wars." As long as the consciousness of civilization strengthens in relation to other identities, "a 'hate dynamics' emerges comparable to the 'security dilemma' in international relations, in which mutual fears, distrust, and hatred feed on each other."[2]

I conclude this book with some reflections on Huntington's prediction that the fault lines between civilizations, and not between nation-states, will be the battle lines of the future.[3] In my analysis I do not attempt to establish whether the conflict between civilizations is a historical fact.[4] In response to his critics, Huntington formulated a more compelling question: "If Not Civilization, What?"[5] I inquire why at the end of the Cold War a new regime of representation centered in civilization emerged within the discipline of international relations and what will be its consequences for the development of antagonisms and war. I also delineate some alternatives to the study of civilization that put the issue of identity and difference at the center of analysis and therefore provide room for recognition rather than conflict.

CIVILIZATION: GENEALOGY OF A CONCEPT

In this book I have departed from the study of civilizations as a static concept and focused instead on civilization as a regime of representation. This means, in the first place, that representations of civilization have altered historical narratives of the self and the Other. This is the ontological dimension. Second, colonial practices of domination and the political economy of capitalism are related to the formation of identities and differences between civilizers and those to be civilized. This is a political dimension. Third, civilization is a space where violence can be either originated or solved, and therefore it is a place of both conflict and recognition. This is a normative dimension.

Norbert Elias's history of the civilizing process allows us to appreciate how structures of recognition and desire have been played out in the construction of European civilization.[6] He poses the center of the transformation of civilization in the transition from warriors to courtier in the eleventh century when warriors lost their economic and military self-sufficiency and were forced to go to the courts to seek service. Once dependent on the king, what motivated them was the desire to preserve their class prestige. Elias compares the court to a stock exchange where the estimated "value" of each individual was being formed. Each person's value was "in the favor he enjoy[ed] with the king."[7] The transformation in "civilized" behavior was a result of this political economy of exchange of favors and influence. The individual attuned his behavior to his position in the network of courtly opinion. Therefore, self-control was exercised "for social reasons." This adjustment of the self to the Other's desire is what Elias calls "psychologization," observation of others and oneself, "because it is here that vigilant self-control and perpetual observation of others are among the elementary prerequisites for the preservation of one's self position."[8]

According to Elias, the concept of civilization grew as a concept expressing a single human civilization, and until the eighteenth century it still referred to the progress of humanity. Civilization was forward-looking. Furthermore, in early arguments for capitalism, the spread of commerce and the attainment of civilization were seen together.[9] Economic doctrines equated civilization with trade. This change allowed Adam Smith to put forward the idea that "economics can go it alone." Karl Marx shared this optimism about the civilizing consequences of expanding capitalist relations of production.

As Elias illustrates, toward the middle of the nineteenth century the forward-looking and universal orientation of civilization was lost. The ruling classes founded their ideal images of themselves on the past rather than on the future. This change brought with it a consciousness of superiority and a justification of Western rule over the non-European world. Civilization was exerted by "civilized" countries over their colonies. Externally, the concept of civilization played an important role in the drawing of borders among nation-states. Internally, it made possible the displacement of violence toward an outside Other, in the form of either an anarchical interstate system or a "barbaric" Third World. Therefore, civilization organized the relations between nations as hierarchical differences and those within a nation as similarities. At this moment the concept lost its universal connotation and referred to particularized ethnic or historical civilizations. Civilization was articulated to refer to race, and nations were graded according to their degree of civilization. Those peoples who were not European were depicted as manifestly in need of civilization.

Mid-nineteenth-century colonial and postindependence elites in Colombia encountered this metropolitan understanding of civilization. The European vision struck directly at their right to govern the recently liberated country. To accept the European vision would mean to surrender to governance by the civilized nations. The "most embarrassing dilemma," as Simón Bolívar referred to it, was that the Colombian elite could not call into question the desire for civilization since they passionately wanted to be recognized by Europe. Their solution to this dilemma was to take upon themselves the task of completing the European project. A creole elite, born in Nueva Granada of Spanish parents, consolidated their power over mestizos, blacks, women, and Indians in the name of civilization. Out of this encounter between European and local visions, the will to civilization was born as the predominant regime of representation.

In the will to civilization a different political economy was organized. The market or field of this "capital" was characterized by the accumulation of those civilizing qualities that male creole literati appreciated: the law, grammar, and morality. Male creole literati reserved their own place in the regime of representation as the ones knowledgeable enough to direct the new republic on the proper road. The literati were the architects of civilization, and their power stemmed from their capacity to produce, circulate, and value their most precious commodity: words.

Unlike the situation in the early stages of capitalism when civilization and laissez-faire principles were articulated, in Colombia they entered into contradiction. With the will to civilization as the predominant regime of representation, laissez-faire principles were subordinated. The uneven development of capitalism was the result of the contradictory encounter between the will to civilization and laissez-faire capitalism as conceived in Europe. The construction of hierarchical identities also explained the absence of a regime of representation in which the economy could "go alone," and interests were universalized. Not only were blacks, Indians, and local artisans seen as barbarians needing the employment of force, but also the pursuit of self-interest was seen as contrary to the principles of morality and civilization.

WHY WAR?

Throughout this book I have argued that civilization and violence are not necessarily antagonists. In the nineteenth century, civilization and violence intertwined and supported each other. Although this experience could support Huntington's proposal that civilization is a cause of violence, their relationship is not the one sustained by him. His proposition is that a multicivilizational world is more likely to result in "identity wars." In his view, antagonisms arise from the rivalry between Western and non-Western civilizations. Let us review his argument.

First it is important to remark that for Huntington "civilization" is constructed intersubjectively: "Civilizations are the biggest 'we' within which we feel culturally at home as distinguished from all others 'thems' out there."[10] Therefore, differences are brought in as part of the quest for identity. To assert my identity, I differentiate myself from those outside myself. As I have argued, civilization played a key role as a marker of difference. Second, for Huntington the search for identity presupposes the identification of enemies: "For people seeking identity and reinventing ethnicity, enemies are essential."[11] Therefore, knowing the self depends on negating the Other and being against it: "We know who we are only when we know who we are not and often only when we know whom we are against."[12] Against a pluralistic vision of identity, Huntington poses that antagonism is at the center of politics. His argument has important flaws. One is a radicalization of antagonism where "us" and "them" are seen as "enemies" without a common ground.[13] As I have demonstrated, situations of antagonism do not necessarily end in open conflict. It is clear with respect to class antagonism, for example, that proletarian and capitalist can coexist without open conflict. To solve this problem I distinguish between the formation of antagonism, the violence of representation, and *manifested violence*, which refers to physical confrontation, as in war. A radicalization of antagonism calls for a solution based on force rather than a struggle for representation. No wonder that Huntington's proposals to preserve Western civilization involve defense and security mechanisms, despite his attempt to politicize identities by making them relational.

A second flaw in Huntington's argument refers to the construction of the civilized "us" and the issue of power over the uncivilized "them." Huntington is right with regard to the need to renounce the concept of Western civilization as a universal concept. The imperialist expansion in the name of civilization has witnessed the violent consequences of the desire to convert the Other into an entity the same as oneself. As he recognizes, "imperialism is the necessary logical consequence of universalism."[14] Huntington's solution lies in particularism, "to preserve, protect, and renew the unique qualities of Western civilization."[15]

The question to be asked is this: "Is the recognition of a 'unique' civilization a safeguard against war?" I answer in the negative as long as to be unique is to dispense with the Other. On the one hand, a unique civilization contradicts the relational character of identities. If identities are constructed through difference, it means that there is not a sovereign identity independent of the identity of the Other. As Bakhtin recognized, identities are on the "boundary." On the other hand, to pose a "unique" civilization meant to ignore the internal fragmentation of identity.

The search for a coherent identity makes sure that internal differences are not only not recognized, but also feared. Therefore, a society is more likely to project into the Other its own fragmentation.[16] The bigger the need to construct a unique civilization, the more important the need to protect this identity from the Other. This position voices the feeling of hostility that originated in the projection of Western fragmentation into the non-Western Other. If the West appears to be the source of its own civilization, non-Westerners appear to be the ones preventing the West from achieving this identity. Conflict arises from the feeling that non-Westerners want to deprive the West of its rightful enjoyment of civilization.

One conclusion to be drawn from this understanding is that the source of antagonism is internal rather than external. As Žižek points out, antagonism does not arise from an external enemy, but rather arises from the subject's self-hindering experience. The important issue is to detect why Western countries are experiencing a self-blockage in their own civilization and why this fragmentation is projected into the Other as a feeling of aggressiveness not from the self, but from the Other. Undoubtedly the fear of a fragmented and declining West underlies Huntington's proposal of a clash of civilizations, confirming the postulate that the clash of civilizations has to do more with Western self-perception of fragmentation than with the real threat emanating from non-Westerners. Huntington sees a decline of the power of the West as measured by the smaller proportion of its share in the world's population, territory, and economic product. As a consequence, he predicts that after the "golden age" of Western hegemony there is a possibility of decay and a danger of invasion from barbarian Others. This will happen, Huntington says, quoting Carroll Quigley, "when civilization, no longer *able* to defend itself because it is no longer *willing* to defend itself, lies wide open to 'barbarian invaders,' who often come from "another, younger, more powerful civilization"(emphasis in original).[17]

Huntington also sees problems of "moral decline, cultural suicide, and political disunity in the West."[18] Increasing antisocial behavior, family decay, a decline in "social capital," and weakening of the "work ethic," are some of these problems. A more "dangerous challenge," according to him, comes from intellectuals who, in the name of multiculturalism, deny the existence of "a common American culture, and promote racial, ethnic, and other subnational cultural identities and groupings."[19]

This internal fragmentation is projected onto dangerous Others that threaten the West. Muslims in Europe and Hispanics in the United States, in Huntington's view, are endangering Western values and threaten to render the United States a "cleft country" potentially disunited and torn by internal strife. In Europe, "Islamization" will be followed by "Africanization" and its dangers of "AIDS and other plagues."[20] This social fantasy extends as well to poor countries in Africa, as reflected in Robert Kaplan's article "The Coming Anarchy," which followed Huntington's publication. Under the heading "A Premonition of the Future" Kaplan depicts the future of civilization as mirrored within West Africa.[21]

Therefore, it is no coincidence that Huntington fears an active non-Western people, as they become makers of their own history. In his words, "[In] the politics of civilizations, the peoples and governments of non-Western civilizations no longer remain the objects of history as *targets* of Western colonialism but join the West as *movers* and *shapers* of history."[22] This perception of non-Westerners as a threat is reflected in the epithet of "challenger civilizations." They exhibit increasing rates of economic growth and a tendency to value their own culture. It is this perception of a similar non-West that is feared the most. The threat originates not in non-Westerners' feelings of hate toward Western countries, but rather in a feeling of self-fragmentation that Western countries project onto the Other.

A second conclusion is that the dichotomization of civilization into universalism or particularism is not the solution to violence. Both can support strategies leading to war and domination. Rather, as Ernesto Laclau reminds us, the "universal emerges out of the particular not as some principle underlying and explaining it, but as an incomplete horizon suturing a dislocated particular identity."[23]

Violence can be resolved only in representation, by refixing meanings and recreating original relations of identity and difference. It is in representation that antagonisms have to be reconstituted, first by recognizing a dialogical constitution of identities where the Other is internal to the self and that looking at the self is to look through the eyes of the Other. This framework has allowed authors such as Tzvetan Todorov to formulate the possibility of a "nonviolent communication" and Ashis Nandy that of a "dialogue of cultures."[24] In their view, an encounter with the Other within the self is requisite for a dialogue between civilizations. Nandy's dialogue of cultures not only differs from Huntington's vision of the Other as the enemy, but also advances the proposal that the Other is an ally in the discovery of the self. In Nandy's view, a dialogue of cultures needs "the ability to involve the often recessive aspects of other civilizations as allies in one's struggle for cultural self-discovery."[25]

But as Fernando Coronil reminds us, it is not enough to incorporate the Other into the self.[26] He calls for an approach where the Other unsettles the self.[27] Walter D. Mignolo goes even further by suggesting a border thinking that restores what the restrictive concept of civilization suppressed: "the self-appropriation of all the good qualities that were denied to the barbarians."[28]

Michael Shapiro states that what a nation "represents as a hostile object of an aggressive aim is in part a stand-in for an inward aim."[29] This is an important distinction that highlights a need to change theoretical perspectives for the study of conflict and violence from a concern with the Other as the aggressor to one where the focus is on the desire of the self for the Other. As the case of Colombia demonstrates, the desire to civilize the Other is one of the main causes of violence. Furthermore, the suppression of alternative histories overruled the creation of a space of recognition, and therefore violence has not been superseded.

Notes

INTRODUCTION

1. Norbert Elias, *The Civilizing Process: The History of Manners and State Formation and Civilization* (Oxford and Cambridge: Blackwell, 1994), 41.

2. Quoted in Elias, *The Civilizing Process,* 41.

3. Samuel P. Huntington, *The Clash of Civilizations: Remaking of World Order* (New York: Touchstone Book, 1996), 51.

4. Mary Louise Pratt, *Imperial Eyes: Travel Writing and Transculturation* (London and New York: Routledge, 1992).

5. The best known publication is Domingo F. Sarmiento, *Civilización y Barbarie: Vida de Juan Francisco Quiroga* (México: Editorial Porrúa, 1985).

6. For this analysis I am indebted to Michel Foucault's understanding of "normalization," or the systematic division of subjects into dichotomous categories such as mad and sane, sick and healthy, criminals and "good boys." According to Foucault, the isolation and identification of anomalies allows a transfer of fear to the abnormal and the development of technologies to control these anomalies through the enactment of laws or institutional settings or the drawing of boundaries between populations. See especially Michel Foucault, *The History of Sexuality,* vol. I (New York: Vintage Books, 1990), 100. See also Hubert L. Dreyfus and Paul Rabinow, *Michel Foucault: Beyond Structuralism and Hermeneutics* (Chicago: University of Chicago Press, 1982), 195.

7. In Europe the practices leading to laissez-faire capitalism were articulated within discourses of European civilization. In early arguments for

171

capitalism, the spread of commerce and the attainment of civilization were seen together. Lucien Febvre's study on the origin of the word *civilization* argues that the belief in the benign effect of commerce coincided with the emergence of the concept of *civilization*. According to Febvre, the word *civilization* appeared toward the middle of the eighteenth century, taking the place that *police* had occupied at the top of a ladder whose bottom was occupied by savages and its middle by barbarians. Lucien Febvre (1930), "*Civilization:* Evolution of a Word and a Group of Ideas," in *A New Kind of History from the Writings of Febvre,* ed. Peter Burke (London: Routledge and Kegan Paul, 1973), 225. The relationship between early arguments about capitalism and the formation of identities is also clearly stated in Albert Hirschman's book *The Passions and the Interests: Political Arguments for Capitalism before Its Triumph* (Princeton, N.J.: Princeton University Press, 1977). The book illustrates how the idea of the expansion of the capitalist economy coincided with a positive attitude toward economic activities, especially commerce. According to Hirschman, there was talk about the *douceur* of commerce, which conveyed the idea of sweetness, softness, and gentleness and was the antonym of *violence* (p. 59). Marx's *Manifesto* shared the book's optimism about the civilizing consequences of expanding capitalist relations of production. This "evolution" was expected to result from the bourgeoisie's desire to imitate capitalism's leaders: "The bourgeoisie, by the rapid improvement of all instruments of production, by the immensely facilitated means of communication, draws all, even the most barbarian, nation into civilization." Karl Marx (1888), "Manifesto of the Communist Party," in *Karl Marx Political Writings: The Revolutions of 1848,* ed. David Fernbach, vol. 1 (New York: Vintage Books, 1974), 71.

8. Rosa Luxemburg, *The Accumulation of Capital—An Anti-Critique* (New York and London: Monthly Review Press, 1972), 145.

9. Pierre Philippe Rey, *Les Alliances de Classes* (Paris: François Maspero, 1973), 158.

10. Barbara Bradby and Aidan Foster-Carter are critical of the way Rey elevates a common contingency to the status of an inexorable law. Barbara Bradby, "The destruction of natural economy," in *Economy and Society* 4, no. 2 (1975); Aidan Foster-Carter, "The Modes of Production Controversy," *New Left Review* 17 (1978).

11. André Gunder Frank, *Capitalism and Underdevelopment in Latin America: Historical Studies of Chile and Brazil* (New York: Monthly Review Press, 1969).

12. Gilberto Mathias and Pierre Salama, *L'Etat Surdéveloppé: Des Métropoles au Tiers Monde* (Paris: François Maspero, 1983).

13. Guillermo O'Donnell, *Modernization and Bureaucratic-Authoritarianism: Studies in South American Politics* (Berkeley: University of California, 1973).

14. According to Bakhtin, a "monological" interpretation is one that "closes down the represented world and the represented persons." Mikhail M. Bakhtin, *Problems of Dostoevsky's Poetics* (Minneapolis: University of Minnesota Press, 1984), 293.

15. Dorothy Smith, "The Social Construction of Documentary Reality," *Sociological Inquiry* 44, no. 4 (1974), 267.

16. Edward Said, *Orientalism* (London: Routledge and Kegan Paul, 1978); Arturo Escobar, "Discourse and Power in Development: Michel Foucault and the Relevance of His Work for the Third World," *Alternatives* 10 (1984–85); see also Homi K. Bhabha, "Difference, Discrimination, and the Discourse of Colonialism," *The Politics of Theory,* Proceedings of the Essex Conference on the Sociology of Literature, ed. Frances Barker (Colchester: University of Essex, 1983).

17. David Slater, "The Geopolitical Framework and the Enframing of Development Theory," *Transactions of the Institute of British Geographics* 10 (1993).

18. Gayatri Chakravorty Spivak, "Three Women's Texts and a Critique of Imperialism," *Critical Inquiry* 12, no. 1 (1985).

19. For a comprehensive revision of the importance of the construction of identities to state practices, see E. Fuat Keyman, *Globalization, State, Identity / Difference* (Atlantic Highlands, N.J.: Humanities Press, 1997).

20. Samuel Huntington, *Political Order in Changing Societies* (New Haven: Yale University Press, 1968), 41.

21. Chalmers Johnson, *Revolutionary Change* (Boston: Little Brown, 1966), 57.

22. Huntington, *The Clash of Civilizations.*

23. Ibid., 129.

24. The complicity of history and denial of difference was put forward by Michel Foucault. He identifies a total history as one in which all differences of society are reduced to a single form—a world-view, a system of values, and a coherent system of civilization. In Foucault's view, a total history presupposes that the same historicity operates upon all social institutions and produces the same kinds of transformations. His proposal is for a general history of discontinuities, series, and relations. Other histories should not be treated as subject to the same law or as heading toward the same pattern of development and progress. The change of analysis from totality to discontinuity leads to an epistemological turn from one where words designate things to discourses as practices that form objects. Representation is not a duplicate of things, but is constitutive of them. Michel Foucault, *The Archeology of Knowledge and The Discourse on Language* (New York: Pantheon Books, 1972). In this direction, Foucault argues that the discourse on reason created and constituted a representation of both reason and unreason. He illustrates this point with reference to the object madness. "This cannot be

known by interrogating 'madness itself,'" nor its secret content and self-enclosed truth. Rather, this mental illness "was constituted by all that was said in all the statements that named it, divided it up, described it, explained it, traced its development" (p. 32).

25. Edward Said's *Orientalism* goes beyond Foucault's analysis in his grasping of the history of non-Western civilization. As he contends, Orientalism is a "way of coming to terms with the Orient that is based on the Orient's special place in European Western experience"(p. 1). Therefore, Orientalism is Said's reading of the way Western culture "managed" and "produced" the Orient politically, ideologically, and militarily. What circulates in discourse is not "truth," but representations that do not depend on the Orient: "That Orientalism makes sense at all depends more on the West than on the Orient, and this sense is directly indebted to various Western techniques of representation that make the Orient visible, clear, 'there' in discourse about it" (p. 23).

26. Michael J. Shapiro, *Reading the Postmodern Polity* (Minneapolis: University of Minnesota Press, 1992), 54.

27. Mikhail M. Bakhtin, *The Dialogic Imagination* (Austin: University of Texas Press, 1984).

28. Ernesto Laclau reminds us that representation is a *fictio iuris;* representation presupposes the presence of someone in a place from which he or she is actually absent, and as such representation organizes actual social relations. Because representation is "something new," it has the character of an "unlimited horizon of inscription of *any* social demand and *any* possible dislocation." Ernesto Laclau, *New Reflections on the Revolution of Our Time* (London and New York: Verso, 1990), 38 and 65.

29. In the words of Slavoj Žižek, "The subject of the signifier is precisely this lack, this impossibility of finding a signifier which would be 'its own': the failure of its representation is its positive condition." Slavoj Žižek, *The Sublime Object of Ideology* (London and New York: Verso, 1998), 175.

30. Fantasy and desire form the background of civilizing missions, as has been illustrated by tales of cannibalism, which, as Peter Hulme argues, "remain below the surface, ready to reappear when civilizational influence showed signs of waning." Peter Hulme, "Introduction: The Cannibal Scene," in *Cannibalism and the Colonial World*, ed. Francis Barker, Peter Hulme, and Margaret Iversen (Cambridge: Cambridge University Press, 1998), 3.

31. This recognition by the Other is the locus of desire; "nowhere does it appear more clearly than that man's desire finds its meaning in the desire for the Other, not so much because the Other holds the key to the object desired, as because the first object of desire is to be recognized by the Other." Slavoj Žižek, *The Plague of Fantasies* (London and New York: Verso, 1998), 58.

32. Ibid., 312.

33. Slavoj Žižek, *The Sublime Object of Ideology*, 115.

34. Charles Tilly, *From Mobilization to Revolution* (New York: Random House, 1978), 176.

35. "Multivariety" is an expression used by A. Camacho in "La violencia en Colombia: Elementos para una Interpretación," *Revista Foro* (June 1988).

36. Comisión de Estudios sobre la Violencia *Colombia: Violencia y democracia: Informe presentado al Ministerio de Gobierno* (Bogotá: Universidad Nacional de Colombia, Centro Editorial, 1987).

37. Carlos Miguel Ortiz Sarmiento, *Estado y subversión en Colombia* (Bogotá: Fondo Editorial CEREC, 1985), 22.

38. Gabriel García Márquez, *La Mala Hora* (Bogotá: Editorial la Oveja Negra, 1978).

39. Helen Delpar, *Red against Blue: The Liberal Party in Colombian Politics 1863–1899* (University: University of Alabama Press, 1981). See also Helen Delpar, "Aspects of Liberal Factionalism in Colombia, 1875–1885," *Hispanic American Historical Review* (May 1971).

40. *Hereditary hatred* has been the expression most commonly used to characterize the enmity between Liberals and Conservatives. Two recent examples are Daniel Pecaut, *Orden y Violencia: Colombia 1930–1954*, 2 vols. (Bogotá: Siglo XXI, 1987), and Jonathan Hartlyn, *The Politics of Coalition Rule in Colombia* (Cambridge: Cambridge University Press, 1988).

41. The expression *unchallenged hegemony* belongs to Frank Safford and is used in his study "The Emergence of Economic Liberalism in Colombia," in *Guiding the Invisible Hand*, ed. Joseph L. Love and Nils Jacobsen (New York: Praeger, 1988).

42. Tariffs on imports were reduced and simplified in the reform of 1847 and in subsequent reforms carried out in 1861, 1870, and 1873. In 1847, the government promoted the privatization of tobacco, a state monopoly since colonial times. The Liberal government installed in 1849 accelerated the pace of reform. Legislation passed on May 21, 1851, abolished slavery. The law on decentralization of Indian communal land (1850) allowed Indians to sell their land. These measures were considered crucial to liberate the factors of production. In 1850 and 1851, the laws on "decentralization of rent and expenditures" were approved in favor of the provinces. Most provinces abolished the *diezmos* tax and the monopoly of *aguardiente*. These reforms are summarized in Jorge O. Melo, "Las vicisitudes del Modelo Liberal (1850–1899)," in *Historia Económica de Colombia*, ed. José. A. Ocampo (Bogotá: Siglo XXI, 1987). See also G. Molina, *Las Ideas Liberales en Colombia 1849–1914* (Bogotá: Editorial Tercer Mundo, 1970), and Frank Safford, "The Emergence of Economic Liberalism in Colombia," in Safford, *Guiding the Invisible Hand*.

43. The most important representatives of this generation within the Liberal Party are Miguel Samper (1825–99), his brother José María Samper (1828–88), José Hilario López (1789–1869), Manuel Ancízar (1812–82), Florentino González (1805–74), Salvador Camacho Roldán (1827–1900), Aníbal Galindo (1834–1901), Manuel Murillo Toro (1816–80), and José María Rojas Garrido (1824–83). This generation is also known as los radicales del Siglo XIX because of their ideological and political contribution to the period of liberal radicalism linked to the constitution of 1863. The best representatives of the Conservative Party are José Eusebio Caro (1817–53), Miguel Antonio Caro (1843–1909), Sergio Arboleda (1822–1888), and Rafael Núñez (1825–94).

44. According to historian Fabio Zambrano, this fear is central for understanding the contraction of the political system in Colombia, explaining one of the characteristics of Colombian politics: la *democracia sin pueblo* (democracy without people). Fabio Zambrano Pantoja, "El miedo al pueblo," in *Análisis: Conflicto social y violencia en Colombia,* Documento 53, Centro de Investigación y Educación Popular (CINEP) (1989).

45. A characteristic of the Colombian party system is the all-embracing distinction between Liberals and Conservatives. Although most of Latin America developed Liberal and Conservative parties, only in Colombia, and perhaps Uruguay, have the original parties dominated to the present. Partisan affiliation has provided not only an element of continuity between nineteenth-century violence and the period of *La Violencia,* but also a sense of identity.

1. THE WILL TO CIVILIZATION

1. In liberal analyses laissez-faire is generally defined as a policy prescription that sought to free economic activity from all constraints on the market and to promote the international division of labor. Joseph L. Love and Nils Jacobsen, eds., *Guiding the Invisible Hand: Economic Liberalism and the State in Latin American History* (New York: Praeger, 1988), vii.

2. Although there are differences in the analysis of it, most of nineteenth-century Colombian history centers on the economic relations during the laissez-faire period: William P. McGreevey, *Historia Económica de Colombia 1845–1930* (Bogotá: Ediciones Tercer Mundo, 1971); José A. Ocampo, *Colombia y la Economía Mundial 1830–1910* (Bogotá: Siglo XXI, 1984); Charles Berquist, *Labor in Latin America: Comparative Essays on Chile, Argentina, Venezuela and Colombia* (Stanford, Calif.: Stanford University Press, 1986); Salomón Kalmanovitz, "Desarrollo Capitalista en el Campo Colombiano," in *Colombia Hoy,* ed. Mario Arrubla et al. (Bogotá: Siglo XXI, 1978); Marco Palacios, *El Café en Colombia 1850–1970* (México: El Áncora Editores, 1983).

3. To capture the ambivalence in representation, Bhabha develops the concept of "mimicry." The colonial mimicry "is the desire for a reformed, recognizable Other, *as a subject of difference that is almost the same, but not quite.*" Homi K. Bhabha, *The Location of Culture* (London and New York: Routledge, 1994), 86. This concept, in Bhabha's view, allows a representation of difference that is also a process of disavowal. There is no full presence; the representation of the self and the Other is "partial." Through the use of mimicry, Bhabha also avoids the problem of power's being placed on the side of the colonizer and thus preventing resistance. The ambivalent place of mimicry, as reflected in the expression "almost the same, but not quite," expresses both the power of regulation and discipline but also their incoherence; this allows the authority of the colonizer to be disrupted. The partial presence creates a space from which colonial authority can be eroded. Colonial discourse is "a discourse at the crossroads of what is known and permissible and that which, though known, must be kept concealed. As a discourse uttered between the lines it operates both against the rules and within them"(p. 89). Bhabha calls the discourse on civilization "sly civility" to reflect the ambivalence of a discourse uttered between the lines. Even liberals such as J. S. Mill have transformed the defense of Western liberal principles to one of policing those culturally and racially differentiated colonial subjects. This ambivalence as expressed in contradictory beliefs (democracy and despotism, just and unjust) is what threatens colonial authority.

4. Marco Palacios, *Coffee in Colombia, 1850–1970* (Cambridge: Cambridge University Press, 1980). For those parts that do not appear in the English edition, I have referred to the Spanish version: Marco Palacios, *El Café en Colombia 1850–1970* (Mexico: El Áncora Editores, 1983).

5. Frank Safford, *The Ideal of the Practical: Colombia's Struggle to Form a Technical Elite* (Austin: University of Texas Press, 1976); Frank Safford, "The Emergence of Economic Liberalism in Colombia," in Safford, *Guiding the Invisible Hand.* See also Frank Safford, "Reflexiones sobre la Historia Económica de Colombia, 1845–1930, de William McGreevey," in *Aspectos del Siglo XIX en Colombia,* ed. Frank Safford (Medellín: Ediciones Hombre Nuevo, 1977).

6. Marco Palacios, "La Fragmentación Regional de las Clases Dominantes en Colombia: Una Perspectiva Histórica," *Revista Mexicana de Sociología,* 42 (1980), 1675.

7. Marco Palacios, *Coffee in Colombia 1850–1970,* 77.

8. Ibid., 83.

9. Safford, *The Ideal of the Practical,* 229. Safford mentions that in 1867, the National University was created with an emphasis on the natural sciences and engineering. In 1877, the school of engineering was converted to the military School of Civil and Military Engineering. The National Institute of Agriculture was established in 1880; in the same year, the National

Congress approved the creation of several mining engineering programs. In their pursuit of the practical, Colombians also sent their sons abroad for technical training.

10. Among these projects were the reestablishment of the Casa de Refugio ("workhouse") in 1833: "Like its American counterpart, the House of Refuge represented an attempt to endow a semi-penal institution with constructive and corrective functions that emphasize the instruction of youth in basic literacy as well as artisan skills." Frank Safford, *The Ideal of the Practical*, 59. A similar intent was the establishment of forced apprenticeship *(concertaje)* for vagrant or homeless youths. A law of April 1836 defined as vagrant prostitutes and persons who were unemployed or partially employed. It also included minors who scandalized society and those students who refused to obey their teachers. Vagrants were forced into the army or forced to do public labor. This law was used mainly to control manumitted blacks.

11. Safford mentions three important changes that were implemented: the law of May 8, 1848, undermined the centralist system by making it unnecessary for *colegios* to meet Bogotá-prescribed standards as to faculty and curriculum. In a law of May 15, 1850, the "freedom of instruction" was carried to the extreme of making it unnecessary to obtain an academic degree to practice law or medicine. The law also abolished the three national universities, renaming them *colegios nacionales,* in order to reduce the distance between the cultural centers and the *colegios* in poorer provinces.

12. Safford, *The Ideal of the Practical,* 139.

13. This is the description of Gerardo Molina in *Las Ideas liberales en Colombia, 1849–1914* (Bogotá: Ediciones Tercer Mundo, 1970). The myth of the "angelical" character of the Liberal reforms is common in the interpretation of nineteenth-century history. A widespread legend was that when Victor Hugo read the Colombian constitution of 1863, he declared that it was "a constitution for angels." See Jorge O. Melo, "Del federalismo a la Constitución de 1886," *Nueva Historia de Colombia,* vol. 1 (Bogotá: Editorial Planeta Colombiana, 1989), 18. Marxists have not escaped from this utopian vision, as Berquist's analysis shows: "Imbibing an integral world view which had become dominant in the industrializing nations of the West, Liberals ultimately sought to write down into law a philosophy of man and society fundamentally at odds with the structure of the society they live in." Charles Berquist, *Coffee and Conflict in Colombia, 1886–1910* (Durham, N.C.: Duke University Press, 1978), 11.

14. A regime of representation is the space where meanings are articulated. As such, it extends in time by means of the construction of systems of meanings that are relatively fixed and distinct. This system never manages to be fully fixed. Ernesto Laclau and Chantal Mouffe, *Hegemony and*

Socialist Strategy: Towards a Radical Democratic Politics (London: Verso, 1985), 111. Hegemony is an articulatory practice facilitating negotiation among discursive surfaces. This is possible only in a system where identities are not fixed. Articulation makes possible the constitution of nodal points, which are equivalent to Lacan's *point de capiton,* "which partially fix the meaning of the social in an organized system of differences" (p. 135). To "hegemonize" is to fix meaning around a nodal point. This accounts for the open-ended character of history. For a different description of representation as linking practices, see Antanas Mockus, *Representar y Disponer* (Bogotá: Universidad Nacional, 1988).

15. Mariano Ospina Rodríguez, "La Civilización se Define," *La Civilización* 1 (August 9, 1849). Reprinted in Mariano Ospina Rodríguez, *Escritos sobre Economía Política* (Bogotá: Universidad Nacional de Colombia), 73.

16. Ibid., 74.

17. According to Norbert Elias, the concept of *civilization* grew as an absolute concept of a single coherent human civilization and not as a relative concept of particularized and individualized ethnic or historical civilizations. The opposition between European "polished nations," and "rude and barbarous ones" became common toward the second half of the nineteenth century. Norbert Elias, *The Civilizing Process: The History of Manners and State Formation and Civilization* (Oxford: Blackwell, 1994), 232. This period questioned the civilizing power of capitalism. In this narrative, civilization is coupled with racial difference rather than with commonality. As Elias noted, in its early usage the concept of civilization played down the national differences between peoples and emphasized what is common to all human beings (p. 5). This phase concluded, in Elias's view, when the consciousness of "civilization" served colonial conquerors as a justification of their rule (p. 41). During the last two decades of the nineteenth century and up to 1914, the expansion of capitalism (known as imperialism) was accomplished by the search for markets and colonies. In the period from 1878 to 1914, Magdoff estimated "that the rate at which foreign lands were seized was *three times higher* than it had been during the preceding seventy-five years. . . . Before 1880 colonial possessions in Africa were relatively few and limited to some coastal areas; twenty years later, almost the entire African continent was split into separate territories owned by Europeans nations." H. Magdoff, "Imperialism: A Historical Survey," in *Sociology of "Developing Societies,"* ed. Hamza Alavi and Teodor Shanin (London: MacMillan Press, 1982), 19–20.

18. Mariano Ospina Rodríguez, "La Civilización se Define," 76.

19. As Lacan states, the ego constitutes itself in relation to the image in a mirror. The ego is outside itself and, as a consequence, the subject attempts to discover a confirming image of the self in the response of the Other.

Jacques Lacan, *Écrits: A Selection* (New York: London, 1977). This dialectic of recognition does not dispense with language (p. 85). By recognizing a triad between the imaginary, the symbolic, and the real, the subject is not an effect of language, nor is it a unitary, self-constituted subject. At the level of the imaginary, the subject is identified with the external mirror image. The mirror image unifies the fragmented "I," but in the process the subject alienates its own image. The level of the symbolic allows the subject to adapt to new situations and change his or her perceptions. This is possible because the symbolic includes *empty signifiers* that can be filled with particular new contents. Žižek, *The Plague of Fantasies,* 94.

20. Mary Louise Pratt, *Imperial Eyes: Travel Writing and Transculturation* (London and New York: Routledge, 1992).

21. Ibid.

22. Ibid., 51.

23. Ibid., 126.

24. José María Samper, *Ensayo sobre las Revoluciones Políticas i la Condición Social de las Repúblicas Colombianas (Hispanoamericanas)* (París: Imprenta de E. Thunot y C., 1861). In this essay, Samper calls the reader's attention to the name *Colombia,* which he uses as synonym of *Hispanoamérica* to mean the geographical extension from Cape Horn to northern Mexico. The reason is to avoid confusion with the word *America* which had been appropriated by the United States after Washington's Confederation of American States. The American Civil War created more confusion by introducing the concept of South and North to denominate the parts of the country in conflict.

25. Ibid., 3.

26. Ibid., 6.

27. Pratt, *Imperial Eyes,* 268.

28. Miguel Samper, "Libertad y Orden," in Miguel Samper, *Escritos Político-Económicos de Miguel Samper,* vol. 2 (Bogotá: Editorial Cromos, 1986), 9–10.

29. Benjamin Kidd, quoted in Samper, "Libertad y Orden," 10.

30. Homi K. Bhabha, "Of Mimicry and Man: The Ambivalence of Colonial Discourse," in Bhabha, *The Location of Culture,* 89. In Bhabha's view, it is in the ideological construction of Otherness in colonial discourse where the problem of the mode of *representation* of otherness (p. 68). This discourse attempts to "fix" differences between what is rigid, unchanging, and always in place and what is disordered and repetitious. Colonial discourse has to deal with this ambivalence between an "Otherness" that is the object of both desire and derision. The problem lies in the construction of these discourses as opposites, thereby introducing a bipolarity. The presence of multiple power relations is obscured by the opposition between the self and the

Other or between master and slave. Bhabha's proposal is for "representation as a concept that articulates the historical and the fantasy (as the scene of desire) in the production of the 'political' effects of discourse" (p. 72). Making a reference to Fanon's "Black Skin, White Masks," Bhabha comments, "It is not the colonialist self or the colonized Other, but the disturbing distance in-between that constitutes the figure of the colonial otherness—the white man's artifice inscribed on the black man's body"(p. 45).

31. Sergio Arboleda, *La República en la América Española* (Bogotá: Biblioteca Popular de Cultura Colombiana, 1951), 36.

32. Ibid., 39.

33. Evelyn J. G. Ahern, "Desarrollo de la Educación en Colombia, 1820–1850," *Revista Colombiana de Educación* 22–23 (1991).

34. Jane Meyer Loy, "Primary Education during the Colombian Federation: The School Reform of 1870," *Hispanic American Historical Review* (May 1971), 276. Meyer mentions that in 1870, of the nation's 563,000 children, only 32,000 attended school of any kind.

35. Benedict Anderson, *Imagined Communities: Reflections on the Origin and Spread of Nationalism* (London: Verso, 1983), 58.

36. Anthony McFarlane, *Colombia before Independence: Economy, Society, and Politics under Bourbon Rule* (Cambridge: Cambridge University Press, 1993), 278.

37. Homi Bhabha believes that to state that colonial power is possessed entirely by the colonizer is a historical and theoretical simplification. Homi K. Bhabha, "Difference, Discrimination, and the Discourse of Colonialism," in Francis Barker et al., *The Politics of Theory* (Colchester: University of Essex, 1983), 199. The contradictory articulation of reality and desire also explains the feeling of menace that "civil" discourse takes on in its attempt to normalize the Other: "The ambivalence of colonial authority repeatedly turns from *mimicry*—a difference that is almost nothing but not quite—to *menace*—a difference that is almost total but not quite." Homi K. Bhabha, *The Location of Culture*, 91. The consideration of ambivalence opens a space for resistance to colonial power, as no single side possesses the entire power of representation.

38. Quoted in Renán Silva, "Presentación: El Ambito Intelectual de la Expedición Botánica," *Revista Colombiana de Educación* 11 (1983), 134–36.

39. Ibid.

40. On the role that the *Papel Periódico* played in the preindependence period, see Renán Silva, *Prensa y Revolución a Finales del Siglo XVIII* (Bogotá: Banco de la República, 1988). Colombia's capital was founded in 1538 with the name Santafé in memory of the city built by King Ferdinand and Queen Isabel during the siege of Granada. Colombia was named Nueva Granada because of its resemblance to the Spanish territory. In 1548 King

Charles V renamed the city Santafé de Bogotá in memory of the Muiscas' capital. After independence was achieved, the Law of the Constitution of the Republic (Ley Fundamental de Constitución de la República) of December 17, 1819, renamed the capital Bogotá. The same year New Granada was renamed República de Colombia, known as La Gran Colombia, which included Ecuador and Venezuela. The name Nueva Granada was restored in 1831, and a new constitution was issued in 1832. The federalist Constitution of 1863 changed the name to Estados Unidos de Colombia. The centralist character of the constitution of 1886 is reflected in the use of República de Colombia, which survived the decentralized character of the 1991 constitution. This was not the case of Bogotá, which returned to its colonial name, Santa Fe de Bogotá, though it was soon again to be renamed Bogotá. In this book I employ the names used by the authors as an additional recognition of the difficult struggle for representation.

41. Silva mentions a case where an article was rejected because it named specific subjects, whereas the policy was rather to promote general ideas "without mentioning known individuals" ("las reflexiones de [el papel periodico] . . . irán formadas sobre unas ideas generales que de ningún modo se pueden glosar respecto a personas conocidas"). Ibid., 37.

42. Quoted in Renán Silva, *Prensa y Revolución a Finales del Siglo XVIII*, 34–35.

43. The large percentage of *mestizaje* made New Granada (Colombia) different from its Andean neighbors with their large Quechua- and Aymara-speaking populations, as well as from the province of Caracas, where creole planters dominated a society that rested on African slavery. Anthony McFarlane, *Colombia before Independence* (Cambridge: Cambridge University Press, 1993), 34–38.

44. Quoted in Frank Safford, "Race, Integration, and Progress: Elite Attitudes and the Indian in Colombia, 1750–1870," in *Hispanic American Historical Review* 71, no. 1, (1991), 8.

45. Pablo Rodríguez, *Seducción, Amancebamiento y Abandono en la Colonia* (Santa Fe de Bogotá: Fundación Simón y Lola Guberek, 1991).

46. Hans-Joachim König has documented this period in *Camino hacia la Nación: Nacionalismo en el Proceso de Formación del Estado y de la Nación de la Nueva Granada, 1750–1856* (Santafé de Bogotá: Banco de la República, 1994).

47. Quoted in ibid., 238.

48. Quoted in ibid., 243.

49. Quoted in ibid., 206.

50. Ibid., 218.

51. Evelyn Cherpak, "Las Mujeres en la Independencia," in *Las Mujeres*

en la Historia de Colombia: Mujeres, Historia y Política, vol. 1, ed. Magdala Velásquez Toro (Santa Fe de Bogotá, 1995).

52. Quoted in ibid., 94.

53. The Europeans also represented America using the image of an Indian. The most famous is the engraving by Theodor Galle after a drawing by Jan van der Straet (ca. 1575). In his discussion of the engraving, Louis Montrose illustrates the dynamic of gender and power characteristics in the encounter of European with alien cultures. He concludes that the composition "gives iconic form to the oscillation characterizing Europe's ideological encounter with the New World: an oscillation between fascination and repulsion, likeness and strangeness, desires to destroy and to assimilate the Other; an oscillation between the confirmation and the subversion of familiar values, beliefs, and perceptual norms." Louis Montrose, "The Work of Gender in the Discourse of Discovery," in Stephen Greenblatt, *New World Encounters* (Berkeley: University of California Press, 1993), 181–82.

54. Marta Traba, *Historia Abierta del Arte Colombiano* (Cali: Ediciones del Museo La Tertulia, 1974), 48.

55. Jesús Martín Barbero, *De los Medios a las Mediaciones: Comunicación, Cultura y Hegemonía* (México: Editorial Gili, 1987), 15.

56. Safford, "Race Integration and Progress," 14. On the reforms of the Congress of Cúcuta, see also David Bushnell, *The Making of Modern Colombia. A Nation in Spite of Itself* (Berkeley: University of California Press, 1993). On the reaction among the Páez, see Joanne Rappaport, *The Politics of Memory: Native Historical Interpretation in the Colombian Andes* (Cambridge: Cambridge University Press, 1990).

57. Quoted in Safford, "Race Integration and Progress," 14.

58. Ibid., 12.

59. For a description, see Harold A. Bierck Jr., "Las Pugnas por la abolición de la esclavitud en la Gran Colombia," in *El Siglo XIX Visto por Historiadores Norteamericanos,* ed. Jesús A. Bejarano (Bogotá: Editorial la Carreta, 1977), 76–77.

60. Quoted in Álvaro Tirado, *Aspectos Sociales de las Guerras Civiles en Colombia* (Bogotá: Instituto Colombiano de Cultura, 1976), 98. This passage is from the year 1843, the same year repressive measures were taken against the threat of insurrection of slaves.

61. The disputes around the abolition of slavery at that time appear in Bierck, "Las Pugnas por la Abolición de la Esclavitud en la Gran Colombia," 309–44.

62. Quoted in Salomón Kalmanovitz, *Economía y Nación: Una Breve Historia de Colombia* (Bogotá: Siglo XXI, 1985), 156.

63. König, *En el Camino Hacia la Nación,* 263. As he reminds us, the

1813 coins with the Indian woman were known as the "Indian coin" or the "china coin"; *china* was a derogatory term used for the Indian domestic servant (p. 262).

64. Samper, *Ensayo sobre las Revoluciones Políticas i la Condición Social de las Repúblicas Colombianas*, 99.

2. CIVILIZATION AND VIOLENCE

1. Paul Oquist, *Violence, Conflict and Politics in Colombia* (New York: Academic Press, 1980), 169.

2. David Bushnell, "Politics and Violence in Nineteenth-Century Colombia," in *Violence in Colombia: The Contemporary Crisis in Historical Perspective,* ed. Charles Berquist, Ricardo Peñaranda, and Gonzalo Sánchez (Wilmington, Del.: SR Books, 1992), 24.

3. Daniel Pecaut, *Orden y Violencia en Colombia, 1930–1954* (Bogotá: Siglo XXI, 1987), 20.

4. Ibid., 534.

5. Ibid., 535–37.

6. Carlos Mario Perea, *Porque la Sangre Es Espíritu: Imaginario y Discurso Político en las Elites Capitalinas 1942–1949* (Santa Fe de Bogotá: Editorial Santillana, 1996), 20.

7. Regarding the argument that "every relation of identity is established in relation to differences," see William R. Connolly, *Identity/Difference: Democratic Negotiations of Political Paradox* (Ithaca: Cornell University Press, 1991), 67. According to Connolly, relations of identity/difference carry a paradoxical element: "To possess a true identity is to be false to difference, while to be true to difference is to sacrifice the promise of a true identity."

8. Ernesto Laclau and Chantal Mouffe, *Hegemony and Socialist Strategy* (London and New York: Verso, 1985). In their view, "society does not exist." Antagonisms (class, gender, and ethnic) are at the limit of the social. In Laclau and Mouffe's concept of antagonism, "The presence of the 'Other' prevents me from being totally myself" (p. 125). It is also what constitutes "me." Therefore, in the case of class antagonism, when I define myself as "proletarian," I fight against the "capitalist" who prevents me from realizing my potential. Slavoj Žižek radicalizes this relationship by inverting the two terms: "It is not the external enemy who is preventing me from achieving identity with myself, but every identity is already in itself blocked, marked by an impossibility, and the external enemy is simply the small piece, the rest of reality upon which we 'project' or 'internalize' this intrinsic, immanent

impossibility." Slavoj Žižek, "Beyond Discourse—Analysis," in Ernesto Laclau, *New Reflections on the Revolution of Our Time* (London and New York: Verso, 1990), 251–52.

9. Jacques Lacan, *Écrits: A Selection* (New York: London, 1977), 19.

10. According to Lacan, this is the cause of frustration, "not frustration of a desire of the subject but frustration by an object in which his desire is alienated." Ibid., 42.

11. René Girard, *Violence and the Sacred* (Baltimore and London: Johns Hopkins University Press, 1979). Girard's thought on the mimetic and triangular view of desire is close to Lacan's in that both are influenced by Kojeve's theme of the "desire of the desire of the other." On this point, see Mikkel Borch-Jacobson, *Lacan the Absolute Master* (Stanford, Calif.: Stanford University Press, 1991), 254, n. 22.

12. As Lacan states, "What the subject finds in this altered image of his body is the paradigm of all the forms of resemblance that will bring over on to the world of objects a tinge of hostility, by projecting on them the manifestation of the narcissistic image, which, from the pleasure derived from meeting himself in the mirror, becomes when confronting his fellow man an outlet for his most intimate aggressivity." Lacan, *Écrits*, 307.

13. Óscar Masotta, *Lecturas de Psicoanálisis: Freud, Lacan* (Madrid: Paidós, 1992).

14. Girard, *Violence and the Sacred*, 79.

15. Michael Shapiro, *Violent Cartographies: Mapping Cultures of War* (Minneapolis: University of Minnesota Press, 1997), 59. Security studies are not alien to ontological considerations, as it has been David Campbell's endeavor to explain. As he states, "A notion of what 'we' are is intrinsic to an understanding of what 'we' fear." David Campbell, *Writing Security: United States Foreign Policy and the Politics of Identity* (Minneapolis: University of Minnesota Press, 1992), 85. Every relation of colonist and colonizer is also traversed by the ontological quest for identity and difference. Tzvetan Todorov's narrative *The Conquest of America* argues that the discovery of America was not only the most astonishing encounter, but also the most intense example in terms of being the greatest genocide in human history. Columbus's attitude toward the Indians was based on his perception of the Other as a projection of the self. He saw the Indians as identical to himself, and this behavior led to assimilationism, where his values were identified with values in general. This illustrates the identification "of our I with the universe—in the conviction that the world is one." Tzvetan Todorov, *The Conquest of America* (New York: Harper and Row, 1984), 43.

16. This point is raised by Peter Dews in *Logics of Disintegration:*

Post-structuralist Thought and the Claims of Critical Theory (London and New York: Verso, 1987), 105.

17. Jacques Lacan, *Séminaire 3*, 50, quoted in Dews, *Logics of Disintegration*, 60.

18. Laclau and Mouffe, *Hegemony and Socialist Strategy*, 128–29.

19. Slavoj Žižek, *The Sublime Object of Ideology* (London and New York: Verso, 1998), 124.

20. The liberating aspect of the law appears in the following passage: "The status of desire presents itself as autonomous in relation to mediation of the Law, for the simple reason that it originates in desire, by virtue of the fact that by a strange symmetry it reverses the unconditional nature of the demand of love, in which the subject remains in subjection of the Other, and raises it to the power of the absolute condition (in which 'absolute' also implies 'detachment')." Lacan, *Écrits*, 311.

21. As stated by Žižek, "What the subject obeys is no longer the Other's will but a Law which regulates its relationship to the Other—the Law imposed by the Other is simultaneously the Law which the Other itself must obey." Slavoj Žižek, *For They Know Not What They Do: Enjoyment as a Political Factor* (London and New York: Verso, 1996), 266.

22. "Law is the agency of prohibition which regulates the distribution of enjoyment on the basis of a common, shared renunciation (the 'symbolic castration'), Ibid., 237.

23. José M. Samper, *Apuntamientos para la Historia Política i Social de la Nueva Granada desde 1810 i especialmente de la administración del 7 de Marzo* (Bogotá: Imprenta del Neo-Granadino, 1853), 25.

24. Quoted in José E. Caro, "Declaratoria Politica," reprinted in *Escritos Histórico-Político de José Eusebio Caro,* ed. Simón Aljure Chalela (Bogotá: Fondo Cultural Cafetero, 1981), 183.

25. Ibid., 78.

26. Samper, *Apuntamientos para la Historia Política i Social de la Nueva Granada,* 10.

27. Louis Montrose, "The Work of Gender in the Discourse of Discovery," in *New World Encounters,* ed. Stephen Greenblatt (Berkeley: University of California Press, 1993), 192.

28. José María Samper, *Ensayo sobre las Revoluciones Políticas i la Condición Social de las Repúblicas Colombianas (Hispanoamericanas)* (París: Imprenta de E. Thunot y C, 1861), 24.

29. Ibid., 32.

30. Sergio Arboleda, *La República en América Española* (Bogotá: Biblioteca Popular de Cultura Colombiana, 1951), 194.

31. Ibid.

32. The antagonism between Spaniard and *criollo* was central during the

process of emancipation. *Criollos* were those children of Spanish parents who were born in the American territory. They were considered *"mancha-dos de la tierra,"* with an "earth stigma." See José A. Ocampo, "El Proceso Político, Militar y Social de la Independencia," in *Nueva Historia de Colombia,* vol. 2 (Bogotá: Editorial Planeta, 1989); see also Jaime Jaramillo, "Mestizaje y Diferenciación Social en el Nuevo Reino de Granada en la Segunda Mitad del Siglo XVII," in *La Nueva Historia de Colombia,* ed. Darío Jaramillo Agudelo (Bogotá: Instituto Colombiano de Cultura, 1976).

33. Miguel Samper, "Libertad y Orden," in *Escritos Político-Económicos de Miguel Samper,* vol. 2 (Bogotá: Editorial Cromos, 1986), 353.

34. Samper, *Ensayo Sobre las Revoluciones Políticas i la Condición Social de las Repúblicas Colombianas,* 158.

35. Ibid., 156.

36. Ibid., 157.

37. Ibid.

38. On the importance of geographical representations for power relations, see Walter D. Mignolo, "The Movable Center: Geographical Discourses and Territoriality During the Expansion of Spanish Empire," in *Coded Encounters: Writing, Gender, and Ethnicity in Colonial Latin America,* ed. Francisco Javier Ceballos-Candau (Amherst: University of Massachusetts Press, 1994).

39. Samper, *Ensayo Sobre las Revoluciones Políticas,* 156.

40. Ibid., 83 and passim.

41. Ibid., 98.

42. See Frank Safford, "Race, Integration and Progress: Elite Attitudes and the Indian in Colombia, 1750–1870," in *Hispanic American Historical Review* 71, no. 1 (1991).

43. Antonio J. Restrepo, *El Cancionero de Antioquia* (Barcelona: Editorial Lux, 1929), 177.

44. Samper, *Ensayo sobre las Revoluciones Políticas i la Condición Social de las Repúblicas Colombianas,* 79.

45. Social fantasy consists precisely in constructing a vision of society that is not split by antagonistic divisions, such as the corporatist vision of society. In this vision the figure of the Other denies and embodies the impossibility of this society. It is the reason why, for Žižek, fantasy is the way "the antagonist fissure is masked." Žižek, *The Sublime Object of Ideology,* 126.

46. Quoted in Jaime Jaramillo Uribe, *El Pensamiento Colombiano en el Siglo XIX* (Bogotá: Editorial Temis, 1982), 180.

47. Renán Silva, *Prensa y Revolución a Finales del Siglo XVIII* (Bogotá: Banco de la República, 1988), 115.

48. For an account of this process, see Virginia Gutiérrez de Pineda, *La*

Familia en Colombia: Estudio Antropológico (Oficina Internacional de Investigaciones Sociales *FERES,* 1962); Virginia Gutiérrez de Pineda, *La Familia en Colombia: Transfondo Histórico,* vol. 1 (Bogotá: Universidad Nacional, Facultad de Sociología, 1963).

49. Quoted in Gutiérrez de Pineda, *La Familia en Colombia: Transfondo Histórico,* vol. 1, 187.

50. One form of servitude during the colonial period was the system of *naboria,* described by Gutiérrez de Pineda as a system in which nonslave Indians (most of them women) were compelled to work for the rest of their lives in domestic service. Ibid., 200. "The property right between the owner *(amo)* and the women was similar to the right that war gave over the Indian slave." Ibid., 203. On the disappearance of Indian groups, see Germán Colmenares, "La Sociedad Indígena y su Evolución Posterior a la Conquista," in *La Nueva Historia de Colombia,* ed. Darío Jaramillo Agudelo (Bogotá: Instituto Colombiano de Cultura, 1976), 167. Colmenares mentions that at the beginning of the seventeenth century "the proportion of women working in the houses of Spaniards was so high that the Jesuit priest Diego de Torres wrote with a big concern about the harm to the Indian society since in the towns there were no women to be married by the Indians."

51. Gutiérrez de Pineda, *La Familia en Colombia: Transfondo Histórico,* 193.

52. Joan Wallach Scott, *Gender and the Politics of History* (New York: Columbia University Press, 1988), 45.

53. Emiro Kastos, "Algo Sobre las Mujeres," in *Colección de Artículos Escogidos* (Bogotá: Imprenta de Pizano i Pérez, 1859), 137.

54. Ibid., 136.

55. Ibid.

56. Ibid., 137.

57. Salvador Camacho Roldán, "preface" to the first edition of Eugenio Díaz's novel *Manuela* (1889), reprinted in Salvador Camacho Roldán, *Escritos Varios,* tomo 2 (Bogotá: Editorial Incunables, 1983), 506.

58. Ibid., 513.

59. Patricia Londoño, "El Ideal Femenino en el Siglo XIX" and "Publicaciones Periódicas Dirigidas a la Mujer en Colombia 1858–1930," in *Las Mujeres en la Historia de Colombia: Mujeres y Cultura,* tomo 3, comp. Consejería Presidencial para la Política Social (Santa Fe de Bogotá: Grupo Editorial Norma, 1992).

60. Rufino José Cuervo, "Las Mujeres," quoted in Patricia Londoño, "El Ideal Femenino en el Siglo XIX," 314–15.

61. Ibid., 315.

62. Medardo Rivas, "Conferencia sobre Educación de la Mujer leída en

el Colejio de la Merced por el inspector Medardo Rivas" (Bogotá, 1871), quoted in Patricia Londoño, "El Ideal Femenino en el Siglo XIX," 316.

63. Manuel Ancízar, Peregrinación de Alpha (Bogotá: Biblioteca Banco Popular, 1970), 139.

64. This history appears in Jesús C. Torres Almeida, Manuel Murillo Toro, Caudillo Radical y Reformador Social (Bogotá: Ediciones El, 1984), 210.

65. Caro, "Declaratoria Politica," 183.

66. Eugenio Díaz, Manuela (Bogotá: Biblioteca Popular de Cultura, 1895), 24–26.

67. Ezequiel Rojas, El Aviso (July 26, 1848). Quoted in Gerardo Molina, Las Ideas Liberales en Colombia—1849–1914 (Bogotá: Tercer Mundo, 1975), 23–24.

68. Jorge Villegas, Colombia: Enfrentamiento Iglesia Estado 1819–1887 (Bogotá: Editorial La Carreta, 1981).

69. Quoted in ibid., 33. The state also claimed an increased participation on the part of the state in the apportionment of taxes (diezmos) and a more equal participation on the part of the population in paying these taxes. The diezmos were collected mainly from agriculture, and four-fifths of its benefits went to the church to sustain priests.

70. Florentino González, El Neo Granadino (March 25, 1853), quoted in Villegas, Colombia, 43.

71. These measures are a summary of the content of Villegas, Colombia.

72. Letter of the president of Colombia, Tomás Cipriano de Mosquera, to Pope Pius IX in 1862 explaining the reasons for the Liberal reforms. The pope, in response, excommunicated the president and also those priests who had obeyed the government laws. Quoted in Villegas, Colombia, 59.

73. The importance given to constitutions has occasioned what a Colombian author calls "the Constitutional Battle." Hernando Valencia Villa, Cartas de Batalla: Una Crítica del Constitucionalismo Colombiano (Bogotá: Universidad Nacional de Colombia, 1987).

74. Álvaro Tirado Mejía, Descentralización y Centralismo en Colombia (Bogotá: Editorial La Oveja Negra, 1983), 47.

75. Quoted in Valencia, Cartas de Batalla, 136.

76. The powers delegated to the federal government were jurisdiction over foreign affairs, national defense, the monetary system, and the regulation of interoceanic and river routes. The federal government shared with the provinces control of the postal service and public education.

77. Justo Arosemena, Constituciones Políticas, quoted in Samper, Escritos Político-Económicos de Miguel Samper, vol. 2, 351.

78. Germán Colmenares, "La Ley y el Orden Social: Fundamento Profano y Fundamento Divino," Boletín Cultural y Bibliográfico 27, no. 22 (1990), 17. Historian Gerardo Molina also identifies the "kingdom of the

law" as a main characteristic of the thinking of mid-nineteenth-century Liberals. He attributes to this belief one of the main failures of liberalism: "Its adherence to the principle that written texts had a magical power, made Liberals believe that a perfect Constitution will ensure collective happiness. They did not realize that the social constitution is more important, the amalgam of habits, beliefs, material realizations, structures, and everyday life." Gerardo Molina, *Las Ideas Liberales en Colombia 1849–91* (Bogotá: Editorial Tercer Mundo, 1970), 122.

79. Justo Arosema was one of the authors of the constitution of 1853. He also wrote a treatise on the Colombian constitutions in the nineteenth century.

80. José Eusebio Caro, "La libertad y el partido Conservador," *La Civilización* 5 and 6, Septiembre (1849), reprinted in Caro, *Escritos Histórico-Políticos de José Eusebio Caro,* 59.

81. José E. Caro, "La Cuestión Moral," in *Antología Verso y Prosa* (Bogotá: Bilbioteca Popular de Cultura Colombiana, 1951), 297.

82. Caro, "La libertad y el partido conservador," 59.

83. Ibid., 59.

84. Gonzalo Sánchez, *Guerra y Política en la Sociedad Colombiana* (Bogotá: El Áncora Editores, 1991), 33.

85. José M. Samper, *Apuntamientos para la Historia Política i Social de la Nueva Granada desde 1810, i Especialmente de la Administración del 7 de Marzo* (Bogotá: Imprenta del Neo-Granadino, 1853), 13. The denomination "Gran Colombia" referred to the union of New Granada, Venezuela, and Ecuador. Venezuela withdrew from Gran Colombia in 1829 and Ecuador in 1830. In the constitution of 1863 the name New Granada changed to Estados Unidos de Colombia and later to Colombia.

86. José Eusebio Caro, "El 7 de Marzo de 1849," in Caro, *Escritos Histórico-Político de José Eusebio Caro,* 197.

87. As Foucault states, "The successes of history belong to those who are capable of seizing the [rules of history] to replace those who had used them, to disguise themselves so as to pervert them, invert their meaning, and redirect them against those who had initially imposed them; controlling this complex mechanism, they will make it function so as to overcome the rulers through their own rules." Michel Foucault, "Nietzsche, Genealogy, History," in *Interpreting Politics,* ed. Michael Gibbons (New York: New York University Press, 1987), 229.

88. Samper, *Apuntamientos para la Historia Política i Social de la Nueva Granada,* 37.

89. Miguel A. Caro, "La Fundación de Bogotá," quoted in Jaime Jaramillo, *El Pensamiento Colombiano en el Siglo XIX* (Bogotá: Editorial Temis, 1982), 82. Jaramillo offers a broad vision of Caro's call for a return to the Spanish heritage.

90. Caro, *La Fundación de Bogotá,* quoted in Jaramillo, 82.

91. Octavio Quiñones Pardo, *Interpretación de la Poesía Popular* (Bogotá: Editorial Centro, 1945), 40–41.

92. Ibid.

93. Ibid.

3. THE POLITICAL ECONOMY OF CIVILIZATION

1. Robert Cox, "Production and Hegemony: Toward a Political Economy of World Order," in H. K. Jacobson, ed., *The Emerging International Economic Order* (Beverly Hills: Sage Publications, 1982). See also the chapters in Craig Murphy and Roger Tooze, eds., *The New International Political Economy* (Boulder, Colo.: Lynne Rienner Publishers, 1991).

2. See Michael J. Shapiro, "Political Economy and Mimetic Desire in *Babette's Feast,*" in Michael J. Shapiro, *Reading the Postmodern Polity* (Minneapolis: University of Minnesota Press, 1992), 54.

3. Charles Berquist, *Labor in Latin America: Comparative Essays on Chile, Argentina, Venezuela and Colombia* (Stanford, Calif.: Stanford University Press, 1986), 290.

4. Charles Berquist, *Coffee and Conflict in Colombia, 1886–1910* (Durham, N.C.: Duke University Press, 1976), and "The Political Economy of the Colombian Presidential Election of 1897," *Hispanic American Historical Review* 1 (February 1976).

5. Frank Safford, "Aspectos Sociales en la Política de la Nueva Granada 1825–1850," in Frank Safford, *Aspectos del Siglo XIX en Colombia* (Medellín: Ediciones Hombre Nuevo, 1977), 178 and passim.

6. According to Frank Safford, "[In Colombia] the private sector was as poor [as the public sector]. As compared with the standards of Rio de Janeiro, Mexico, or Lima, the wealthiest class in Colombia was an indigent class. The upper-class rent during the first part of the nineteenth century reached $5,000 per person per year, and those with capital of more than $100,000 could be counted on the fingers of one hand." Frank Safford, "Empresarios Nacionales y Extranjeros en Colombia durante el Siglo XIX," in Safford, *Aspectos del Siglo XIX en Colombia,* 31. See also his "Aspectos Sociales de la Politica en la Nueva Granada, 1825–1850," in ibid., 153–200.

7. Malcom Deas, "Miguel Antonio Caro y Amigos: Gramática y Poder en Colombia," in *Del Poder y la Gramática* (Santa Fé de Bogotá: Tercer Mundo Editores, 1993). The article appeared in English as "Miguel Antonio Caro and Friends: Grammar and Power in Colombia," in *History Workshop Journal* 34 (1992). My overall argument differs from the one sustained

by Deas. In his view, the Conservatives' concern with grammar did not form part of a project of domination, nor was it explained by nationalist interests. He explains their interest in grammar in terms of the linkages that language established with the Spanish past, which provided the model for the kind of republic they wanted for Colombia.

8. Pierre Bourdieu acknowledges the existence of "symbolic" and "cultural" capital, which are structured differently than "economic" capital. See Pierre Bourdieu, *Outline of a Theory of Practice* (Cambridge: Cambridge University Press, 1977).

9. See Mikhail M. Bakhtin, *The Dialogical Imagination* (Austin: University of Texas Press, 1981), 251.

10. "Surplus of vision" refers to things that I see but you cannot because of our relative positions. See Mikhail M. Bakhtin, *Problems of Dovstoievski Poetics* (Minneapolis: University of Minnesota Press, 1984).

11. José M. Samper, *Apuntamientos para la Historia Política i Social de la Nueva Granada desde 1810 i Especialmente de la Administración del 7 de Marzo* (Bogotá: Imprenta del Neo-Granadino, 1853), 186–87.

12. Florentino González (1863), quoted in Laurence E. Prescott, *Candelario Obeso y la Iniciación de la Poesía Negra en Colombia* (Bogotá: Publicaciones del Instituto Caro y Cuervo, 1985), 59.

13. José M. Samper, *Historia de un Alma,* vol. 1 (Bogotá: Biblioteca Popular de Cultura Colombiana, 1848).

14. Michael Shapiro, "Spatiality and Policy Discourse: Reading the Global City," in Shapiro, *Reading the Postmodern Polity,* 88.

15. Ángel Rama, *La Ciudad Letrada* (Hanover: Ediciones del Norte, 1984).

16. In Colombia only 1.4 percent of the total population lived in the capital. By the same year in Uruguay, 25 percent of the national population was located in the capital; in Argentina's capital, 10.8 percent; in Paraguay's capital, 7.6 percent; in Ecuador's capital, 7.1 percent; in Peru's capital, 3.7 percent, in Bolivia's capital, 3.5 percent; in Venezuela's capital, 2.8 percent. Regarding the diversification of power, a similar situation also existed in Ecuador, which had two centers of power, Quito and Guayaquil. See James R. Scobie, "The Growth of the Cities," in *Latin America Economy and Society, 1870–1930,* ed. Leslie Bethel (Cambridge: Cambridge University Press, 1989), 149–81.

17. Marco Palacios, "La Fragmentación Regional de las Clases Dominantes en Colombia: Una Perspectiva Histórica," *Revista Mexicana de Sociología* 42 (1980).

18. Felipe Pérez, *Geografía General Física y Política de los Estados Unidos de Colombia y Geografía Particular de la Ciudad de Bogotá* (Bogotá: Imprenta de Echeverría Hermanos, 1883). The census of 1871 estimated that

there were 6,181 literati out of a population of almost three million people, distributed as follows: educators, 1,728; priests, 1,573; lawyers, 1,037; nuns, 767; medical doctors, 727; engineers, 275; and intellectuals, 82.

19. Ibid., 178–79.

20. Pérez, *Geografía General Física y Política de los Estados Unidos de Colombia*, 281.

21. Doris Sommer, *Foundational Fiction: The National Romances of Latin America* (Berkeley: University of California Press, 1991).

22. Malcolm Deas, "Miguel Antonio Caro and Friends: Grammar and Power in Colombia," *History Workshop Journal* 34 (1992).

23. Jaime Jaramillo Uribe, *El Pensamiento Colombiano en el Siglo XIX* (Bogotá: Editorial Temis, 1982), 341. According to Jaramillo, in Bolívar's correspondence there are several letters from Bentham and two responses from Bolívar. In one of them, Bolívar mentioned that he ordered the translation and printing of his *Catecismo de Economía* because it was "obra digna de conocerse" (work which deserved to be known). Nevertheless, in 1828 Bolívar forbad the use of Bentham's books.

24. Ibid., 136.

25. The best example is José M. Samper, *Ensayo Sobre las Revoluciones Políticas i la Condición Social de las Repúblicas Colombianas* (París: Imprenta de E. Thunot, 1861).

26. Carlos Martínez Silva, "El Gran Ciudadano," reprinted in Carlos Martínez Silva, *Escritos Varios* (Bogotá: Ministerio de Educación Nacional / Ediciones de la Revista Bolívar, 1954), 173.

27. The *patronato* refers to the special power conceded by the pope to the Spanish Crown. The Spanish Crown had the jurisdiction to orient Christian evangelization. Religion was used as the main instrument to bring Indians and blacks under Spanish domination. Clerics were part of the royal administration, deriving their income and nomination from the Spanish Crown. During the years of the independence movement and the republic, the *patronato* was not abolished, but was incorporated into the structure of the state; the state retained the right to control clerical appointments.

28. José María Vergara y Vergara, *Historia de la Literatura en Nueva Granada desde la Conquista hasta la Independencia (1538–1820)* (Bogotá: Librería Americana, 1905), 31.

29. Miguel Samper, "La Miseria en Bogotá," in Samper, *Escritos Político-Económicos de Miguel Samper,* 27. An excellent description of the struggles over intellectual formation in diverse professions and the divergences between Liberals and Conservatives appears in Frank Safford, *The Ideal of the Practical: Colombia's Struggle to Form a Technical Elite* (Austin and London: University of Texas Press, 1976).

30. Samper, *Apuntamientos para la Historia Política i Social de la Nueva Granada desde 1810*, 476.

31. Ibid., 496.

32. Miguel A. Caro, "Libertad y Orden," in *Estudios Jurídicos y Constitucionales* (Bogotá: Instituto Caro y Cuervo, 1986), 208.

33. José M. Samper, *Apuntamientos para la Historia Política i Social de la Nueva Granada desde 1810*, 476.

34. Ibid., 485.

35. An overview of the opposition between the Liberals and the Conservatives with respect to freedom of the press appears in Miguel Antonio Caro, *Estudios Jurídicos y Constitucionales*. The chapters were published originally as articles in several issues of the newspaper *La Nación*.

36. Ibid., 199–200.

37. Ibid., 232.

38. Miguel A. Caro, "¡Ni en Rusia!" *El Orden* (Bogotá, April 12, 1887), 18, reprinted in Miguel A. Caro, *Escritos Políticos* (Bogotá: Instituto Caro y Cuervo, 1990), 157.

39. Ibid., 159.

40. Cuervo, "Apuntaciones Críticas sobre el Lenguaje Bogotano," quoted in Deas, 9.

41. Ibid.

42. Ibid., 5.

43. Ibid., 11 [Deas's translation].

44. *Diario de Cundinamarca* (Bogotá, vol. 3, no. 732 [May 31, 1872]), quoted in Jane Meyer Loy, "Primary Education during the Colombian Federation: The School Reform of 1870," *Hispanic American Historical Review* (May 1971), 277. Meyer's study fully supports the view of education as part of the quest for civilization. She mentions that newspapers identified education with civilization. According to Meyer, this linkage was strengthened as a result of Prussia's victory over France in 1870, which was interpreted by local newspapers as a result of Prussia's policy of educating the masses.

45. Quoted in Safford, *The Ideal of the Practical*, 50. See also David Bushnell, *El Régimen de Santander en la Gran Colombia* (Bogotá: El Áncora Editores, 1985).

46. The criticism included not only Bentham, but also the Protestant Wattel, an authority on international law. Bushnell, *El Régimen de Santander en la Gran Colombia*, 235.

47. Evelyn J. G. Ahern, "El Desarrollo de la Educación en Colombia: 1820–1850," *Revista Colombiana de Educación*, 22–23 (1991), 51.

48. Aline Helg mentions some of the reasons that could explain the German origin of the mission: the importance of some German pedagogues,

the increasing importance of tobacco exports to Germany, and the importance given by the local press to the German victory over France, which was attributed to education. Aline Helg, *La Educación en Colombia 1918–1957* (Bogotá: Fondo Editorial CEREC, 1987), 25.

49. Quoted in Ángel Cuervo and Rufino José Cuervo, "La Vida de Rufino Cuervo y Noticias de su Epoca" (1892), in *Obras,* vol. 2, ed. Rufino José Cuervo (Bogotá: Instituto Caro y Cuervo, 1954), 1413–14.

50. Salvador Camacho Roldán (1881), "Punto Negro en el Horizonte," *La Unión* (Septiembre 27), reprinted in Salvador Camacho Roldán, *Escritos Varios,* vol. 2 (Bogotá: Editorial Incunables, 1983), 98.

51. Ibid., 98.

52. The main elements of this debate are illustrated in Jane Meyer Loy, "Los Ignorantistas y las Escuelas: La Oposición a la Reforma Educativa durante la Federación Colombiana," in *Revista Colombiana de Educación* 9 (Bogotá: Universidad Pedagógica Nacional, 1982), 9–24.

53. Ibid., 11.

54. Ibid., 15.

4. THE SUBALTERNS' VOICES

1. A recent representative example concludes that "the distinctive experience of Liberalism in Latin America derived from the fact that Liberal ideas were applied in countries which were highly stratified, socially and racially, and economically underdeveloped, and in which the tradition of centralized authority ran deep. In short, they were applied in an environment which was resistant and hostile, and which in some cases engendered a strong opposing ideology of conservatism." Charles A. Hale, "Political and Social Ideas," in *Latin America Economy and Society, 1870–1930,"* ed. Leslie Bethell (Cambridge: Cambridge University Press, 1989), 226.

2. Arturo Escobar, *Encountering Development: The Making and Unmaking of the Third World* (Princeton, N.J.: Princeton University Press, 1995), 59.

3. Edward W. Said "Orientalism Reconsidered," in *Europe and Its Others,* Proceedings of the Essex Conference on the Sociology of Literature, ed. Francis Barker et al., 2 vols. (Colchester: University of Essex, 1985), vol. 1, 22.

4. Ranajit Guha, "The Prose of Counter-Insurgency," in *Cultures, Power, History: A Reader in Contemporary Social Theory,* ed. Nicholas B. Dirks, Geoff Eley, and Sherry Ortner (Princeton, N.J.: Princeton University Press, 1994).

5. Ranajit Guha, "On Some Aspects of the Historiography of Colonial India," in *Subaltern Studies,* vol. 1, ed. Ranajit Guha (Delhi: Oxford University Press, 1982).

6. Gayatri Chakravorty Spivak, "Can the Subaltern Speak?" in *Marxism and the Interpretation of Culture,* ed. Cary Nelson and Lawrence Grossberg (London: Macmillan, 1988), 287.

7. Said, "Orientalism Reconsidered," 7–8.

8. Gayatri Chakravorty Spivak, "Three Women's Texts and a Critique of Imperialism," *Critical Inquiry* 12, no. 1 (1985), 259.

9. Ibid., 254.

10. N. García Canclini, *Culturas Híbridas: Estrategias para Entrar y Salir de la Modernidad* (México: Editorial Grijalbo, 1990), 257.

11. Fernando Coronil, *The Magical State: Nature, Money and Modernity in Venezuela* (Chicago and London: University of Chicago Press, 1997), 16–17. For a similar understanding of encounters between the self and the Other, see the excellent volume edited by Gilbert M. Joseph, Catherine C. Legrand, and Ricardo D. Salvatore, *Close Encounters of Empire: Writing the Cultural History of U.S.–Latin American Relations* (Durham, N.C. and London: Duke University Press, 1998).

12. Bakhtin believes that it is not possible to be outside of relationships linking oneself to the Other, since "man *(sic)* has no internal sovereign territory; he is all and always on the boundary; looking within himself he looks *in the eyes of the other* or *through the eyes of the other.*" Mikhail M. Bakhtin, *Problems of Dostoevsky Poetics,* quoted in Tzvetan Todorov, *Mikhail M. Bakhtin: The Dialogical Principle* (Minneapolis: University of Minnesota Press, 1984), 96 (emphasis in original). Language "lies on the borderline between oneself and the Other." Mikhail M. Bakhtin, *The Dialogic Imagination* (Austin: University of Texas Press, 1981), 293.

13. In Bakhtin's view "there are always two consciousnesses, two language-intentions, two *voices* and consequently two accents participating in an intentional and conscious artistic hybrid." Bakhtin, *The Dialogic Imagination,* 360. In his view, hybridization allows for the intentional presence of the represented and the representer. In this encounter between represented and representers in a single space, both are provided with a space from which to talk. In this sense, the analysis does not privilege the interpretations coming from outside or from a single group of actors; that is, each participant in the dialogue has a "double voice" whose meanings can be contradictory (pp. 358–66).

14. Ibid., 304. According to Bhabha, hybridity allows the questioning of the colonial authority, since it "reverses the effects of colonial disavowal, so that the Other's 'denied' knowledge enters upon the dominant discourse and

estrange the basis of its authority—its rules of recognition. Homi K. Bhabha, *The Location of Culture* (London and New York: Routledge, 1994), 114.

15. Bakhtin, *The Dialogic Imagination,* 254–55.

16. Bakhtin, *Problems of Dovstoevsky's Poetics.*

17. Gayatri Chakravorty Spivak, "Three Women's Texts and a Critique of Imperialism," 251.

18. Medardo Rivas, *Los Trabajadores de Tierra Caliente* (Bogotá: Imprenta y Librería de M. Rivas, 1899), 10.

19. Ibid., 38–39.

20. Ibid., 48.

21. Ibid., 39.

22. Ibid., 48–49.

23. Bhabha, *The Location of Culture,* 89.

24. Rivas, *Los Trabajadores de Tierra Caliente,* 51.

25. Ibid., 48–49.

26. José María Vergara y Vergara, *Historia de la Literatura en Nueva Granada desde la Conquista hasta la Independencia (1538–1820)* (Bogotá: Librería Americana, 1905), 470–71.

27. Ibid., 467.

28. Ibid., 470–71.

29. José M. Restrepo, "De la Poesía Popular en Colombia" (1911) reprinted in José M. Restrepo, *El Cancionero de Antioquia* (Barcelona, Editorial Lux, 1929), 50–51.

30. Jesús Martín Barbero, *De los Medios a las Mediaciones* (México: Gustavo Gili, 1987), 210.

31. Obeso published several books of poems and drama, as well as novels. His most important works are *Cantos Populares de Mi Tierra, Lectura para Tí, Lucha de la Vida, and Secundino el Zapatero* (a comedy in three parts). He translated into Spanish *Curso de Lengua Italiana* and *Nociones de Táctica de Infantería, de Caballería y de Artillería.*

32. Laurence E. Prescott, "'Negro Nací': Authorship and Voice in Verses Attributed to Candelario Obeso" *Afro-Hispanic Review* (Spring 1993), 8.

33. Candelario Obeso, "Advertencia al Lector," in *Cantos Populares de Mi Tierra* (Biblioteca Popular de Cultura Colombiana: 1950), 13. This edition includes *Cantos Populares de Mi Tierra, Lectura para Ti,* and *La Lucha de la Vida.*

34. See Laurence E. Prescott, *Candelario Obeso y la Iniciación de la Poesía Negra en Colombia* (Bogotá: Publicaciones del Instituto Caro y Cuervo, 1985), 72.

35. Richard L. Jackson considers Obeso's work a precursor of *poesía negra*. According to Jackson, in *Cantos Populares de Mi Tierra*, published in 1877, Obeso consciously used "authentic black talk" as a way to accord

"dignity to his black fellow countrymen while advising the local literati that a truly national literary identity could be found only in local popular poetry and song." Richard L. Jackson, *Black Writers in Latin America* (Albuquerque: University of New Mexico Press, 1979), 53–54.

36. *Cachaco* is a pejorative term used for white creole inhabitants from Bogotá.

37. Obeso, *Cantos Populares de mi Tierra*, 32.

38. Ibid., 15–16. The translation of the second verse is from R. L. Jackson, *Black Writers in Latin America*, 56.

39. Obeso, *Cantos Populares de mi Tierra*, 24–26.

40. Ibid., 28.

41. Ibid., 31.

42. Ibid., 28.

43. Ibid., 20.

44. Ibid., 34–36.

45. Candelario Obeso, *La Lucha de la Vida*, in *Cantos Populares de Mi Tierra*, 94–98.

46. Ibid., 108.

47. Ibid., 109 and passim.

48. Quoted in Prescott, *Candelario Obeso y la Iniciación de la Poesía Negra en Colombia*, 71.

49. Monserrat Ordoñez, "Introducción," in *Soledad Acosta de Samper: Una Nueva Lectura,* by Soledad Acosta de Samper (Bogotá: Fondo Cultural Cafetero, 1988).

50. Quoted in ibid., 13.

51. Quoted in ibid., 355.

52. Soledad Acosta de Samper, article in *La Mujer,* no. 59 (1881), quoted in Santiago Samper Trainer, "Soledad Acosta de Samper: El Eco de un Grito," in *Las Mujeres en la Historia de Colombia* (Santa Fe de Bogotá: Editorial Norma, 1995), 141.

53. Soledad Acosta de Samper, "El corazón de la Mujer," in *Soledad Acosta de Samper. Una Nueva Lectura,* 128–29.

54. Ibid., 128.

55. Soledad Acosta de Samper, "La Monja," in *Soledad Acosta de Samper: Una Nueva Lectura.*

56. Ibid., 96.

57. Mikhail M. Bakhtin, *The Dialogic Imagination,* 159.

58. *Guacharacas* are birds of certain regions whose main characteristic is the noise they make.

59. Soledad Acosta de Samper, "Episodios Novelescos de la historia Patria: Un Chistoso de Aldea," in *Soledad Acosta de Samper: Una Nueva Lectura,* 267.

60. Soledad Acosta de Samper, "El Corazón de las Mujeres," in *Soledad Acosta de Samper: Una Nueva Lectura*, 127.

61. Soledad Acosta de Samper, "Matilde," in *Soledad Acosta de Samper: Una Nueva Lectura*, 132.

62. Ibid., 130.

63. Ibid., 131.

64. Spivak, "Three Women's Text and a Critique of Imperialism," 244–45.

65. Soledad Acosta de Samper, *Cartas de París* (1891), quoted in Santiago Samper Trainer, "Soledad Acosta de Samper: El Eco de un Grito," 142.

66. Soledad Acosta de Samper, "Mercedes," in *Soledad Acosta de Samper: Una Nueva Lectura*.

67. Ibid., 159.

68. Ibid., 172.

69. Ibid., 176.

70. Ibid., 177.

5. THE WILL TO CIVILIZATION AND ITS ENCOUNTER WITH LAISSEZ-FAIRE

1. John P. Harrison, "The Evolution of the Colombian Tobacco Trade," *The Hispanic American Historical Review* 32, no. 2 (1952), 172.

2. This process is depicted in José A. Ocampo, *Colombia y la Economía Mundial 1830–1910*, (Bogotá: Siglo XXI, 1984), 294–300.

3. Ibid., chapter 5. Ocampo explains the lack of competitiveness of Colombian tobacco in the external market as a result of the inefficient system for the production, processing, and packaging of tobacco. Colombian tobacco was replaced by exports from Sumatra, whose better quality displaced Colombia from the market. A disease called *amulatamiento* intensified this decrease in quality.

4. Ibid., 295.

5. Joseph L. Love and Nils Jacobsen, *Guiding the Invisible Hand: Economic Liberalism and the State in Latin American History* (New York: Praeger, 1988), vii.

6. William P. McGreevey, *Historia Económica de Colombia 1845–1930* (Bogotá: Ediciones Tercer Mundo, 1971).

7. Ocampo, *Colombia y la Economía Mundial 1830–1910*.

8. Ibid., 345.

9. This is Brenner's main criticism of the world system approach. See Robert Brenner, "The Origins of Capitalist Development: A Critique of Neo-Smithian Marxism," in *Introduction to the Sociology of "Developing Societies,"* ed. Hamza Alavi and Teodor Shanin (London: Macmillan, 1982);

Robert Brenner, "The Social Basis of Economic Development," in *Analytical Marxism,* ed. John Roemer (Cambridge: Cambridge University Press, 1986).

10. See Salomón Kalmanovitz, "Desarrollo Capitalista en el Campo Colombiano," in *Colombia Hoy,* ed. Mario Arrubla et al. (Bogotá: Siglo XXI, 1978), 278.

11. Salomón Kalmanovitz, *El Desarrollo Tardío del Capitalismo: Un Enfoque Crítico de la Teoría de la Dependencia* (Bogotá: Siglo XXI, 1986), 53–55.

12. Salomón Kalmanovitz, "El Régimen Agrario Durante el Siglo XIX en Colombia," in *Manual de Historia de Colombia,* vol. 2, 2nd ed. (Bogotá: Círculo de Lectores, S.A., 1982), 308. Among the differences between true capitalism and feudalism Kalmanowitz mentions the existence of accumulation of capital and profits in those sectors linked to the external market. There is also a major circulation of commodities and a social division of labor. Land and labor have more mobility than in feudalism, and some peasants have rights over land, as was the case in the Antioqueño colonization.

13. Salomón Kalmanovitz, *Economía y Nación: Una Breve Historia de Colombia* (Bogotá: Siglo XXI, 1985), 215.

14. Ibid., 182.

15. Ibid., 237–38.

16. Mikhail M. Bakhtin, *The Dialogic Imagination* (Austin: University of Texas Press, 1981) 276.

17. Roberto Schwarz, "Misplaced Ideas. Literature and Society in Late Nineteenth Century Brazil," in *Misplaced Ideas: Essays on Brazilian Culture* (London and New York: Verso, 1992).

18. Ibid., 20. The originality in Schwarz's argument about Brazil has to do with the complicity between liberalism and the ideology of favor: "Favor assured both parties [proprietor of the *latifundium* and the 'free man'], especially the weaker one. Even the most miserable of those given favor saw his freedom recognized in this act." Ibid., 24.

19. The eradication of violence from the labor contract is a major distinction of capitalism. Contract labor cannot be understood independent of the formation of identities in both its ontological and its normative dimensions. For Marx, capitalist relations of production fostered the notion of "undifferentiated" individuals who were equated under the guise of the search for self-interest. Exchange relations presumed the existence of individuals who are indifferent to one another: in the exchange relationship, "Whatever other individual distinction there may be does not concern them; *they are indifferent to all their other individual peculiarities*" [emphasis in original]. Karl Marx, *Grundrisse* (Harmondsworth, U.K.: Penguin Books, 1973), 242. Even more, "In the developed system of exchange . . . the ties of personal de-

pendence, of distinction of blood, education, etc., are in fact exploded, ripped" (p. 63). In Marx's *Grundrisse,* the linkage between construction of identities and the extrusion of force from the relations of production is established. According to Marx, in relations of exchange, individuals appear as *equals,* making it impossible to find any trace of distinction between them: "They are, as equals, at the same time also indifferent to each other." This form of equality becomes the condition that makes it possible to perceive of the relation of exchange as an exchange of equivalents and hence as unforced: "Out of the act of exchange itself, each individual is reflected in himself as its exclusive and dominant (determinant) subject. With that, then, the complete freedom of the individual is posited: voluntary transaction, no force on either side" (p. 244).

20. Quoted in David Bushnell, *El Régimen de Santander en la Gran Colombia* (Bogotá: El Áncora Editores, 1985), 233.

21. A discussion of the debate in the first half of the nineteenth century appears in Evelyn J. G. Ahern, "El Desarrollo de la Educación en Colombia: 1820–1850," *Revista Colombiana de Educación* 22–23 (1991).

22. J. M. Restrepo (1828), quoted in Rufino J. Cuervo (1892), "Vida de Rufino J. Cuervo y Noticias de su Epoca," in Rufino J. Cuervo, *Obras,* ed. Simón Aljure Chalela, vol. 2 (Bogotá: Instituto Caro y Cuervo, 1954), 1278.

23. See Ahern, "El Desarrollo de la Educación en Colombia: 1820–1850," 53.

24. Jaime Jaramillo Uribe, "El Proceso de la Educación, del Virreinato a la Época Contemporánea," in Jaime Jaramillo Uribe, *Manual de Historia de Colombia,* vol. 3 (Bogotá: Círculo de Lectores, 1982).

25. José E. Caro (1849), "La libertad y el Partido Conservador," in José E. Caro, *Escritos Histórico-políticos* (Bogotá: Ediciones Fondo Cultural Cafetero, 1980), 61.

26. Ezequiel Rojas, *El Aviso* (Bogotá, 1848), reprinted in Gerardo Molina, *Las Ideas Liberales en Colombia—1849–1914* (Bogotá: Editorial Tercer Mundo, 1970), 23.

27. Mariano Ospina Rodríguez, "La Civilización se Define" (1849), reprinted in *Escritos sobre Economía Política* (Bogotá: Universidad Nacional de Colombia, 1969), 73.

28. Ibid., 78.

29. Ibid., 79.

30. José E. Caro, "La Falsedad del Laissez Faire" (1849), reprinted in *Antología Verso y Prosa* (Bogotá: Biblioteca Popular de Cultura Colombiana, 1951), 386.

31. Quoted in Molina, *Las Ideas Liberales en Colombia—1849–1914,* 54.

32. The 1851 figure is derived from official data quoted in J. León

Helguera, "Antecedentes Sociales de la Revolución de 1851," in *El Sur de Colombia: Anuario Colombiano de Historia General y de la Cultura,* vol. 5 (1970), 59. The figure for the end of the century is taken from Jorge Palacios Preciado, "La Esclavitud y la Sociedad Esclavista," *Manual de Historia de Colombia,* vol. 1, ed. Jaime Jaramillo Uribe (Bogotá: Círculo de Lectores, 1982).

33. Murillo's radicalism is reflected in the Constitution of the province of Santander, authored by him. In Murillo's own words, "The Constitution of Santander has abolished, as was supposed to be the case, the government." Quoted in Jesús C. Torres Almeida, *Manuel Murillo Toro: Caudillo Radical y Reformador Social* (Bogotá: Ediciones El Tiempo, 1984), 210.

34. Manuel Murillo, "Dejad Haced" (1853), published in Molina, *Las Ideas Liberales en Colombia—1849–1914,* 319–33.

35. Ibid., 321.

36. Historian Delpar refers to Samper as "the most articulate and consistent exponent of classical economic liberalism." Helen Delpar, *Red against Blue: The Liberal Party in Colombian Politics, 1863–1899* (Tuscaloosa: University of Alabama Press, 1981), 72. The two main historians of ideas in Colombia, Gerardo Molina and Jaime Jaramillo Uribe, also believe that Samper is the clearest representative of economic liberalism in Colombia. See Molina, *Las Ideas Liberales en Colombia—1849–1914* and Jaramillo Uribe, "El Proceso de la Educación, del Virreinato a la Época Contemporánea," in *Manual de Historia de Colombia,* vol. 3.

37. Miguel Samper, "La Miseria en Bogotá" (1867), in Miguel Samper, *Escritos Político-Económicos de Miguel Samper,* vol. 1 (Bogotá: Editorial Cromos, 1925), 94.

38. Ibid.

39. Ibid., 77.

40. This was Samper's reaction to Núñez's attempt to introduce measures limiting imports. Miguel Samper, "La Protección" (1880), in Samper, *Escritos Político-Económicos de Miguel Samper,* vol. 1, 213.

41. Miguel Samper, "Libertad y Order" (1895), in Samper, *Escritos Político-Económicos de Miguel Samper,* vol. 2, 10 and 11.

42. Ibid., 259.

43. Ibid., 81.

44. José M. Samper, *Apuntamientos para la Historia de Colombia* (Bogotá: Imprenta del Neo-Granadino, 1853), 5. See also José M. Samper, *Ensayo sobre las Revoluciones Políticas i la Condición Social de las Repúblicas Colombianas* (Paris: Imprenta de E. Thunot Y., 1861).

45. Samper, *Apuntamientos para la Historia de Colombia,* 10.

46. Ibid., 46.

47. José E. Caro, "La Cuestión Moral," in José E. Caro, *Antología, Verso y Prosa* (Bogotá: Biblioteca Popular de Cultura Colombiana, 1951), 304.

48. Ibid., 298–99.

49. Miguel A. Caro, "Estudios sobre el Utilitarismo" (1869), in Miguel A. Caro: *Obras Completas* (Bogotá: Instituto Caro y Cuervo, 1962), 159.

50. Ibid., 166.

51. Miguel A. Caro, "Carta al Doctor Ezequiel Rojas" (1869), in *Miguel A. Caro: Obras Completas*, 390.

52. Miguel A. Caro, "Estudios sobre el Utilitarismo" (1869), reprinted in *Miguel A. Caro: Obras Completas*, 224.

53. Ibid., 270.

54. According to the 1870 census, the labor force of Colombia was 1.5 million people (over half of its 2.9 million total population). Artisans were the second group in importance after those employed in the agricultural sector. There were 350,000 artisans (23 percent of the labor force). A high proportion of artisans was women (249,000 or 71 percent). In some regions, such as the province of Santander, the proportion of women working in the artisan sector was as high as 88 percent of the labor force. The main activities carried out by women were textile and hat manufacture. Hats accounted for 9.5 percent of the total exports, a proportion not surpassed by current manufactured exports.

During the colonial period, the country had been self-sufficient in cotton and wool textiles. At the beginning of the nineteenth century, the national production of textiles balanced the amount of imports. The production of textiles lost its importance and experienced decay during the 19th century: by midcentury the local production represented 40 percent of the internal demand; by 1880, the local production met only one-fourth of the total demand. José O. Melo, "La Evolución Económica de Colombia, 1830–1900," in *Nueva Historia de Colombia* (Bogotá: Planeta Colombiana Editorial, 1989). José A. Ocampo, "Comerciantes, Artesanos y Política Económica en Colombia, 1830–1880," in *Boletín Cultural y Bibliográfico*, vol. 27, no. 2 (Bogotá: Banco de la República, 1990), 43–45.

55. Ibid., 3.

56. According to the historian Luis Ospina Vásquez, hand weaving was also common in Europe until the beginning of the twentieth century. The gap was mainly in the mechanization of cotton spinning. The mechanization of wool spinning took place even later than did that of cotton. This technology began in Europe in 1820 and spread to Colombia forty or fifty years later. Luis Ospina Vásquez, *Industria y Protección en Colombia 1810–1930* (Medellín: FAES, Biblioteca Colombiana de Ciencias Sociales, 1987), 159–60.

57. Florentino González, *Memoria de Hacienda de 1847,* quoted in Ospina Vasquez, *Industria y Protección en Colombia,* 237.

58. This letter was published by other liberal contenders to prove González's rejection of purely laissez-faire principles. See Gerardo Molina, *Las Ideas Liberales en Colombia—1849–1914,* 56.

59. Artisans had been mobilized as a group since 1831, when they requested the full prohibition of competitive goods. In 1846 the organization was known as the Society of Artisans; in 1849 the society's name was changed to the Democratic Society of Artisans or Democratic Society. The history of the artisans' movement appears in David Sowell, "'La Teoría y la Realidad': The Democratic Society of Artisans of Bogotá, 1847–1854," *Hispanic American Historical Review* 67, no. 4 (1987). See also Francisco Gutiérrez Sanín, *Curso y Discurso del Movimiento Plebeyo 1849–1854* (Bogotá: Instituto de Estudios Políticos y Relaciones Internacionales y El Áncora Editores, 1995).

60. José M. Samper, *Historia de un Alma 1834 a 1881,* vol. 1 (Bogotá: Biblioteca Popular de Cultura Colombiana, 1946), 237–39.

61. Ibid.

62. Cruz Ballesteros, "La Teoría i la Realidad" (1851), reprinted in Carmen Escobar, *La Revolución Liberal y la Protesta del Artesanado* (Bogotá: Ediciones Fondo Editorial Suramérica, 1990), 351–56. For a view of the struggle between artisans and Liberals, see Sowell, "'La teoría y la Realidad," 611–30.

63. Ballestros, "La Teoria i la Realidad," 355.

64. Candelario Obeso, *Secundino el Zapatero* (Bogotá: Imprenta de Zalamea, 1880), reprinted in *Teatro Colombiano del Siglo XIX de Costumbres y Comedias,* ed. Carlos Nicolás Hernández (Bogotá: Tres Culturas Editores, 1989), 301–2.

65. Miguel Samper, "La Miseria en Bogotá" (1867), in Samper, *Escritos Económico-Políticos de Miguel Samper,* 89 and passim. According to Samper, artisans were both victims and causes of Bogotá's poverty.

66. Ibid., 46.

67. Camachá's letters were published in the newspaper *La República* the 2nd, 16th, and 30th of October 1867.

68. José Leocadio Camacho, "Al Señor Doctor Miguel Samper, Carta Primera," *La República* (October 16, 1867), 55.

69. Quoted in David Sowell, "La teoría y la Realidad," 620. According to Sowell, "The artisans stressed that their petition was based on social reality not economic theory."

70. José Leocadio Camacho, "Al Señor Doctor Miguel Samper, Carta Cuarta," *La República* (October 30, 1867).

71. José Leocadio Camacho, "Al Señor Doctor Miguel Samper, Carta Tercera," *La República* (October 16, 1867) (emphasis added).

72. Samper, "La Miseria en Bogotá," 95.

73. *Acuarelas de la Comisión Corográfica: Colombia 1850–1859* (Bogotá: Litografía Arco, 1986).

74. "Los Democráticos" (Bogotá, August 6, 1854), reprinted in Carmen Escobar, *La Revolución Liberal y la Protesta del Artesanado* (Bogotá: Fundación Universitaria Autónoma de Colombia, 1990), 357–58.

75. Antonio José Restrepo, *El Cancionero de Antioquia* (Barcelona: Editorial Lux, 1929), 252–53.

76. José M. Samper, *Ensayo sobre las Revoluciones Políticas i la Condición Social de las Repúblicas Colombiana*, 318–19.

77. Joaquín Piñeros Corpas, *Acuarelas de Mark: Colombia 1843–1856* (Santafé de Bogotá: Litografía Arco, 1992), 145.

78. Octavio Quiñones Pardo, *Interpretación de la Poesía Popular* (Bogotá: Editorial Centro, 1947), 102.

79. Ibid., 131.

6. REPRESENTATION, VIOLENCE, AND THE UNEVEN DEVELOPMENT OF CAPITALISM

1. Kelvin Santiago-Valles, *"Subject People" and Colonial Discourses: Economic Transformation and Social Disorder in Puerto Rico, 1898–1947* (Albany: State University of New York Press, 1994), 6.

2. For the case of the Third World in general, see Robert Brenner, "The Origins of Capitalist Development: A Critique of Neo-Smithian Marxism," in *Introduction to the Sociology of "Developing Societies,"* ed. Hamza Alavi and Teodor Shanin (London: Macmillan, 1982).

3. The Latin American debate appeared in Ernesto Laclau, "Feudalism and Capitalism in Latin America," in Ernesto Laclau, *Politics and Ideology in Marxist Theory* (London and New York: 1977). In Colombia Kalmanovitz aligned with the defenders of the feudalism position. In his view, after independence there was a tendency toward the *enfeudamiento* of the relations of production. Salomón Kalmanovitz, "El Regimen Agrario Durante el Siglo XIX en Colombia in *Manual de Historia de Colombia*" (Bogotá: Círculo de Lectores S.A., 1982). When addressing the dilemma, historian Palacios preferred to use a third category. In his view, the relations of production "do not look like capitalism, but neither is it feudalism"; rather, they look like "semiservitude." Marco Palacios, *Coffee in Colombia, 1850–1970* (Cambridge: Cambridge University Press, 1980), 119–20. José A. Ocampo

did not doubt the capitalist character of the economy in the nineteenth century. He thought that its peripheral location within the world capitalist system gave Colombian capitalism a speculative character. The main drive was not to reinvest in the productive capacity, but to obtain easy gains. José A. Ocampo, *Colombia y la Economía Mundial, 1830–1910* (Bogotá: Siglo XXI, 1984).

4. The following regions and their territorial divisions into states were distinguished in 1870: the Caribbean coast, the first region of Spanish colonization, which includes Bolívar, Magdalena, and Panamá; the eastern cordillera region, the most densely populated and urbanized part of Colombia, where Boyacá, Cundinamarca, and Santander are located; the western region, where Antioquia is located; and Southern Colombia, where Cauca is located.

5. I recognize that a regional analysis is still a generalization. As Catherine LeGrand suggested in a personal communication, it is possible to analyze subregional regimes of representation. For example, the Antioqueño self-image as white, homogenous, and racially undifferentiated applied only to the mountainous areas (coffee areas), not to the lowland mining and cattle ranching frontiers in the northern and eastern parts of the region, which were viewed by the elites as racially mixed, "dangerous" places.

6. Marco Palacios, "La Fragmentación Regional de las Clases Dominantes en Colombia: Una Perspectiva Histórica," *Revista Mexicana de Sociología* (1980), 42 1684. On the regional question, see also Álvaro Tirado Mejía, *Centralización y Centralismo en Colombia* (Bogotá: Fundación Friedich Naumann, 1983), and Jorge Orlando Melo, "Etnia, Región y Nación: El Fluctuante Discurso de la Identidad (Notas para un Debate)," in *Predecir el Pasado: Ensayos de Historia de Colombia* (Santa Fé de Bogotá: Fundación Simón y Lola Guberek, 1992).

7. Salvador Camacho Roldán, "Manuela, Novela de Costumbres Colombianas por Eugenio Díaz" (1889), in Salvador Camacho Roldán, *Escritos Varios*, vol. 2 (Bogotá: Editorial Incunables, 1983).

8. Peter Wade, "The Language of Race, Place, and Nation in Colombia," in *America Negra* 2 (Bogotá: Pontificia Universidad Javeriana, December 1991), 46.

9. For an overview of partisan alignment, see Helen Delpar, *Red against Blue: The Liberal Party in Colombia Politics 1863–1899* (Tuscaloosa: University of Alabama Press, 1981).

10. Ibid., 34–35.

11. Ibid., 39.

12. This argument follows Carol A. Smith, "Local History in Global Context: Social and Economic Transitions in Western Guatemala," in Daniel H.

Levine, ed., *Constructing Culture and Power in Latin America* (Ann Arbor: University of Michigan Press, 1993).

13. Frank Safford, "Significación de los Antioqueños en el Desarrollo Económico Colombiano," in *Aspectos del Siglo XIX en Colombia,* ed. Frank Safford (Medellín: Ediciones Hombre Nuevo, 1977).

14. A small number of families had more than a thousand slaves employed on plantations and in mines. Michael Taussig, "The Evolution of Rural Wage Labour in the Cauca Valley of Colombia, 1700–1970," in *Land and Labour in Latin America: Essays on the Development of Agrarian Capitalism in the Nineteenth and Twentieth Centuries,* ed. Kenneth Duncan and Ian Rutledge (Cambridge: Cambridge University Press, 1977).

15. José Escorcia, *Sociedad y Economía en el Valle del Cauca: Desarrollo Político, Social, y Económico,* vol. 3 (Bogotá: Biblioteca Banco Popular: 1983), 73.

16. León Helguera, "Antecedentes Sociales de la Revolución de 1851 en el Sur de Colombia (1848–1849)," in *Anuario Colombiano de Historia Central y de la Cultura,* 5 (1970).

17. Anthony McFarlane, *Colombia before Independence: Economy, Society, and Politics under Bourbon Rule* (Cambridge: Cambridge University Press, 1993), 274. See also Anthony McFarlane, "*Cimarrones* and *Palenques*: Runaways and Resistance in Colonial Colombia," in *Out of the House of Bondage: Runaways, Resistance, and Marronage in Africa and the New World,* ed. Gad Heuman (London: Cass, 1986).

18. The concept of the "culture of terror" is from Michael Taussig, *Shamanism, Colonialism, and the Wild Man* (Chicago: University of Chicago Press, 1987).

19. Gutiérrez de Pineda gives some examples of this code: if a slave walked at night around the estate without the owner's permission, he should have two hundred lashes in public; if one stole a pig, he should receive one hundred lashes; if he disappeared for ten days, he should receive two hundred lashes; if for twenty days, he must die or his genitals must be cut off. The same punishment was allowed for robbery in the mines. Virginia Gutierrez de Pineda, *La Familia en Colombia,* vol. 1 (Bogotá: Editorial Iqueima, 1963), 204–5.

20. Catherine LeGrand, *Frontier Expansion and Peasant Protest in Colombia, 1830–1936* (Albuquerque: University of New Mexico Press, 1986), 20.

21. José E. Caro, "La polémica de los Rojos" (1849), in José E. Caro, *Escritos Histórico-políticos* (Bogotá: Fondo Cultural Cafetero, 1981), 125.

22. Article 6 states: "The emancipated young, children of slaves . . . will be inducted into the army, or sent to new villages within the Republic, according to the Executive, in whose jurisdiction it is to prescribe and order in accord."

23. José E. Caro, "La Polémica de los Rojos" (1849), in Caro, *Escritos Histórico-políticos,* 124 (emphasis added).

24. Ibid., 125.

25. Michael T. Taussig, *The Devil and Commodity Fetishism in South America* (Chapel Hill: University of North Carolina Press, 1980).

26. Ibid., 36.

27. Ibid., 139.

28. Joanne Rappaport, *The Politics of Memory: Native Historical Interpretation in the Colombian Andes* (Cambridge: Cambridge University Press, 1990).

29. Ibid., 91.

30. Francisco Gutiérrez Sanín, *Curso y Discurso del Movimiento Plebeyo 1849–1854* (Bogotá: El Áncora Editores: 1995).

31. Ibid., 140.

32. For a description, see J. León Helguera, "Antecedentes Sociales de la Revolución de 1851 en el Sur de Colombia (1848–1849)," in J. León Helguera, *Anuario Colombiano de Historia Social y de la Cultura* 5 (1970).

33. Quoted in Ibid., 212.

34. "Punitive expeditions" is Gutiérrez's term; ibid., 143.

35. The laws aimed to control the provinces' electoral processes and the provincial armies. Felipe Pérez, *Anales de la Revolución Escritos Según sus Propios Documentos* (Bogotá: Imprenta del Estado de Cundinamarca, 1862).

36. The complete text of Mosquera's declaration appears in ibid., 513.

37. Mariano Ospina, "Alocución a los Granadinos," in ibid., 575 and passim.

38. Ibid., 577.

39. A detailed description of these systems appear in Michael Taussig, "The Evolution of Rural Wage Labour in the Cauca Valley of Colombia, 1700–1970," in *Land and Labour in Latin America,* ed. Duncan and Rutledge.

40. Taussig, *The Devil and Commodity Fetishism in South America.*

41. Quoted in Taussig, "The Evolution of Rural Wage Labour in the Cauca Valley," 410.

42. Taussig, *The Devil and Commodity Fetishism in South America.*

43. Ibid., 53.

44. Quoted in José Antonio Ocampo, *Colombia y la Economía Mundial 1830–1910* (Bogotá: Siglo XXI editores, 1984), 253.

45. John P. Harrison, "The Evolution of the Colombian Tobacco Trade, to 1875," in *The Hispanic American Historical Review* 32, no. 2 (1952), 173.

46. Quoted in Taussig, *The Devil and Commodity Fetishism in South America,* 55.

47. Quoted in Jesús C. Torres Almeida, *Manuel Murillo Toro: Caudillo*

Radical and Reformador Social (Bogotá: Ediciones El Tiempo, 1984), 210. The first article stated that the province was constituted of all men in the territory, no matter their nationality. The 1857 assembly of the province abolished the death penalty and granted a general amnesty for political prisoners.

48. John Leddy Phelan, *The People and the King: The Comunero Revolution in Colombia, 1781* (Madison: University of Wisconsin Press, 1978), 89.

49. The description of this situation appears in Orlando Fals Borda, *El Hombre y la Tierra en Boyacá* (Bogotá: Editorial Antares, 1957).

50. Quoted in Jorge Orlando Melo, *Indios y Mestizos de la Nueva Granada a Finales del Siglo XVIII* (Bogotá: Biblioteca del Banco Popular, 1985), 31.

51. Phelan, *The People and the King*, 92. On the policies of abolition of *resguardos* put in place by Moreno y Escandón, visitor to the eastern region, see also Melo, *Indios y Mestizos de la Nueva Granada.*

52. Manuel Ancízar, *Peregrinación de Alpha* (Bogotá: Biblioteca Popular, 1942). The translation is from Frank Safford, "Race, Integration, and Progress: Elite Attitudes and the Indian in Colombia, 1750–1870," *Hispanic American Historical Review* 71, no. 1 (1991), 28.

53. Ancízar, *Peregrinación de Alpha*, 32.

54. Ibid., 109.

55. Fals Borda, *El Hombre y la Tierra en Boyacá*, 44–50.

56. Horacio Rodríguez Plata, *La Inmigración Alemana al Estado Soberano de Santander en el Siglo XIX* (Bogotá: Editorial Kelly, 1968), 33.

57. Salvador Camacho Roldán, *Mis Memorias,* vol. 1 (Bogotá: Biblioteca Popular de Cultura Colombiana, 1946), 162–69.

58. José Antonio Ocampo, "Comerciantes, Artesanos, y Política Económica en Colombia, 1830–1880," *Boletín Cultural y Bibliográfico* 27, no. 2 (1990), 38.

59. These figures has been taken from Helen Delpar, *Red against Blue,* 36.

60. Ancízar, *Peregrinación de Alpha,* 169.

61. Palacios, *Coffee in Colombia, 1850–1970,* 80.

62. The situation differed in the case of the extraction of quinine, which took place in forests where empty lands were granted to private individuals or companies *(compañías)*. The latter defended the land using private armies, and fights between *compañías* were common. The relationship between the *compañía* and the *cascarillero* was one of distrust; finally, the *compañía* employed collective exploration with a hierarchical internal structure. See Ocampo, *Colombia y la Economía Mundial,* 297 and passim.

63. Ancízar, *Peregrinación de Alpha,* 95.

64. Ibid., 167.

65. Ibid., 145.

66. This right lasted only three years. Women's right to vote was recognized in 1957.

67. Emiro Kastos, "Algo sobre las Mujeres," reprinted in Emiro Kastos, *Colección de Artículos Escogidos* (Bogotá: Imprenta de Pizano i Pérez, 1859), 124.

68. Emiro Kastos, "Industria: Tabaco y Sombreros," in Kastos, *Colección de Artículos Escogidos*, 175.

69. Ancízar, *Peregrinación de Alpha* (1942), 443. *Nacuma* was a plant used to manufacture the hats.

70. *Acuarelas de la Comisión Corográfica. Colombia 1850–1859* (Bogotá: Litografía Arco, 1986).

71. According to some data, in the city of Bucaramanga the number of artisans dedicated to the production of hats diminished from three thousand in 1850, to sixteen hundred in 1878; in the province of Soto, production diminished from three hundred sixty thousand hats in 1873 to one hundred twenty thousand in 1878. The number continued to diminish through 1880. David Church Johnson, *Santander: Siglo XIX—Cambios Socioeconómicos* (Bogotá: Carlos Valencia Editores, 1984), 279.

72. Frank Safford, "On Paradigms and the Pursuit of the Practical: A Response," *Latin America Research Review,* 13, no. 2 (1978), 253.

73. See Gerardo Molina, "El Pensamiento Político de Murillo Toro," in *Las Ideas Liberales en Colombia, 1849–1914* (Bogotá: Ediciones Tercer Mundo, 1975), 70–83.

74. The article, entitled "Dejad Hacer," is reprinted in ibid., 319–33.

75. Murillo Toro, "Dejad Hacer," 327.

76. Ibid., 329.

77. M. Murillo Toro, *Informe del Jefe Superior del Estado de Santander a la Asamblea Legislativa, Bucaramanga* (1858), 19–20, quoted in Church Johnson, *Santander: Siglo XIX—Cambios Socioeconómicos,* 97.

78. Ibid., 59.

79. Gonzalo Tavera, "Circular Llamando la Atención de los Funcionarios Públicos al Estudio de las Instituticiones del Estado, para que Identifiquen con Ellas Su Conducta Oficial" (Bucaramanga, January 14, 1858), quoted in Church Johnson, *Santander: Siglo XIX—Cambios Socioeconómicos,* 75.

80. Molina, *Las Ideas Liberales en Colombia,* 18.

81. Quoted in Robert Louis Gilmore, "Nueva Granada's Socialist Mirage," *Hispanic American Historical Review* 26, no. 2 (1956), 205.

82. Quoted in Church Johnson, *Santander: Siglo XIX—Cambios Socioeconómicos,* 56.

83. Ibid., 101.

84. Horacio Rodríguez Plata, *La Inmigración Alemana al Estado Soberano de Santander* (Bogotá: Editorial Kelly, 1968), 15.

85. Lengerke obtained from the government the concession to build the following: the road from Zapatoca to Barrancabermeja, the road from Cañaverales (the midpoint between Bucaramanga and Rionegro) to Puerto de Botijas in the Lebrija River, the road from Girón to La Ceiba, the road that linked the Sogamoso and Barrancabermeja Roads, the road from Girón to Puerto de Mata, and the bridge over the Suárez River, named Bridge Lengerke. Ibid., 110.

86. Manuel Alberto Garnica Martínez, "Guarapo, Champaña, y Vino Blanco: Presencia Alemana en Santander," *Boletín Cultural y Bibliográfico, Biblioteca Luis Angel Arango* 29, no. 29 (1992), 49.

87. Ibid.

88. Church Johnson, *Santander: Siglo XIX—Cambios Socioeconómicos,* 282.

89. Garnica Martínez, "Guarapo, Champaña, y Vino Blanco," 55.

90. Geo von Lengerke, "Memorial del Señor Geo von Lengerke a la Asamblea del Estado," reproduced in Horacio Rodríguez Plata, *La Inmigración Alemana en el Estado Soberano de Santander en el Siglo XIX,* 225–53.

91. Quoted in Rodríguez Plata, *La Inmigración Alemana,* 244–45.

92. Quoted in ibid., 229–33.

93. Quoted in ibid., 234.

94. Ibid., 240.

95. Ibid.

96. Ibid., 47.

97. In 1865 the province published the *Codígos Político i Municipal, de Policía, Penal, i Militar del Estado Soberano de Santander,* which included regulations not only about government and justice, but also about land distribution, use of water, fisheries, control of epidemic diseases, and behavior during celebrations. The code also regulated the construction of roads. According to the code, roads were a state's responsibility. According to the law, prisoners should work in public works. This information is from David Church Johnson, whose conclusion was that "it was difficult to find an aspect of social relations which was not regulated in the codes." Church Johnson, *Santander: Siglo XIX—Cambios Socioeconómicos,* 181, 203–4.

98. José Antonio Ocampo, "Comerciantes, Artesanos y Política Económica en Colombia, 1830–1880," *Boletín Cultural y Bibliográfico,* Banco de la República, XXVII, 22 (1990), 41.

99. Ibid., 41.

100. Ocampo, *Colombia y la Economía Mundial 1830–1910.*

101. These changes are documented in Jesús Antonio Bejarano and Orlando Pulido, *El Tabaco en una Economía Regional: Ambalema Siglos*

XVIII y XIX (Bogotá: Empresa Editorial Universidad Nacional de Colombia, 1986).

102. Salomón Kalmanovitz, "El Régimen Agrario durante el Siglo XIX en Colombia," in *Manual de Historia de Colombia* (Bogotá: Círculo de Lectores, 1982).

103. Malcom Deas, "A Colombian Coffee State: Santa Barbara," in *Land and Labour in Latin America,* ed. Duncan and Rutledge.

104. Ibid, 279.

105. Ibid., 280.

106. Ibid., 282.

107. Michael Jiménez, "Class, Gender, and Peasant Resistance in Central Colombia, 1900–1930," in Forrest D. Colburn, *Everyday Forms of Peasants Resistance* (Armonk and London: M. E. Sharpe Inc., 1989).

108. Salvador Camacho Roldán, "Introducción," in Eugenio Díaz Castro, *Manuela* (Bogotá: Biblioteca Popular de Cultura, 1895), 503.

109. Medardo Rivas, *Los Trabajadores de Tierra Caliente* (Bogotá: Imprenta y Librería de M. Rivas, 1899).

110. Díaz Castro, *Manuela.*

111. For an alternative interpretation of *Manuela,* see Raymond Leslie Williams, *The Colombian Novel, 1844–1987* (Austin: University of Texas Press, 1991). For Williams, the novel symbolizes the encounter and conflict between the written and the oral culture in Colombia. He sees Manuela as representing oral (preliterate) culture, whereas the male characters are associated with the highly rational culture of writing.

112. Rivas described the typical situation in the lowlands around the 1870s. According to Catherine LeGrand, the land struggles emerged in a legal-institutional context. *Colonos* (settlers) resisted land entrepreneurs using judicial and administrative channels, appealing to bureaucrats, congressmen, and hiring lawyers. The press and pamphlets were also used as means to express different viewpoints. The selective use of violence was also employed in the land struggles. Catherine LeGrand, *Frontier Expansion and Peasant Protest in Colombia, 1850–1936* (Albuquerque: University of New Mexico Press, 1986), chapter 4.

113. Rivas, *Los Trabajadores de Tierra Caliente,* 230.

114. José M. Samper, *Ensayo sobre las Revoluciones Políticas i la Condición Social de las Repúblicas Colombianas,* 95–96.

115. Quoted in Palacios, *Coffee in Colombia, 1850–1970,* 72. Palacios added that probably the *Bogotano* felt more at home with the Bostonian than with the Indian or the Magdalena boatman.

116. During the tobacco crisis, Colombia invested in indigo, whose price had increased in the world market. The national exports increased from 4 tons in 1864 to 182 tons in 1870. Ten years later, the exports decreased to

the same level as in 1863, 6 tons. The decrease in Colombian exports was related to soil exhaustion and the low-technology conditions of production and packing, which were unable to respond to a increase in world demand. Ocampo, *Colombia y la Economía Mundial,* 364–69.

117. Rivas, *Los Trabajadores de Tierra Caliente,* 306.

118. Michael Jiménez, "Class, Gender, and Peasant Resistance in Central Colombia, 1900–1930," 132.

119. Eugenio Díaz Castro, *Manuela,* 207.

120. *Amulatamiento* means "degeneration into mulatto." Ocampo, *Colombia y la Economía Mundial.*

121. Anthony McFarlane, *Colombia before Independence,* 138.

122. James J. Parsons, *The Antioqueño Colonization in Western Colombia* (Berkeley and Los Angeles: University of California Press, 1968).

123. Reported in ibid., 51.

124. José M. Samper, *Ensayo sobre las Revoluciones Políticas i la Condición Social de las Repúblicas Colombianas,* 85.

125. An account of the dynamic of population in Antioquia is found in James Parsons, *The Antioqueño Colonization in Western Colombia.*

126. James Parsons, *La Colonización Antioqueña en el Occidente de Colombia* (dissertation).

127. Everett E. Hagen, *El Cambio Social en Colombia: El Factor Humano en el Desarrollo Económico* (Bogotá: Ediciones Tercer Mundo, 1963).

128. Frank Safford, "Significación de los Antioqueños en el Desarrollo Económico Colombiano," in *Aspectos del Siglo XIX en Colombia,* ed. Frank Safford.

129. Álvaro López Toro, *Migración y Cambio Social en Antioquia durante el Siglo Diez y Nueve* (Bogotá: Centro de Estudios para el Desarrollo Económico, Universidad de los Andes, monografía 25, 1968), 52.

130. At the end of the eighteenth century the gold and silver produced in Cauca represented 43 percent of Colombia's production, as compared with 31 percent in Antioquia. Their shares of the Colombian population in mid–nineteenth century were 15 percent and 11 percent, respectively. Popayán, Cauca's capital, played an important political and social role, sometimes comparable to that of the capital, Bogotá. During the period after independence Cauca was the most important political center. The presidency of the country was often occupied by men from important families of Popayán.

131. José María Vergara y Vergara, *Historia de la Literatura en la Nueva Granada desde la Conquista hasta la Independencia (1538–1820)* (Bogotá: Librería Americana, 1905), 480.

132. Alejandro López, *Problemas Colombianos* (Paris: Editorial París-América, 1927).

133. Quoted in ibid., 25. Juan Antonio Mon y Velarde was a Spanish visitor in Antioquía from 1785 to 1798.

134. Marco Palacios, "La Fragmentación Regional de las Clases Dominantes en Colombia," 1678.

135. Salomón Kalmanowitz, "El Régimen Agrario Durante el Siglo XIX en Colombia," in *Manual de Historia de Colombia,* vol. 2, 293 and passim.

136. Ibid., 297.

137. Helen Delpar, *Red against Blue,* 94–95.

138. An expression used by Conservative José María Quijano Otero. Quoted in ibid., 96.

139. Luis Javier Villegas Botero, *Aspectos de la Educación en Antioquia durante el Gobierno de Pedro Justo Berrio 1864–1873* (Medellín: Ediciones de Educación y Cultura, 1991).

140. Gregorio Gutiérrez González, "Memoria Científica sobre el Cultivo del Maíz en los Climas Cálidos del Estado de Antioquia por uno de los Miembros de la Escuela de Ciencias y Artes Dedicado a la misma Escuela," reprinted in Eduardo Camacho Guizado, "La Literatura Colombiana entre 1820 y 1900," in *Manual de Historia de Colombia,* vol. 2 (Bogotá: Círculo de Lectores S.A., 1982), 638.

141. Mariano Ospina Rodríguez, "Los Israelitas y Sus Detractores" (1875), published with the title "Los Israelitas y los Antioqueños" in *Escritos sobre Economía y Política en Mariano Ospina Rodríguez* (Bogotá: Biblioteca Universitaria de Cultura Colombiana, 1969), 207–10.

142. Mariano Ospina Rodríguez a Pedro Alcántara Herrán, August 28, 1854, quoted in Frank Safford, "Significación de los Antioqueños en el Desarrollo Económico Colombiano," in Safford, *Aspectos del Siglo XIX en Colombia,* 87. According to Safford, this was not the only occasion when Antioqueños thought in that way: in the conflicts of 1860–63 this antipolitical feeling appeared again.

143. López Toro, *Migración y Cambio Social en Antioquia durante el Siglo Diez y Nueve,* 32–33.

144. The previous remarks do not mean that the colonization was democratic and equitable. Palacios referred to this interpretation as a "white legend"; on the contrary, land distribution was far from egalitarian, and social conflict also existed among the colonizers. Palacios, *Coffee in Colombia, 1850–1970,* especially chapters 8 and 9. López Toro, in *Migración y Cambio Social en Antioquia Durante el Siglo Diez y Nueve,* also mentions that in new waves of colonization a number of vagrants, poor people, and criminals were displaced to the areas of colonization. Conflicts were also caused by the appropriation of land on the part of big landowners and the displacement of independent peasants.

CONCLUSION

1. Sigmund Freud, "Why War?," reprinted in *Classical Readings in Culture and Civilisation,* ed. John Rundell and Stephen Mennell (London and New York: Routledge, 1998), 145.

2. Samuel Huntington, *The Clash of Civilizations: Remaking of World Order* (New York: Touchstone Book, 1997), 266.

3. Samuel P. Huntington, "The Clash of Civilizations?" *Foreign Affairs,* Summer 1993.

4. Some have already taken this road, and Huntington has dismissed them with the argument that it is not possible for a paradigm to be falsified with accounts of anomalous events. In his own words, the debate on the civilizational paradigm "either accords with reality as people see it or it comes close enough so that people who do not accept it have to attack it." Ibid., 187.

5. Samuel P. Huntington, "If Not Civilization, What?" *Foreign Affairs,* November–December 1993.

6. This description follows Norbert Elias, *The Civilizing Process: The History of Manners and State Formation and Civilization* (Oxford and Cambridge: Blackwell, 1994).

7. Ibid., 476.

8. Ibid., 478.

9. Albert Hirschman, *The Passions and the Interests: Political Arguments for Capitalism before Its Triumph* (Princeton, N.J.: Princeton University Press, 1977).

10. Huntington, *The Clash of Civilizations,* 43.

11. Ibid., 20.

12. Ibid., 21.

13. I take this argument from Slavoj Žižek, "Carl Schmitt in the Age of Post-Politics," in *The Challenge of Carl Schmitt,* ed. Chantal Mouffe (London and New York: Verso, 1999).

14. Ibid., 310.

15. Huntingon, *The Clash of Civilizations,* 311.

16. Following Slavoj Žižek, "The negativity of the Other which is preventing me from achieving my full identity with myself is just an externalization of my own auto-negativity, of my self-hindering." Slavoj Žižek, "Beyond Discourse Analysis," in Ernesto Laclau, *New Reflections on the Revolution of Our Time* (London and New York: Verso, 1990), 252–53. Žižek illustrates this point for the case of anti-Semitic ideology: The functioning of anti-Semitic ideology works by constructing the Jew as a *point de capiton,* a terrifying subject who enables an explanation of the experiences of economic crisis, "moral decadence," "national humiliation," and so on. This process is described as an inversion by means of which a textual operation—the "quilting" into a unified

ideological field—is perceived as a stable point of reference that acts as a hidden cause. In his view, the efficacy of this mechanism cannot be reduced to an organizational device. Enjoyment is the surplus on which this mechanism relies, writing of "the fact that we impute to the 'Jew' an impossible, unfathomable enjoyment, allegedly stolen from us." Slavoj Žižek, *For They Know Not What They Do* (London: Verso, 1991), 18–19.

17. Quoted in Huntington, *The Clash of Civilization,* 303.

18. Ibid., 304.

19. Ibid., 305.

20. Ibid., 204.

21. According to Kaplan, "West Africa is becoming *the* symbol of worldwide demographic, environmental, and societal stress, in which criminal anarchy emerges as the real "strategic" danger. Disease, overpopulation, unprovoked crime, scarcity of resources, refugee migrations, the increasing erosion of nation-states and international borders, and the empowerment of private armies, security firms, and international drug cartels are now most tellingly demonstrated through a West African prism. West Africa provides an appropriate introduction to the issues, often extremely unpleasant to discuss, that will soon confront our civilization." Robert D. Kaplan, "The Coming of Anarchy," *The Atlantic Monthly,* February 1994, 46.

22. Huntington, "The Clash of Civilizations?" 23.

23. Ernesto Laclau, "Universalism, Particularism, and the Question of Identity," *October* 61 (1992), 90.

24. Tzvetan Todorov, *The Conquest of America* (New York: Harper and Row, 1984), and Ashis Nandy, *Traditions, Tyranny, and Utopias: Essays in the Politics of Awareness* (Delhi: Oxford University Press, 1987). For a review of both proposals, see David Blaney and Naeem Inayatullah, "Prelude to a Conversation of Cultures in International Society? Todorov and Nandy on the Possibility of a Dialogue," *Alternatives* 19 (1994).

25. Ashis Nandy, quoted in David Blaney and Naeem Inayatullah, "Prelude to a Conversation of Cultures in International Society?" 39.

26. Fernando Coronil, "Beyond Occidentalism: Toward Non-Imperial Geohistorical Categories," *Cultural Anthropology* 2, no. 1 (1996).

27. In the case of Western representation, *Occidentalism* means to unsettle "a mode of representation that produces polarized and hierarchical conceptions of the West and its Others." Fernando Coronil, *The Magical State: Nature, Money, and Modernity in Venezuela* (Chicago and London: University of Chicago Press, 1997), 14–15.

28. Walter D. Mignolo, *Local Histories/Global Designs: Coloniality, Subaltern Knowledges, and Border Thinking* (Princeton, N.J.: Princeton University Press, 2000), 304.

29. Michael Shapiro, *Violent Cartographies* (Minneapolis and London: University of Minnesota Press, 1997), 59.

Index

CRISTINA ROJAS teaches Latin American politics and international political economy at the Norman Paterson School of International Affairs at Carleton University, Canada. She has been a visiting scholar at Harvard University and professor of political science at Javeriana University, Colombia.